Spalding Gray was born in Barrington, Rhode Island, in 1941, and began his career as an actor in regional and Off-Broadway theatre. In 1969 he joined the Wooster Group, a performance theatre in SoHo, where he continues to appear several times each year. Over the past decade he has written and performed a series of autobiographical monologues to critical acclaim throughout the United States, as well as in Canada, Europe and Australia. He is the recipient of several fellowships, including a 1985 Guggenheim.

Gray's appearance in his first major motion picture, *The Killing Fields*, was the basis for the monologue 'Swimming to Cambodia', which was first published in book form in 1985. He has a major role in David Byrne's movie *True Stories*.

SWIMMING TO CAMBODIA

THE COLLECTED WORKS OF SPALDING GRAY

Published by Pan Books

Acknowledgements

Poem extract on page 64 from 'Of Mere Being', in *The Palm at the End of the Mind* by Wallace Stevens, copyright c 1967, 1969, 1971 by Holly Stevens; New York: Alfred A Knopf, Inc; used by permission of the publisher. Quotations on page 100 from *The Cocktail Party* by T.S.Eliot, copyright © 1950, 1978 by Esme Valerie Eliot; New York: Harcourt Brace Jovanovich (US) and Faber and Faber (Great Britain); used by permission of the publishers. Lines on page 46 from 'Killing Me Softly with His Song' used by permission of Charles Fox and Norman Gimbel, copyright ©1972 by Charles Fox and Norman Gimbel. All rights reserved.

Excerpts from *The Message in the Bottle* by Walker Percy copyright © 1954, 1956, 1957, 1958, 1959, 1961, 1967, 1972 and 1975 by Walker Percy. Reprinted by permission of Farrar, Straus & Giroux, Inc.

Grateful acknowledgement is made to Folkways for permission to reprint an excerpt from the lyrics to 'Sounds of the Annual International Sportscar Grand Prix of Watkins Glen, N.Y.', by Henry Mandler and Robert Strome. Folkways Record FX6140. Used by Permission.

Swimming to Cambodia first published in the United States of America 1985 by Theatre Communications Group, Inc.

Copyright ©1985 by Spalding Gray

Sex and Death to The Age 14 first published in the United States of America 1986 by Vintage books, a division of Random House, Inc.

Copyright ©1986 by Spalding Gray

This collection first published in Great Britain 1987
by Pan Books Ltd, Cavaye Place, London, SW10 9PG
9 8 7 6 5 4 3 2
Copyright ©1985, 1986 by Spalding Gray
ISBN 0 330 29947 6

Printed in Great Britain by
Richard Clay Ltd, Bungay, Suffolk

CONTENTS

PREFACE

Stories seem to fly to me and stick. They are always out there, coming in. We exist in a fabric of personal stories. All culture, all civilization is an artful web, a human puzzle, a colorful quilt patched together to lay over raw indifferent nature. So I never wonder whether, if a tree falls in the forest, will anyone hear it. Rather, who will tell about it?

While I was a student at Emerson College in Boston, I worked at The Katherine Gibbs School at night. I got into the habit of telling the story of my day, at the end of each day, while I ran the dishwasher or worked the garbage truck. So my first audience was made up of reformed alcoholic ex-Merchant Marines, a bevy of female Irish Catholic cooks and a few Emerson students who, luckily for me, were good listeners.

When I went to work at a small theater in Saratoga, New York, this habit of telling stories from my daily life continued. We all lived in a converted old whorehouse with sagging brown silk ceilings, wall-to-wall carpeting and no furniture. The whole situation was so wild that I fled to the sanctuary of Skidmore College, just up the road. There I met Elizabeth LeCompte, an arts major, and began telling her my stories in her studio while she worked and listened. It felt as if I was peeling them off and dropping them in her lap so I could breathe again.

In 1967 Liz and I began living together on Sixth Street and Avenue D on the Lower East Side of Manhattan. I was collecting thirty-two dollars a week in unemployment and Liz worked selling postcards at the Metropolitan Museum of Art. I survived on these personal stories. At the time I never thought of writing them down. We didn't even have a desk in the apartment and I wasn't a very good speller.

During my first years in New York I fell into a free theater workshop run by Joyce Aaron, a member of the Open Theatre. One day she asked us to do an exercise where we stood up and told a personal story as far as we could. If we blanked out or ran out of personal memories we were to jam, like a jazz musician, on a particular word or phrase until a new passage came. To my surprise, when it was my turn I experienced a memory film, a series of rather mundane events that had occurred during the previous week. I had no trouble editing or selecting which material to use as I spoke. The images came into my mind in vivid frames and I was able to describe it all in perfect detail. When I sat down, Joyce said, 'Very interesting. Who wrote that monologue for you?'

It was ten years before I returned to that form. In the meantime, I became more and more involved with the underground experimental theater world of the late sixties and seventies, which was heavily influenced by Artaud and Grotowski; narrative form was given little space to flourish. It was a time of deconstruction of texts. We worked with occasional words sandwiched between a piece of howl and a slice of grunt. I loved it. It opened me up in a completely new way and words went into deep hibernation.

In 1970 I joined up with Richard Schechner and the Performance Group. Liz LeCompte joined shortly thereafter. After five very productive years working with the group, Liz and I and several others broke off to form The Wooster Group. The work of The Wooster Group was radically different but Richard still remained a strong influence for me. He was the first director to tell me to be myself first, before I thought of acting a role or taking on a character. This was both a real challenge and very therapeutic. I was ready now to express myself and that is what I did with and under the direction of Liz LeCompte in our trilogy, *Three Places in Rhode Island*. The first work, *Sakonnet Point*, performed in 1975, was a silent mood piece which represented the child before speech. The next work, *Rumstick Road*, was about the child learning to speak by listening and imitating. It was based on a series of audio tapes I'd made of my family. The work evolved as a docudrama in which we improvised a series of actions using the family audio tapes as background text. Eventually these improvisations were set and scored.

During my performances in *Rumstick Road* I took on no outside character. I referred to myself as Spalding Gray. I actually stepped forward to address the audience directly and told a few personal stories, not unlike the wonderfully mundane Haikus in John Cage's

A Year from Monday. In *Nayatt School*, the third part of the trilogy, the monologue form I'd been developing found its full expression. Much of *Nayatt School* was based on a deconstruction of T.S. Eliot's *The Cocktail Party*, and at the beginning of the piece I performed a short monologue about my relationship to that play while sitting at a long wooden table. The other members of The Wooster Group were my first audience. Each day when I'd come in for rehearsal they would ask me to tell it again, and I did, while Liz taped it. Each day it was embellished and edited and grew as a text until at last we transcribed it.

After we completed *Three Places in Rhode Island* I felt I had come to the end of the group collaborative process. It had been a turbulently productive time, during which I began to keep a daily diary. The performances became my public autobiography and my private thoughts went into diary form. I felt the diary might be a way of taking full responsibility for my life, and also a more therapeutic way of splitting off a part of my self to observe another part. It was the development of a writer's consciousness. I tried to write mainly about detail of fact and action, rather than emotions. This report became like a Christmas tree, the structure upon which I could later hang my feelings, like ornaments.

I kept this diary for seven years without missing a day. It was invaluable training for recording personal detail, but also seemed the perfect assurance against slipping into a life of regret. I could refer back to it and see a clear map of the consequences of my actions.

In 1978 I went to the University of Santa Cruz to teach a summer workshop in performance. Until that time I'd been working with a group in a windowless art house, a world that to some extent referred only to itself. Now I saw vivid stories coming at me from the outside. While in Santa Cruz, I began to sit in on a class taught by Amelie Rorty, called 'The Philosophy of Emotions'. It was her enthusiasm and energy that attracted me. One day after class I was talking to Amelie about my diary and about how I felt that I'd come to the end of a way of working, that I didn't know where to turn next. Because my work had stopped I had a feeling that the world was also coming to an end. I told her I thought we had come to the end of the white middle-class world as we knew it. She took me at my word and said, 'Well, Spalding, during the collapse of Rome, the last artists were the chroniclers.' And all the bells went off inside me. Of course, I thought. I'll chronicle my life, but I'll do it orally, because to write it down would be in bad faith, it would mean I believed in a future. Also, it would be just another product cluttering up the world, not to mention destroying all the trees needed to make paper for the books. Each performance was to be a personal epitaph. Each night my personal history would disappear on a breath.

I returned to The Performing Garage in 1979, imbued with this *Sturm und Drang* spirit, perhaps a Germanic reaction to sunny California. I began my first monologue, 'Sex and Death to the Age 14', but this time I was performing solo, and I took the idea of that long table from *Nyatt School* and shrank it down to the size of a desk. I sat behind that desk with a little notebook containing an outline of all I could remember about sex and death up until I was 14 years old.

The first night maybe fifteen people came to the Garage and the monologue ran about forty minutes. The next night the audience was a little larger and so was the monologue. I tape-recorded each performance, played it back the following morning and made adjustments in my outline. It wasn't as though I was having new memories as much as remembering things I had long forgotten. The monologue grew to an hour and twenty minutes, and when I stopped it there, my memories continued into a second monologue, 'Booze, Cars, and College Girls'.

This process led to the creation of ten monologues. None of them had been written down prior to performance; they always came together in front of the audience, and perhaps they never would have been written at all if Melanie Fleishman from Random House hadn't approached me. At first I was intimidated by the idea and thought that I would have to take the stories in each monologue and rewrite them. When I tried to do this I found I no longer had my own voice. My writing was derivative and imitative. It was then that Melanie and I decided to rework the transcripts from my performances and turn them into writing. She wanted to preserve the original breath and rhythm of my voice, which had its own life in the transcripts. Melanie's input was very valuable to me. She came at this sprawling mess of words with the sharp eye of a skilled editor, and I thank her for that.

These seven monologues are a section of an ongoing oral history, within which I include myself, of course, and all the others who have been a part of 'our' history along the way. All of my stories are a reporting of actual events, sometimes slightly embellished, a memory of the memory. As much as I would have liked to maintain actual names (I do feel that a rose by any other name would smell quite different), I have changed most names and adjusted some circumstances to protect the privacy of certain individuals. While rewriting the manuscript I was careful to meditate on the memory of the actual person in order to find the right fictional name to represent what I felt to be his or her essence.

The whole process of writing these stories down has been very healing, to the extent that it has projected me into a future. And although this cannot fully assure a future, it has at least created one for me to move toward, as I watch it race ahead before me.

Spalding Gray
December 1985

SWIMMING
TO CAMBODIA

TO THE CAMBODIANS AND CAMBODIA,
A COUNTRY BEYOND MY IMAGINATION AND
MUCH TOO FAR TO SWIM TO.

I would like to thank Peter Wollen for telling Susie Figgis to look me up when she came to New York, and Bob Carrol for giving Susie my phone number once she arrived. My thanks, also, to Roland Joffe, a fine director, and David Puttnam, a courageous producer, for giving me the opportunity to be a part of the incredible experience that became *The Killing Fields*; to the more than 150 people who were part of that project; and especially to those either directly mentioned by name or referred to in *Swimming to Cambodia* – my appreciation for their indulgence and willingness to be included in this most unlikely by-product of the film. I would also like to give credit and thanks to William Shawcross for his tremendously informative book *Sideshow* (Simon & Schuster, 1979), from which I drew much of my historic material. I am also indebted to Sidney Schanberg and Elizabeth Becker for their personal contributions.

PART ONE

It was the first day off in a long time, and all of us were trying to get a little rest and relaxation out by the pool at this big, modern hotel that looked something like a prison. If I had to call it anything I would call it a 'pleasure prison'. It was the kind of place you might come to on a package tour out of Bangkok. You'd come down on a chartered bus – and you'd probably not wander off the grounds because of the high barbed-wire fence they have to keep you in and the bandits out. And every so often you would hear shotguns going off as the hotel guards fired at rabid dogs down along the beach on the Gulf of Siam.

But if you really wanted to walk on the beach, all you had to learn to do was to pick up a piece of seaweed, shake it in the dog's face and everything would be hunkydory.

So it was our first day off in a long time and there were about 130 of us out by the pool trying to get a little rest and relaxation, and the Thai waiters were running and jumping over hedges to bring us 'Kloster! More Kloster!' Everyone was ordering Kloster beer. No one was ordering the local brew because someone had said that the beer, which is exported to the United States, has formaldehyde in it. The waiters were running and jumping over hedges because they couldn't get to us fast enough. They were running and jumping and smiling – not a silly smile but a profound smile, a deep smile. There was nothing idiotic about it because the Thais have a word, *sanug*, which, loosely translated, means 'fun'. And they never do anything that isn't *sanug* – if it isn't *sanug* they won't touch it.

Some say that the Thais are the nicest people that money can buy, because they like to have fun. They know how to have fun and, perhaps due to their very permissive strain of Buddhism, they don't have to suffer for it after they have it.

It was a lovely day and we were all out by the pool and some of the crew were out there with their Thai wives. They had had the good sense – or bad sense, depending on how you look at it – as soon as they arrived in Bangkok, to go down to Pat Pong and buy up women to travel with them. I was told that each man bought two women so as not to risk falling in love. And there they were, lying like 250-pound beached whales while their ninety-pound 'Thai wives', in little two-piece bathing suits, walked up and down on them giving them Shiatsu massages as a Thai waiter ran, jumped over the hedge, tripped and fell, hurling his Klosters down to explode on the cement by the pool. And looking up with a great smile he said, 'Sorry sir, we just ran out of Kloster.'

Ivan (Devil in my Ear), a South African and head of the second camera unit – and a bit of a Mephistophelian figure – said, 'Spalding, there's a party tonight up on the Gulf of Siam. Could I come over and borrow your toenail clippers?'

'Sure.'

'Shall I bring some Thai stick? Do you want to smoke a joint before we go?'

I thought, why not? It's a day off and I haven't smoked since I've been here. Why not give it a try?

Now, every time I've been in a country where the marijuana is supposed to be really good – Mexico, India, Northern California and now Thailand – I've always felt that I should try it. Maybe this time it would be different. Maybe this time I would be able to sleep, like so many people say they do. Maybe this time I'd have a sense of well-being and feel at one with the world. You see, marijuana tends to unlock my Kundalini in the worst way and all the energy just gets stuck in my lower Chakra. It just gets stuck and spins there like a snake chasing its tail, or a Studebaker stuck in sand.

So I said, 'Sure, bring it over.'

Then I thought, maybe I should have waited until I'd spoken with Renée first. Renée was over there visiting me for fourteen days and we planned to go back to New York together as soon as I finished the film. We had rented a summer house together in upstate New York, in Krummville, and Krummville was looking less and less exotic to me the longer I stayed in Thailand. You see, I hadn't had a Perfect Moment yet, and I always like to have one before I leave an exotic place. They're a good way of bringing things to an end. But you can never plan for one. You never know when they're coming. It's sort of like falling in love . . . with yourself.

Also, I was beginning to get this image of myself as a kind of wandering poet-bachelor-mendicant beating my way down the whole coast of Malaysia, eating magic mushrooms all the way, until I finally reach Bali and evaporate into the sunset in a state of ecstasy. But I wasn't telling Renée that. I was only telling her that I wasn't sure when I would be coming back, and that was enough to enrage her. We fell into a big fight on the way to the party that lasted all the way down to the Gulf of Siam. And there we were, arguing on this fantastic beach where, unlike the Hamptons, there was no boat and a bigger boat, no ship and a bigger ship, no carrot and the carrot and desire and desire. It was just one big beach with no boats. Nothing to buy. Just one big piece of calendar art.

And Renée and I were walking down the beach arguing and I said, 'Stop, Renée. Stop with the fighting. Look at this beautiful sunset. Look! Look! I might be able to have a Perfect Moment right now and we could go home.'

But Renée would have none of it. She's very confrontational and always wants to talk about what is going on in the relationship, not the sunset. So she went off to cry on Therese's shoulder and talk to Julian, and I went to Ivan (Devil in My Ear) who said, 'Spalding, don't let her get the upper hand, man. I mean, after all, how many straight, single men your age are there left in New York City anyway? What's she going to do?'

And I said, 'Ivan, no, don't say things like that.'

Then Renée and I came out of our respective corners and went back at it for another round, until at last she said, 'Listen, I'll give you an ultimatum. Either you marry me or you give me a date when you're coming back.'

I thought for a minute and said, 'July 8. I'll be back on July 8.'

Then it was time for the pleasure. We had fought and made up and it was time for the *sanug*. That's the order in which we do it in our culture. So we went down to the beach with Ivan and sat at the water's edge. By then it was dark and gentle waves were lapping as party sounds drifted in the distance. We were the only ones down on the beach, under the stars, and it was almost too much, too beautiful to bear. Ivan lit the Thai stick and passed it down.

I took three deep tokes and as I held the smoke in, this over-whelming wave of anxiety came over me. I closed my eyes and saw this pile of black and brown shit steaming on the edge of a stainless steel counter. The shit was cold and yet it was steaming, and I somehow knew that it represented all of the negative energy in my mind. I could see a string extending from between my eyes to the shit and I knew that if I pulled that string with my head I could pull all that shit right off the edge of that stainless steel counter. I started to pull and as I was pulling I could see that next to the shit was this pile of bubbly pastel energy floating about two inches off the stainless steel counter. I saw that this pastel energy was connected to the shit through these tendrils that ranged from pastel to shit-brown. It was then I realized that if I pulled the negative energy off the counter I would pull the positive off with it, and I'd be left with nothing but a stainless steel counter, which I was not yet ready for in my life. And at the moment I realized that, the counter turned into a tunnel I was going down at the speed of the Santa Cruz roller coaster. But the tunnel was not black this time so I knew I was getting healthier. It was gold-leaf, and the leaves were spreading like palm leaves or like the iris of a big eye as I picked up speed and headed for the center of the Earth, until I was going so fast that I couldn't stand it anymore and I pulled back, opened my eyes, grabbed the beach and let out a great WHOOOA . . .

When I opened my eyes Ivan was there but Renée was gone. She must have wandered off down the beach. I had no real sense of where I was. It all looked and felt like a demented Wallace Stevens poem with food poisoning, and in the distance I saw what looked like a group of Thai girl scouts dancing around a campfire. I thought that if I could get in that circle and hold hands with them I would be whole again. I would be cured and back in real time. I got up and tried to walk toward the fire and found that I was falling down like a Bowery bum, like a drunken teenager or the fraternity brother I'd never been. And all of a sudden I realized I was going to be very sick and I crawled off like a Thai dog to a far corner of the beach.

Up it came, and each time the vomit hit the ground I covered it over with sand, and the sand I covered it with turned into a black gauze death mask that flew up and covered my face. And so it went; vomit-cover-mask, vomit-cover-mask, until I looked down to see that I had built an entire corpse in the sand and it was my corpse. It

was my own decomposing corpse staring back at me, and I could see
the teeth pushing through the rotting lips and the ribs coming
through the decomposing flesh of my side. I looked up to see Renée
standing over me saying, 'What's wrong, Hon?'

'I'm dying, that's what's wrong.'

'Oh. I thought you were having a good time building sand castles.'
She had been looking on at a distance.

Two men, I don't know who, carried me out of there, one arm
over one shoulder and one arm over another, like a drunken, cruci-
fied sailor. And I was very upset because the following day I was
scheduled to do my big scene in the movie.

In February of '83 I met this incredible British documentary film-
maker, Roland Joffe. He was very intense – a combination of Zorro,
Jesus and Rasputin – body of Zorro, heart of Jesus and eyes of
Rasputin. Roland had come to New York to cast a new film called
The Killing Fields, produced by David Puttnam, and I was called in
for an audition. Peter Wollen had seen one of my monologues and
told Susie Figgis, who was helping cast the film, about me and she
had set up an audition with Roland.

It was unlike any audition I'd ever been to before. Roland didn't
have me read; he didn't even ask me any questions. He did all of the
talking while I listened, and he talked and talked. He talked for about
forty minutes nonstop. Roland told me the story of *The Killing
Fields*.

It was the story of a *New York Times* reporter named Sidney
Schanberg and his sidekick, Dith Pran, who was a Cambodian
photographer. It was about how they covered and reported the story
of the Americans' secret bombing of Cambodia, and how Schanberg
and Pran stayed behind in Phnom Penh after the American embassy
was evacuated because they wanted to cover what happened when
the Khmer Rouge marched in. They wanted to find out if there was
going to be a 'bloodbath' or not, so they fled to the French embassy
to hide out, and when the Khmer Rouge marched into the city they
went directly to the French embassy and demanded, 'All Cambodians out or everyone dies.' So Dith Pran had to be expelled to
almost certain death because the Khmer Rouge were killing any
Cambodian who was connected with Americans. Pran was given up
for dead by most, but Schanberg never gave up hope and kept
searching until, after three years, he located Pran in a Thai refugee

camp. He brought him to New York City where Pran now works for *The New York Times*.

'Great story,' I said. 'Sounds fantastic. Sounds like someone made it up. I want to tell you that I would love to play any role in this film, just to be in it. But I must also confess that I know nothing about what you've told me. I'm not very political – in fact, I've never even voted in my life.'

And Roland said, 'Perfect! We're looking for the American ambassador's aide.'

He went on, 'But I'm not saying you have the role. I have a lot of other people to see and I have to see how it all shapes up and fits together with casting. I'm going out to the Coast to see some people and I'll be back in a couple of months. Let's chat again then.'

I said goodbye and left, and as I went out of the room I thought, I really want to be in that film. In fact, I want to be in that film more than any project I've ever been approached for. At the same time, I had no idea what I could actively do to get the role. That was a large part of why I had stopped trying to be a professional actor in the first place; I couldn't stand all the waiting while that big, indifferent machine made up its so-called mind. I wanted power and influence over the events of my life.

I couldn't stand leaving it all to chance, and the first idea that occurred to me was *prayer*. But I thought, it's been so long, God would know I was in bad faith.

The next thing that occurred to me was *contacts*. Well, no, maybe *contacts* was first and *prayer* was second . . . But anyway, I didn't have any contacts within the British film industry. So the next voice that came to me was that old logical, coping voice we all know so well: 'Well, if I get it, I get it. If I don't, I don't. I'll do something else. After all, I can still *see* and *walk*.' And my mother had always said, 'Think of the starving Koreans.' I was trying to do that.

But my illogical, preconscious voice would have none of this, and set up a condition I would have to call Compulsive Magical Thinking, which soon got quite out of control.

It all started innocently enough in my living loft. I found that I was unable to leave my loft without turning my little KLH radio off on a positive word. And do you know how difficult those words are to find these days? I would just stand there by the radio with my hand on the little knob so I could turn it off real fast when I heard the positive word.

'The stock market is *rising*.' (click)

' . . . consider moving Marines to *safer* . . . ' (click)

'You may go to a doctor that belongs to the AMA but it doesn't necessarily mean you're going to the *best*.' (click)

And then I could leave my loft. And as I went out I found that I would turn the doorknob three times. Threes became very important, as did right shoe in front of left shoe. I always made sure that I put my right shoe ahead of my left shoe when I left them by the bed. I led with my right foot as I started up the street, snapping my fingers three times, then in sets of three, then three fingers in sets of six, as I walked up to the supermarket to buy soup, where every third can was fine. The first two had botulism.

Then I went on to Barnes & Noble, snapping all the way, in search of books on Cambodia. When I got there I went to the piles of books in the Annex and, pulling out every third book, I whispered to myself, 'Now this has power.'

Then I turned and saw a man behind me fleeing from stack to stack. I knew he didn't work for Barnes & Noble because of his overcoat and the wads of newspaper stuck in his ears and I thought, this is one of the therapeutic joys of living in New York City. It always works. As soon as you think you're crazy, all you have to do is look over your shoulder.

It wasn't long before these little compulsions got more elaborate and the condition more complex. I was walking down the street and I saw a man coming toward me and I thought, I've got to keep this lamppost on my right and the man on my left and have us all line up perpendicular just at the end of the third snap in a series of six finger snaps. Then I thought, wait a minute, lamppost on right or man on right? Which is more important, man or lamppost? And, wham. I ran into the man.

It was then that I realized it was getting out of hand. I thought, I'd better slow down with this stuff or I'll get put away before I even get the role in the movie. I guess it was then that the 'Little King' took over. The superego figure took charge and set up an alternative condition that was very new for me. I'd have to call it a Will. And the Little King superego figure proclaimed that if I willed my Will to stop this Magical Thinking then this act of will, willing Will, would have more power toward getting me the role in the film.

*

Around the time I was developing my Will I was invited out to Los Angeles to perform my monologues. I got good reviews so Warner Brothers Television called me up and said, 'Could you come in and read? Anything, just come in and read.'

'Come up and see my monologue, why don't you? It's just up the street.'

'Well, we haven't got time for that, we go to bed early out here. But could you come in?'

And what they chose for me to read was a sitcom – a pilot that had been 'axed' or 'cut' or whatever the technical term is for a show that's been put on the shelf because it's no good. So that was the text.

I was to be reading the role of Howard and my wife was Harriet. I started out, 'But I don't want to spend my Sundays eating mixed nuts in the company of your sister and her jerky husband.'

Harriet answered, 'Oh come on. You know you really like Norman.'

'Harriet, the idea of Norman doesn't put a smile on any part of my body.'

'Get ready. Put your shoes on.'

'Why? They know I have feet.'

'Come on, you know it's become a tradition to have them over on Sundays.'

'Tradition? Now listen Harriet. Decorating a Christmas tree is a tradition. Fireworks on the Fourth is a tradition. But having your sister and her jerky husband over here to park their carcasses on my couch, watch my TV and scarf down all the cashews from the mixed-nut bowl is not my idea of a tradition!'

I didn't get the role. I think I read it with too much of an edge, actually. Too East Coast intellectual. So I was on my way out and – the Lord works in strange ways – lo and behold, I ran into Roland Joffe, who was there casting *The Killing Fields*. Warner Brothers was putting money into the film and they were going to distribute it, so they were letting him use an office. Roland said, 'Let's chat again.'

I went home and put on my white shirt and my pink tie and my tweed jacket and went back to the studio. Once again Roland talked to me, this time for forty-five minutes. He did all the talking again, about what an incredible country Cambodia was before it was colonized, that it had a strain of Buddhism so permissive and so sensual that the Cambodians seemed to have done away with unnecessary guilt. Compared to Cambodia, Thailand was a Nordic country – Thailand was like Sweden compared to Cambodia, which was more like Italy. Ninety percent of the Cambodians owned their land – it was dirty land, it was earth, but it was clean. Earth dirt. Clean dirt. And they were so happy.

The Cambodians knew how to have fun. They knew how to have a good time being born; how to have a good time growing up; a good time going through puberty; a good time falling in love and staying in love; a good time getting married and having children; a good time raising children; and a good time growing old and dying. They even knew how to have a good time on New Year's Eve. I couldn't believe it.

The only thing, according to Roland, was that they had lost touch with evil. Because it was such a beautiful, gentle land, they'd lost touch with evil. The situation was something like that of the Tantric colonies on the East Coast of India. They were so open down there that the Huns just came in and ate them up like chocolate-covered cherries. And the same thing was happening to the Cambodians.

The Samoans, on the other hand, have a very pleasurable culture but they've made sure to initiate their children into pain through certain tattoo rituals, so that they have a realistic association with pain.

I couldn't get a clear vision of Cambodia in my mind. I had a map in my head, but I couldn't quite place it among the other countries – so I looked at a map and there it was, about the size of the state of Missouri. In 1965 there were about seven million people in the entire country, six hundred thousand in the capital of Phnom Penh. There's a big freshwater lake right in the middle for all sorts of recreational activities, fishing along the coast, seaports along the Gulf of Siam. And in 1966 that happy, sexy Prince Sihanouk – perhaps because of his Buddhist tolerance and open-mindedness – allowed the Vietnamese a few 'sanctuaries' along the border.

The American Air Force got very upset about this, one general in particular, who was sure that there was a Central Headquarters up there about the size of the Pentagon from which the Vietnamese sent out orders. Maybe it was even a replica of the Pentagon – I think the Air Force thought that.

And if they could just bump off that Central Headquarters by flying in a few B-52s from Bangkok . . . they wouldn't even have to tell the American public about it. 'Who needs to know about it? We can do it in one raid and we'd be done with that Central Head-quarters.' So the general called a secret meeting at the Pentagon, named, of course, Operation Breakfast. At Operation Breakfast they came up with *the menu*.

It was kind of a weird diet, as you can imagine. The bombers came up from Bangkok like big flying motels, dropping their bombs according to some computer program on all the sanctuaries, then up to where they thought the headquarters might be and all along the Ho Chi Minh supply line.

But instead of driving the Vietcong back, Operation Breakfast had the opposite effect. It drove them further into the Cambodian jungles where they hitched up with this weird bunch of rednecks called the Khmer Rouge, run by Pol Pot along with Khieu Samphan and Ieng Sary. They had been educated in Paris in the strict Maoist doctrine, except someone threw a perverse little bit of Rousseau into the soup.

This made for a strange bunch of bandits, hanging out in the jungle living on bark, bugs, leaves and lizards, being trained by the Viet-cong. They had a back-to-the-land, racist consciousness beyond anything Hitler had ever dreamed of. But they had no scapegoat other than the city-dwellers of Phnom Penh. They were like a hundred thousand rednecks rallying in New Paltz, New York, ninety miles above the City, about to march in.

Now, around the time that the VC were up there training the Khmer Rouge, Sihanouk – who was out of town for a day – was deposed, maybe by a CIA plot. No one really knows about that. And Lon Nol was put in his place, General Lon Nol, formerly Prince Sihanouk's prime minister. No one knew anything about Lon Nol in the United States. As one political cartoonist noted at the time, the only thing we knew was that 'Lon Nol' spelled backwards was 'Lon Nol'.

Well, leave it to a Brit to tell you your own history; the next thing that Roland told me was that, at that time, President Nixon was developing this madman theory on the banks of Key Biscayne. He said to Bob Haldeman, 'Listen Bob, just let it be known that I've gone mad, see, and then the Vietcong will think that I'm going to press the button – you know how trigger-happy I am – and they'll stop all of their bombing.'

In order to develop this madman theory he was watching reruns of

Patton in his bedroom every night, over and over again, and taking military advice from Bebe Rebozo and John Mitchell.

The incident at Kent State happened around then as well, as Roland reminded me. He suggested I read up on it in a book called *Sideshow*, by William Shawcross, which I did, later. I remembered Kent State but I had just lumped it in with the Vietnam protest; I'd forgotten that it was a direct protest against the invasion of Cambodia. I also didn't know that most US National Guard troops were not allowed to have live ammunition in their guns, but in Ohio they were. Governor James Rhodes had called them out because the protesters were storming Kent's ROTC building, and on a lovely May day fifteen people were shot, four innocent bystanders were killed. Roland told me that the American public was polled on its reaction to the incident and the majority of people said that the shooting was justified. This caused enormous dissension and one hundred thousand protesters marched on the White House. Haig massed troops in the basement of the White House thinking there was going to be a siege. According to Shawcross, Nixon got no sleep at all; he was up the entire night making phone calls. He made fifty calls, eight to Kissinger, seven to Haldeman, one to Norman Vincent Peale, one to Billy Graham. After one hour of sleep he got up and put on Rachmaninoff's Concerto No. 1 and, with his Cuban valet Manolo Sanchez, he went down to the Lincoln Memorial to talk to the protesters about surfing, football, how travel broadens the mind. In fact, Roland reports that one of the students said, 'I hope it was because our President was tired, but when he asked me what college I was from and I told him, he said, 'How's your team doing this year?'

Now colleagues and friends – actually, I don't know if he had any *friends* – but colleagues of Kissinger wanted him to resign. And Kissinger said, 'What if I resign and then the President has a heart attack? We'll be left with Agnew. That's the only reason I'm staying on. For national security.'

Because of all this, the Cooper-Church Amendment went through. This was an amendment meant to stop any ground support troops from going into a country where war had not officially been declared by the Senate or Congress. But, as Roland reminded me, we're not living in a democracy. I had forgotten all about this: the President is the Commander-in-Chief of the Army and can simply bypass Senate and Congress. Which is just what he did. Nixon kept saying, 'Bomb,

bomb, bomb,' and the bombs kept falling.

The only thing that the protest accomplished was to frighten Nixon enough that he declared, 'No more close ground support troops more than twenty-one miles over the border into Cambodia.' How they controlled that, I don't know, whether the troops had odometers strapped to their legs or what. But twenty-one miles in they had to go right back out, or turn into pumpkins.

During this time they sent Alexander Haig over to speak to Lon Nol because Lon Nol had been told that the American troops weren't going to be in Cambodia anymore. Lon Nol, of course, saw in this the downfall of his country. It was very clear; the handwriting was on the wall. He turned to the window and wept.

And Haig went back and reported this to the American government, that Lon Nol had cried in front of him. The American government was so upset that they sent over an official psychiatrist to examine Lon Nol for crying in public. He came back and reported that Lon Nol was an unstructured, vague individual. Not only that, but that he made astrological, occultist and folkloric references in his addresses to the nation. Can you imagine? 'My fellow Americans, I am not going out for the next two weeks because my moon is in Gemini.'

This freaked the Americans out, so they compiled a whole report on Lon Nol in which they detailed his weird rituals. One was to cut the skin of the troops to let in the spirit of Buddha. Another was to create the illusion that there were more troops than actually existed. (I don't know how they were supposed to have done this – with scarecrows or what – but it caused enormous extortion of American funds.) The third ritual was called 'transference of grass into troops'. I'm not sure what this means; I assume they were sending marijuana to the front, but I don't know why they would refer to marijuana as 'grass' in a government report. Fourth, they faced all statues of Buddha in toward Phnom Penh and away from China in order to revitalize the city. Number five, the Cambodians debated but never settled on. The question was whether they should copy the old Khmer warriors' magical markings from the uniforms in their museums onto the soldiers' outfits. The markings had been meant to stop slings and arrows in the old days, but no one was sure they would be powerful enough to stop bullets. It was still in debate.

While that was being argued, according to Roland, the unsung hero, Donald Dawson, reared his ugly head. He was a Christian

Scientist flying B-52 raids out of Bangkok, but he was home on leave. He was watching *West Side Story* on television but all he could see were bombs falling, people screaming, dying – he was hallucinating. When he got back to flying his missions he found out that a Cambodian wedding party had been wiped out by accident. He held his own wedding to be the most sacred event in his life and he refused to fly anymore, so he was court-martialed.

Dawson got together with three other flyers who refused to fly and, with the help of New York congress-woman Elizabeth Holtzman and the ACLU, they began building a case to be taken to the Supreme Court. The Supreme Court had never dealt with the illegality of this bombing that had been going on for years, but it just so happened that at that time they weren't in session. The ACLU got the case to Thurgood Marshall, who was sympathetic. They then had to get it to William Douglas, who was in Goose Prairie, Washington, in a cabin in the hills, with no telephone. There didn't seem to be any way to reach him. But Burt Neuborn of the ACLU flew out to Goose Prairie, hiked in to the cabin, presented the case and Douglas was sympathetic as well.

The Supreme Court was about to meet and vote on the bombing when Donald Dawson received Conscientious Objector status from the US Air Force, so they never met; the whole five years the bombing went on, the Supreme Court never met about it. And the generals still note with pride that the bombing killed twenty-five percent of the enemy. That's sixteen thousand killed, they say. And there's a military rule: if you kill more than ten percent of the enemy you cause irreversible psychological damage.

So that five years of bombing – along with the traditional diet of lizards, bugs, bark and leaves, education in the Maoist doctrine including a touch of Rousseau, and other things that we will never know about in our lifetimes including, perhaps, an invisible cloud of evil that circles the world and lands at random in Germany, Cambodia, possibly Iran and Beirut, maybe even America – set the Khmer Rouge up to carry out the worst auto-homeo-genocide in modern history.

Whenever I travel, if I have the time, I go by train. Because I like to hang out in the lounge car. I hear such great stories there – fantastic! Perhaps it's because they think they'll never see me again. It's like a big, rolling confessional.

I was on my way to Chicago from New York City when this guy came up to me and said, 'Hi, I'm Jack Daniels. Mind if I sit down?'

'No, I'm Spalding Gray, have a seat. What's up Jack?'

'Oh, nothing much. I'm in the Navy.'

'Really? Where are you stationed?'

'Guantanamo Bay.'

'Where's that?'

'Cuba.'

'Really? What's it like?'

'Oh, we don't get into Cuba, man. It's totally illegal. We go down to the Virgin Islands whenever we want R & R. We get free flights down there.'

'What do you do there?'

'Get laid.'

'Go to whores?'

'No. I never paid for sex in my life. I get picked up by couples. I like to swing, I mean, I'm into that, you know? Threesomes, triangles, pyramids – there's power in that.'

And I could see how he would be picked up. He was cute enough – insidious, but still cute. The only kind of demented thing about him was that his ears hadn't grown. They were like those little pasta shells. It was as if his body had grown but his ears hadn't caught up yet.

So I said, 'Where are you off to?'

'Pittsburgh.'

'Pittsburgh, my God. What's up there?'

'My wife.'

'Really? How long has it been since you saw her?'

'Oh, about a year.'

'I bet she's been doing some swinging herself.'

'No, man, I know her. She's got fucking cobwebs growing between her legs. I wouldn't mind watching her get fucked by a guy once, no, I wouldn't mind that at all.'

'Well that's quite a trip, coming from Cuba to Pittsburgh.'

'No, no. I'm not stationed in Cuba anymore, man. I'm in Philly.'

'Oh, well what's going on in Philly?'

'Can't tell you. No way. Top secret.'

'Oh, come on, Jack. Top secret in Philadelphia? You can tell me.'

'No way.'

And he proceeded to have five more rum cokes and tell me that in

Philadelphia he is on a battleship in a waterproof chamber, chained one arm to the wall for five hours a day, next to a green button, with earphones on. I could just see those little ears waiting for orders to fire his rockets from their waterproof silos onto the Russians. He sits there waiting with those earphones on, high on blue-flake cocaine, a new breed from Peru that he loves, with a lot of coffee because the Navy can't test for cocaine. They can test for marijuana five days after you smoke a joint, but not the cocaine. He sits there high on cocaine, chained to the wall, next to the green button, in a waterproof chamber.

'Why waterproof?' I asked. I thought I'd just start with the details and work out. I know I could have said, 'Why a green button?' but it didn't matter at that point.

'Waterproof, man, because when the ship sinks and I go down to the bottom of the ocean, any ocean, anywhere, I'm still there in my waterproof chamber and I can push that green button, activate my rocket and it fires out of the waterproof silo and up, up, up it goes. I get a fucking erection every time I think of firing a rocket on those Russians. We're going to win! We're going to win this fucking war. I like the Navy, though. I fucking *like* the Navy. I get to travel everywhere. I've been to Africa, Sweden, India. I fucking didn't like Africa, though. I don't know why, but black women just don't turn me on.'

Now here's a guy, if the women in the country don't turn him on, he misses the entire landscape. It's just one big fuzzball, a big black outline and he steps through to the other side of the world and comes out in Sweden.

'I fucking love Sweden, man. You get to see real Russkies in Sweden. They're marched in at gunpoint and they're only allowed two beers. We're drinking all the fucking beer we want. We're drunk on our asses, saying, "Hey, Russkies, what's it like in Moscow this time of year?" And then we pay a couple of Swedish whores to go over and put their heads in the Russkies' laps. You should see those fuckers sweat, man. They are so stupid. We're going to win. We're going to win the fuckin' war. I mean, they are really *dumb*. They've got liquid fuel in their rockets, they're rusty and they're going to sputter, they're going to pop, they're going to land in our cornfields.'

'Wait a minute, Jack. Cornfields? I mean, haven't you read the literature? It's bad enough if they land in the cornfields. We're all doomed.'

'No, they're stupid. You won't believe this. The Russians don't even have electro-intercoms in their ships. They still speak through tubes!'

Suddenly I had this enormous fondness for the Russian Navy. The whole of Mother Russia. The thought of these men speaking, like innocent children, through empty toilet paper rolls, where you could still hear compassion, doubt, envy, brotherly love, ambivalence, all those human tones coming through the tube.

Jack was very patriotic. I thought it only existed on the covers of *Newsweek* and *Time*. But no, if you take the train from New York to Chicago, there it is against a pumpkin-orange sunset, Three Mile Island. Jack stood up and saluted those three big towers, then sat back down.

Meanwhile I was trying to make a mild stand. I was trying to talk him out of his ideas. I don't know what my platform was – I mean, he was standing for all of America and I was just concerned for myself at that point. I really felt as if I were looking my death in the face. I'm not making up any of these stories, I'm really not. And if *he* was making up the story he was telling me, I figure he's white, and if he wants it bad enough and he's in the Navy, if he wasn't down in that waterproof chamber then, he must be down there now.

'Jack, Jack,' I said, 'you don't want to do it. Remember what happened to the guy who dropped the bomb on Hiroshima? He went crazy!'

'That asshole? He was not properly brainwashed. I,' he said with great pride, 'have been properly brainwashed. Also there is the nuclear destruct club. Do you think I'm the only one who's going to be pressing that green button? There's a whole bunch of us going to do it.'

'Wait, wait, wait. You, all of you, don't want to die, do you? You're going to die if you push that button. Think of all you have to live for.' I had to think hard about this one. 'The blue-flake cocaine, for instance. Getting picked up by couples. The Swedish whores. Blowing away the cobwebs between your wife's legs. I mean, really.'

'No, I'm not going to die. We get "pubs".'

Everything was abbreviated, and 'pubs' meant Navy publications that tell them where to go to avoid radiation. And I could see him down there, after the rest of us have all been vaporized. He'll be down there in Tasmania or New Zealand starting this new red-faced, pea-brained, small-eared humanoid race. And I thought, the Mother needs a rest, Mother Earth needs a long, long rest.

If we're lucky he'll end up in Africa.

Anyway, he was beginning to realize that I wasn't totally on his side. It was hard to see that because I didn't have as detailed a platform as he had. Finally, he turned to me and said, 'Listen Mr Spalding,' (I think by then he was calling me Gary Spalding) 'you would not be doing that thing you do, writing, talking, whatever it is you do in the theater, if it were not for me and the United States Navy stopping the Russians from taking over the world.'

And I thought, wait a minute, maybe he's right. Maybe the Russians *are* trying to take over the world. Maybe *I'm* the one who's brainwashed. Maybe I've been hanging out with liberals too long. I mean, after all this time I thought I was a conscientious pacifist but maybe I've been deluding myself. Maybe I'm just a passive-aggressive unconscious coward, and like any good liberal, I should question everything. For instance, when did I last make a stand, any kind of stand, about anything? When did I just stand up for something right? Let alone America. What is America? Every time I try to think of America as a unit I get anxious. I think that's part of the reason I moved to Manhattan; I wanted to live on 'an island off the coast of America'. I wanted to live somewhere between America and Europe, a piece of land with very defined boundaries and only eight million people.

So I had no concept of America or of making a stand. I hated contact sports when I was a kid – I really didn't like the bumps. When I moved to New York City I wanted to be able to make a stand, so I took karate. But I had that horrid feeling of bone bouncing on bone whenever I hit my instructor or he hit me.

When I was in the seventh grade I fell in love with Judy Dorci. Butchy Coca was in love with her too. He lived on the other side of the tracks. He had a black leather motorcyle jacket and I had a camel's hair coat. I was careful never to go into his territory – I stayed in mine, Barrington, Rhode Island – but they didn't have a five-and-dime in Barrington and I had to buy Christmas presents. I went over to Warren, Rhode Island, Butchy's territory, to the five-and-dime, and one of Butchy's gang saw me – put the finger on me. I stepped outside and there they were, eight of them, like in *High Noon*, one foot up against the brick wall, smoking Chesterfield Regulars. I thought, this is it. I'm going to know what it's like to make a stand – but why rush it?

I ducked into the Warren Gazette just to look at Christmas cards, take my time, and there was Mr Walker from Barrington. I said, 'Hi, Mr Walker, are you going my way?'

'I am. My car is out back. Do you mind going out the back door?'

'Nope. Let's go.'

When I arrived in London for the first time, I was jetlagging and I had to rent a car to go up to Edinburgh so I felt a little out of it. All right, I was driving on the wrong side of the road – easily done – you know, no big deal. I cut a guy off first thing, and when I rolled down the window to apologize, he said, 'Take off those glasses, mate, I'm going to punch you out.' Just like a British redcoat announcing his intentions ahead of time.

I just rolled up the window. Why rush it?

Last year I cut a man off on Hudson Street in Manhattan. I cut off a man from New Jersey, which is one of the worst things you can do. A man from New Jersey! And I rolled down the window – why I do this, I don't know – to apologize again. This time I saw the fist coming toward me and I thought, now I'll know what it's like to have my jaw broken in five places. At the last minute, just seconds before making contact with my face, he pulled the punch and hit the side of the van instead. He walked off with his knuckles bleeding, cursing. I rolled up the window and pulled out. Why rush it?

I had a friend who wanted to rush it, because he was going into the Army and he'd never been punched out. So he went to his friend Paul and said, 'Paul, I've never been punched out. But I'm drafted, I'm going into the Army. Please punch me out Paul, quick.' And Paul knocked him out.

I didn't want to go into the Army. I didn't want to get punched out. So I checked all the boxes. I admit it. I did it. I checked 'homosexual' and 'has trouble sleeping'. Where it asked 'What do you do when you can't sleep?' I put that I drank.

My mother was at home at the time having an incurable nervous breakdown and I was studying acting. I thought that if worse came to worse I would just act the way she was acting and I'd get out of the

Army. But there was a guy in front of me who looked very much like me; we both had beards. They touched him first, on the shoulder, and he just went bananas. He flipped out and they took him away screaming.

Now how was I going to follow that? I was depressed on two counts. One, it looked like I was going to be drafted, and two, it looked like I was a bad actor.

Recently in Manhattan, I was up early on a Sunday for some reason. It's rare. If you're up early in New York City on a Sunday, there's a strange overlap between those who are up early and those who haven't gone to bed yet. I was down in the Canal Street subway station – concrete no man's land. There were no subways coming, no law and order down there. There was just this one other guy and he was coming toward me. I knew he wanted something – I could feel the vibes. He needed something from me, wanted something. He was about to demand something.

'Hey man, you got change for a quarter?'

'Uh, yeah, I think I do. Here – wait a minute, I got two dimes here and one, two, three, four pennies. How's that?'

'Nope.'

'Well, what are we going to do?'

'I got a quarter and a nickel. Got three dimes?'

'Yep, I do. Here.' And I counted them out carefully in his hand.

He turned, walked away, then turned back to me and said, 'You only gave me two dimes, man.'

'Wait a minute. I'm very careful about money matters.'

Now, was this where I was going to make my stand?

'Very well. If you feel you need another dime, here.'

Renée has this upstairs neighbor who is a member of the Art Mafia. She has her own gallery in SoHo, along with a drinking problem, and she is unbearable. She plays her quadrophonic machine at all hours, full blast, Bob Dylan's 'Sarah', over and over again. Something must have happened to her way back when that song was popular and she can't get it out of her head. She comes in drunk, puts it on at 1:30 in the morning. Now if it was 1:30 every morning, it would be great. It would be like feeding time, you know. You could get through it. You'd get used to it. But it's 1:35 or it's 2:10 or it's 4:14, You call the police but it does no good. She turns it down, they leave, she turns it up. You call the police again, they come, she turns it down, they leave, she turns it up. What can you do? You can't go to the landlord – he's Italian Mafia and lives in New Jersey.

I don't know which Mafia I dislike the most. I'm leaning toward liking the Italian Mafia because they are just immoral and still believe in mother and child. But the Art Mafia is immoral and, from what I can tell, they've stopped procreating.

So we're in Renée's apartment and I call up, 'Please stop persecuting us.' And she sends down these young, new artists who have gotten rich and famous in New York, but are now camping out in sleeping bags until they find their niches. And they say, 'Hey man. MAN. You know New York is Party City. That's why we moved here. So we could have parties on weekday nights. If you don't like it, move to the country – OLD MAN.'

I try to practice my Buddhist Tolerance – I am turning all my cheeks to the wall at this point. I mean, really, Buddhist Tolerance in New York is just one big pacifist-escapist rationalization. Renée is not practicing it. She is pacing while steam comes screaming out of her navel.

Now there are some people who say that this woman should be killed. And I find that I'm not saying no. I don't protest it. They are talking about vigilantes.

I don't know the language. I knew the language when I was with my people in Boston in 1962, in whitebread homogeneous Boston, brick-wall Boston. In the old days, when I spoke a common language with my people, they had what was called the 'hi-fi'. And when the hi-fi was too loud, all I had to do was call up and say, 'Hi, Puffy. Spuddy Gray, down here. Yeah. You guessed it. The hi-fi is a little loud. Yeah. I wouldn't say anything but I've got an early dance class in the morning. Great. Thanks a lot. Yeah, Merry Christmas to you too, Puff.' Down it would go. You see I knew the language.

Now Renée knows the language because her father was in the Jewish Mafia. So she calls up, 'Bet you want to die, right? Bitch! Bitch! Cunt! I'll beat your fucking face in with a baseball bat. Bitch!' And she slams down the phone. The music gets louder.

One day I was walking out the door carrying an empty bottle of Molson Golden. I guess I was going to get my nickel back. And I heard this party noise coming from upstairs and I was seized with gut rage. Maybe I'd had a few drinks and the rage finally made it to my gut. Not that my intellect wasn't still working – it was going like a ticker tape, repeating that old adage, 'All weakness tends to corrupt, and impotence corrupts absolutely'. I just took the bottle and *hurled* it – my arm practically came out of its socket. It went up the flight of stairs, hit the door and exploded like a hand grenade. They charged out with their bats and guns. I ran. Because it was an act of passion, I had forgotten to tell Renée I was going to do it and she was behind me, picking up some plastic garbage bags or something. She was way behind me so when they got to her door they met up with her. But she was innocent and they recognized that. They recognized that she was truly innocent and they didn't kill her. So there's hope.

But I wonder, how do we begin to approach the so-called Cold War (or Now-Heating-Up War) between Russia and America if I can't even begin to resolve the Hot War down on Northmoor and Greenwich in lower Manhattan?

When I was in therapy about two years ago, one day I noticed that I hadn't had any children. And I like children at a distance. I wondered if I'd like them up close. I wondered why I didn't have any. I wondered if it was a mistake, or if I'd done it on purpose, or what. And I noticed that my therapist didn't have any children either. He had pictures of cats on the wall. Framed.

He may have changed since then, but my therapist was the kind who, if you asked him a personal question, would take the entire session to answer. You had to take the responsibility to stop him. You had to learn to be selfish. So I always said that he was like a drinking partner, except we never went drinking and I paid for the drinks.

I asked him, 'Why didn't you ever have any children?'

And he said, 'Well, I was in Auschwitz when I was nineteen and the death marches were moving out as the Russians moved in. And I said to my friend, who was also nineteen, "I think now we have a beneficent Gestapo. Now we must run for it." And my friend said, "No, I am too tired. I must first rest." So I am watching him sleeping and I see blood from the corner of his mouth and I realize he is dead from exhaustion. So I run and escape and I make it to the border of Poland and Germany, and another death march of twenty thousand goes by, not so beneficent this time. They are shooting from horseback, and I surrender.

'They take us to the edge of this great pit and machine gun the whole lot of us. Everyone falls dead except maybe some twelve or fifteen who fall into the snow and live. I am one. I am shot in and around the genitals so it's a kind of automatic vasectomy. Two days later the Russians find me in the snow.'

I said, 'Two days in the snow and you didn't freeze to death?'

'What . . . ,' he answered, 'it was just *snow*.' (And I was the one in therapy?)

'Listen, this is going to sound weird, but I really envy you.'

'What, are you one of those who think suffering ennobles?'

'No, it's not that. We're all born by chance, no one asked to get born, but to be reborn by chance, to live like that, it must have made your life – you know – much more conscious and vital. Things must have changed enormously for you. Also, you don't have to make a decision about whether or not to have kids. It must have changed your life in a very dynamic . . . '

'No. Uh-uh. Nothing changes, no. We thought that, you see. In the first reunions of the camps everyone was swinging, like a big sex club with the swinging and the drinking and the carrying on as though you die tomorrow. Everyone did what he wanted. The next time, not so much, not so much. The couples stayed together. The next time, we were talking about whether or not we could afford a summer home that year. Now when we meet, years later, people talk about whether or not radioactive smoke-detectors are dangerous in suburban homes. Nothing changes.'

So I got the role and I went to Bangkok. The only thing that I knew about Bangkok was that my hero Thomas Merton had died there. Thomas Merton was a hero of mine because he knew how to shut up. It's not that he wanted other people to stop talking, but he figured that people were chatting so much that someone had to keep the silence. He believed in the silence. And he believed in the power of silent prayer, so he became a Trappist. He got interested in Buddhism and the Trappists sent him to Southeast Asia to research Buddhism. He stepped out of a bathtub, touched an electric fan and died instantly. Judith Malina said it was a CIA plot but I don't know. I don't know.

I arrived in this city, 200 years old, 110 degrees, built on a swamp and sinking, and under my door was pushed this letter from Enigma Films – with the 'a' upside down – addressed to Spalding Gray, Esquire. It was my first major film for a British company – they spoiled me rotten. They referred to all of the actors as 'artists'. They can get you to do anything that way.

The letter was dated May 6, 1983 and was from David Puttnam, the producer:

Dear Spalding,

On Sunday we all start to make a very difficult but worthwhile film. It is by far and away the most ambitious that I have ever attempted to produce, and it will, by the time we get through, have thoroughly tested us all. I'm sure that, like me, you constantly get asked what movies you've worked on. I always *hope* that the one I'm presently working on will instantly top the list when answering that question. All too often it doesn't work out that way. However, by nature, by sheer scope and theme, *The Killing Fields* is one of those few movies by which all our careers will undoubtedly be judged.

Roland and I found a speech of President Kennedy's this week in which he said, 'I realize that the pursuit of peace is not as dramatic as the pursuit of war. And frequently the words of the pursuer fall on deaf ears. But we have no more urgent task.' Those words, spoken twenty years ago, have never been more relevant. We have a unique opportunity with this film to make our contribution. In the years to come, it is my honest belief that *The Killing Fields* will be the very first we mention in explaining and justifying the way we spent the best and most difficult years of our lives.

For my part, I'll always be around to help if things go ugly. But in the final analysis all I can do is stand back, support Roland to the hilt and hope that luck and good sense run with us. All the best to all of us. This story deserves to be told and told well. If we pull that off then every form of possible reward will undoubtedly follow, and we will deserve it.

David Puttnam

My first big scene was to be filmed on a soccer field outside of Bangkok. We were reenacting the 1975 evacuation of the American embassy in Phnom Penh. I was with Ira Wheeler, who was playing John Gunther Dean, the last American ambassador to Cambodia.

Ira is an interesting man – he used to be vice president of American Celanese Chemical. After he retired he was singing in a glee club in New York, where someone saw him and put him in Jane Fonda's

Rollover. Now, at sixty-three years old, he was beginning his film career. If you live long enough I find it all comes full circle. Shortly after I arrived in Bangkok I found out that Ira served on the same ship in World War II as my Uncle Tinky. They were on an LST together in the Pacific.

So Ira was playing John Gunther Dean, the last American ambassador. We got to meet Dean because he is now ambassador to Thailand, right there in Bangkok. Ira and I went over to visit him because we wanted to meet a real ambassador. I was very intimidated by this man. I had met politicians but never a *statesman*. And he was a true statesman, a combination of a ship's captain, say, of the Q.E.II, and a boarding school principal, say, of Phillips or Andover Academy. And he said, 'We saw Cambodia as a ship floundering in high seas. We wanted desperately to bring her safely into port. When we saw we were going to lose her, we wanted to leave the ship with dignity, and I cut down the American flag that you see behind me, wrapped it in plastic and carried it over my arm.'

And there we were, Ira running with the American flag wrapped in plastic over his arm. And me, the ambassador's aide, running beside him, heading for a Cadillac limousine parked on the soccer field. We got to the Cadillac limousine, it was 110 degrees, and the first thing that happened was that the air conditioner broke. We had to spend the whole day in this black torture box – it was going to take that long to shoot the scene – and Ira was sweating, he was dripping. It was cooler outside than in, and Ira is the type who sweats like a, like . . . an *Ira*. He sweats so much that he says he beats his opponents at squash because they slip in his puddles.

Wardrobe was changing his shirt while we sat in the limousine and next the electric windows broke, the radiator boiled over and by the end of the day the entire exhaust system and muffler were dragging on the football field. I was laughing – I found the whole thing very funny. Roland Joffe had told us, 'Look like you're on the verge of tears.' Ira, who was studying Stanislavsky acting for the first time and had read *An Actor Prepares* and *Building a Character*, thought that Roland meant 'on the verge of tears' *all day long*, just in case the camera was turned on. So he was doing an emotional memory and he was in a deep funk. You couldn't even approach him.

I was so bored that I began talking to the driver – an extra. He was an expatriate from San Francisco, an elephant expert, who was spending his time counting elephants in the Thai jungle because he thought, 'America is going crazy. Going nuts, going to the dogs. Going to the wow-wows.' He went to Thailand to get his sanity back, and in Thailand he only trusted elephants. So they were all he was interested in. He slept in the bush at night and in the morning he got up, grabbed his elephant counter and just counted elephants.

He had a limp, a game leg – and he knew that if you frighten elephants at night they will charge. They sleep standing up and he was sure, he confided to me, that he was going to be killed within the following two months by a stampeding elephant.

In the middle of this Ira looked up and cried out, 'WILL YOU STOP TALKING ABOUT WHATEVER IT IS YOU'RE TALKING ABOUT? I'm trying to have an emotional memory.'

'Ira, Ira, this guy is about to be killed by an elephant, for *real*. Think on *that*.'

And we were driving through this black smoke, pouring up off of rubber tires, which were burning to make it look like a real war. We headed for a nonexistent Sikorski – I guess because the American Air Force had not given the Thai Air Force any Sikorskis. They just had little choppers. We were supposed to be getting into the Sikorski but we were just pretending it was there. We drove through Marine guards, lots of extras dressed as American Marines – I don't know who those guys were. I think some of them were Marines who didn't get enough of the war so they went back to join up with Bo Gritz, who had a foreign legion going in Laos to look for MIAs. Others were there to deal drugs, which is extremely lucrative but very dangerous in Thailand. And still others were there basically for the sex. Because on one lower Chakra level Bangkok is one big whorehouse. It's not all our fault, or the fault of the troops on R&R, or the Japanese sex tourists. The tradition existed way back before the war, when there were concubines in all the villages. It just got way out of hand during the war. They had hundreds of prostitutes in quonset huts the size of airplane hangars, to service all the soldiers – and for birth control they took Chinese herbal potions. There were a lot of Amerasian children being born.

After the Vietnam war they put all the prostitutes in Pat Pong. If you've been to Bangkok you've probably seen Pat Pong. (There's nothing else to see in Bangkok but the Gold Buddha. You can see the

Gold Buddha during the day and Pat Pong at night.) If you've seen the film *The Deer Hunter*, you've seen Pat Pong; all of the Saigon sequences were shot there, at the Mississippi Queen. The Mississippi Queen is still there, and walking into it is like stepping into that film.

There is no sense of seduction, as in 'across a crowded room'. The whores just fly to you and stick, and they're small enough that your body can carry six at once, two on an elbow, two on a lap, two here, two there, until you feel like a Christmas tree. You just sit there and they go wild. They smile, giggle, reach into your pockets, and if you can make up your mind which one you're in love with by one o'clock, which is closing time, you can go home with her. Or, if you have enough money, you can go home with all of them. Each one costs 500 Thai *bhat* (about twenty-six dollars) for the entire evening. If you want to buy her out early you can pay another 300 *bhat* and go home anytime. You can even walk to the hotel to save money.

If you don't want to spend the whole night with a giggly, happy Thai whore driving you nuts, or if you're afraid of the intimacies involved and would rather be in control, you can go instead to a massage parlor. The massage parlors are very much like huge department stores; there are three floors. You go in and there are, maybe, thirty-five women on one floor, behind a one-way glass, all fully clothed under fluorescent lighting, sitting on tiers and wearing numbers. All of them are looking at a focal point just under the partition. You don't know what they're looking at, but it's a TV. They're all watching TV.

So you strut up and down in front of that glass like a little Sultan until at last you think you've found the perrrr-fect body, suppose it's Number Eight. You say to the man, 'Could you call Number Eight for me, please?'

And he calls over a microphone, 'Numbah Eight.'

Number Eight stands up and you can tell by her disgruntled expression that it's not going to be as great as you had thought, because you've interrupted her TV show.

You go down into this small room and for a little bit of money you take off all your clothes and she stays dressed, and you get a mild, tweek-tweek massage; nothing Reichian about it. A mild, tweek-tweek surface massage. And for a little bit more money she takes off all her clothes and gives you another mild, tweek-tweek surface massage, and occasionally you might feel her warm, brown Thai body brush-brush up against yours. A little bit more money and you get a hand job. A little bit more money and you get to fuck her. A little bit more money and you get the supremo-supremo . . . the body-body massage. For the body-body massage she puts you in a tub and she completely soaps you up. She doesn't rinse you. She puts you, slippery, on a waterbed. Then she gets in the tub and soaps herself up so she's slippery too, and she doesn't rinse herself either. And she gets on one side of the room and runs and hops on top of you and goes swiggle-swiggle-swiggle, body-body-body, and you slide together like two very wet bars of soap. For the final facial massage she'll let you put your face between her breasts, she'll part them and then let them go and cry out 'Boobily-oobily!'

After you've been fucked, sucked, had your tubes cleaned, toes cleaned and nose cleaned and you're ready for more, you can go rest and relax at a live show. At a live show the women do everything with their vaginas except have babies. One starts with ping-pong balls and a soda fountain glass: Chung, chung, chung, she catches the ball in the glass. Then another brings out a Coca-Cola bottle, a king-size Coke, which she shakes for a long time, really shakes it hard. She works on it and works on it for a long time until – I don't know how, but she does it – she opens it. I don't know if she has a bottle opener in there, or teeth, but the Coke sprays all over the audience (because it's warm, and she's shaken it). Then she pours the rest of the Coke into her womb, squats and – whoosh – refills the bottle like a Coca-Cola bottling machine.

Then comes the banana. First she shoots a few lame shots, just boring shots like those Russian rockets that are going to sputter and pop and land on our cornfields. One, two, three. Then, for the finale, she aims her vagina down the center aisle like a cannon, loads it with a very ripe banana and – FOOP! – fires it. She almost hit me in the eye, almost hit an Australian housewife in the head. The banana hits the back wall and sticks, then slowly slides down to the floor where it is devoured by an army of giant roaches.

For the last act, out comes a Thai couple to do a live sex show. They do all the *kama sutra* poses – and the Thais are the most beautiful race of people I've ever seen. When you see them coming toward you on a Bangkok street you don't know whether they're men or women; there is such androgyny afoot. And when they get closer to you it doesn't matter. The couple does this live fuck show as if they're dancing. They are so beautiful as they go through their poses and positions. And they end with her completely wrapped around him, belly up, in this incredible contortion. And he's got his dick deep in her to hold her up, as she balances in a classic praying position, watching a rerun of *Poltergeist* on the TV over the bar and waving to her friends. Then it's time to go home.

Now some men have no problems with all of this, men who can admit to a longing for the old Henry Miller days. I know I'm too ambivalent about it to count myself in. In fact, some of the British actors said I was resisting tradition, that the whores were there for me and that I should go to them. That was a rule of the culture. But I was ambivalent about it. I found it very difficult to just leap in and not think about it. But the man who wants to, who knows the power balances he would like, who knows that if the bomb doesn't go off, the sun will go out eventually so therefore he's not concerned with history, who knows that after he dies his history will last maybe twenty minutes at most, who just wants to regress a little bit, that man should go to Thailand for a vacation. But he should be careful because it inflates your estrogen and ego in the worst way, making it difficult to reenter the West. He may end up staying on as a school-teacher – many men do. They get stuck in the Lust Ring. I met them there and they were schoolteachers.

Now one of the American actors in the film was determined not to get stuck in this Lust Ring, and to be loyal to his wife back in the States. He just didn't want to get stuck in a situation of lust, so he worked out his libido by jogging and playing tennis. On the third or fourth day out jogging, he pulled a muscle in his right leg very badly, and in our hotel – which was like a Ramada Inn – he saw a sign for massage. He figured it was on the up and up, as it were. He asked for the 'regular massage'.

Later, he said, 'I went in, my God, they worked on the wrong muscle for an hour! For an hour I got a hand job; where am I going to get my leg fixed in this town?' You see, it's subtle.

We were in the posh lounge of this Ramada Inn-like hotel. The only difference between it and a Ramada Inn was that it had those *King and I* round windows to make it Siamese. There was this woman singing with a Thai combo, '*Killing me softly with his song . . .* ' and we were ordering Kloster beers. '*Killing me softly . . .* ' and rats, posh rats, were running across the wall-to-wall car-peted bar to hide up under the furniture. '*Killing me softly . . .* ' and the Art Department was coming through with Cambodian body

parts, artificial limbs for the film. Skeletons, skulls, legs, bones, then
'*Killing me softly* . . .'

The waitress was on her way over with two beers, slinking and
dancing, three inches off the carpet. And she had a slit up the side of
her skirt so you could see her naked leg flashing through. She came to
deliver the two beers, slid in and knelt at our feet, took the beers off
her tray and put them on the coffee table. It's subtle.

We were out by the pool and this woman came out, May. We called
her Chang Mai May. She said, 'Dear sirs, I can't read this writing.
Can you please read this letter to me?'

It said, 'Dear May: I will be arriving from Saudi Arabia on Friday.
I trust your judgment implicitly. I hope you have a lovely escort
waiting for me in my room. If I like her I will marry her. She must be
prepared to return to Saudi Arabia where she'll spend the next six
months, at which time we'll move to London where she will spend
the rest of her life.'

By the way, marriage is a very simple thing in Thailand. It's a
verbal agreement. It can be done in a telephone booth, a swimming
pool, a bed, on the beach, wherever. But I'm told that when Thai
women marry foreigners and get taken out of the country, they don't
stay very long wherever it is that they're taken. They miss Thailand
and go back.

I am also told that Thai wives are very jealous. If one of them ever
catches her husband with another woman, when he least expects it
she cuts off his cock with a straight-edged razor and feeds it to the
ducks. (When I first heard this I thought it was a joke, but since then
I've heard otherwise.) Thai husbands have gotten so used to this
behavior now that they've learned to run and get the severed penis
out of the duck's throat – before it's swallowed up – and get it to a
new plastic surgical penis transplant wing that Thai hospitals have. In
order to beat this, the Thai wives are now beginning to tie the penises
onto gas balloons and send them up in the backyard.

So there we were, driving through the black smoke and Marine
guards, heading for a Sikorski that didn't exist. We got to where the
Sikorski was supposed to be and, 'Cut.' End of shot.

Five months later, when the filming was over, they located the
Sikorskis – at Camp Pendleton in San Diego. That was the only place
they could find any. So we went down there for one last shoot – it was

incredible. The pyrotechies were running around pulling those same rubber tires, sending up black smoke, but this time the crew had tee-shirts on that read 'SKIP THE DIALOGUE, LET'S BLOW SOMETHING UP.'

So there we were on this Marine base, the actors, these Thai kids who were playing Dith Pran's children who had been flown in from Bangkok for the day, and the Marines, who were very excited. It was the day after the Beirut Massacre and they weren't even talking about Beirut. Their flags weren't even at half-mast. (Actually, I figured out why that was. California American flags are the largest American flags in the world. If they were put at half-mast they'd drag on the ground. California also seems to have the smallest flag poles in relation to the size of the flag.)

The Marines were thrilled to have real actors on the base.

'Craig T. Nelson? *Big Chill*, I know it. Don't say no. I saw you in *The Big Chill*.'

'Tom Bird? *Love Is a Many Splendored Thing*. I'm sure I saw you in that. Don't say no.'

So we weren't saying no. We were milling around, talking about what it was like to be a star, giving autographs, when over the horizon came these three giant birds. These Sikorskis are really big. And the Marines turned as though they'd rehearsed it and, on cue, sang the 'tune' from *Apocalypse Now*, you know, *The Ride of the Valkyries*, 'ba-BA-ba-ba-BAA-ba, ba-BA-ba-ba-BAAA-ba . . .' as the helicopters came in and landed. We got on one of them with the wind blowing and the black smoke, and in the finished film it only lasts about thirty seconds. I got on with Ira Wheeler, but then we had to get right off again because we weren't allowed to take off. Only the Marines who were playing Marines were.

One of the Marine guards who had escorted us onto the helicopter got a Polaroid picture of the scene from Continuity and asked us, 'Would you please sign this picture for me? I want to send it to my folks in North Carolina. Because if I never do anything else in my life, at least I can say I have done this.'

The actual evacuation of Phnom Penh took place on April 12, 1975. Lon Nol had long since fled to Hawaii and there were two million people in the capital instead of the usual six hundred thousand. There was no food. Khmer Rouge rockets were coming in and landing in the streets, on schools, randomly. At six o'clock in the morning John

Gunther Dean put out a letter to all American and Cambodian officials, notifying them that the evacuation was taking place: 'You have two-and-a-half hours to make it here to the embassy and then we're taking off.'

The Prime Minister of Cambodia, Long Boret, said, 'Two-and-a-half hours? How are we going to convince the Russians that we're Socialists in two-and-a-half hours? We're ruined.'

Long Boret, Lon Non and Prince Sirik Matak stayed behind. By the way, Lon Nol had two brothers, Lon Non and Lon Nil. Lon Nil was killed in an early insurrection and they cut out his liver and rushed it to a Chinese restaurant, cooked it up in a wok and fed it to the people in the streets. The Khmers were really big on the powers of the human liver.

Prince Sirik Matak sent a letter to the American ambassador informing him that they were not going to evacuate. It read:

Dear Excellency and Friend,
I thank you very sincerely for your letter and for your offer to transport me toward freedom. I cannot, alas, leave in such a cowardly fashion. As for you, and in particular for your great country, I never believed for a moment that you would have the sentiment of abandoning a people which has chosen liberty. You have refused us your protection and we can do nothing about it. You leave, and it is my wish that you and your country will find happiness under the sky. But mark it well, that if I shall die here on the spot, and in the country that I love, it is too bad because we are all born and must one day die. I have only committed this mistake of believing in you, the Americans. Please accept, Excellency, my dear friend, my faithful and friendly sentiments.

Sirik Matak

Five days later their livers were carried through the streets on sticks.

The Americans thought it would be like Danang during the evacuation, but it wasn't. There was no rioting, there were no people hanging off the helicopter runners like in Vietnam. The Cambodians just waved and called, 'Okay, bye-bye. Okay, bye-bye.' They were still smiling. The last helicopter took off and a Khmer Rouge rocket came in and killed one of the people watching. Five days later, April 17, 1975, it was 'Cambodia Year Zero'.

In marched the Khmer Rouge in their black pajamas and Lon Nol's troops threw down their guns and raced to embrace them, thinking that the country would then be reunited. The Khmer Rouge did not smile back. They took strategic points in the city. Some of the kids, because they had grown up in the jungle and never seen cars before, were jumping into cars, getting stuck in first gear and ramming them into buildings. There was chaos for awhile, but soon order reigned. And the Khmer Rouge said, 'Out. Everyone out of the city. The Americans are going to bomb Phnom Penh. Get out. There's no more food, so out. Who will take care of you? Angka will provide. Angka is out there, so get out of the city. Angka . . . ' like some sort of perverse Wizard of Oz figure, 'Angka . . . ' like some Kafkaesque thundercloud raining down manna to feed the people. They emptied a city of two million people in twenty-four hours.

Those who were in hospitals, who couldn't walk, were just chucked out the window, no matter which storey they were on. Out the window. Survival of the fittest. Then the mass murder began. Eyewitnesses said that everyone who had any kind of education was killed. Any artist, any civil servant was butchered. Anyone wearing glasses was killed. The only hope was to convince them that you were a cab driver, so suddenly there were a thousand more cab drivers than cabs. It was just the opposite of New York, where everyone says, 'I'm an artist, I'm an artist. Sure, I drive a cab to make a living, but I'm really an *artist*.' There if you were an artist, boom, you became dead. Little kids were doing the killing, ten-year-olds, fifteen-year-olds. There was very little ammunition left so they were beating people over the head with ax handles or hoses or whatever they could get hold of. Some of the skulls were too tough for sticks and clubs, and because the kids were weak from eating only bark, bugs, leaves and lizards, they often didn't have the strength to kill. So to make it more fun, they were taking bets on how many whacks it would take to cave in a head.

Some eyewitnesses said that the kids were laughing with a demented glee. And if you pleaded for mercy they laughed harder. If you were a woman pleading for mercy they laughed even harder. And if you didn't die the kids just took your half-dead body and threw it in an American bomb crater, which acted as a perfect grave. It was a kind of hell on earth.

You were killed if you had your own cooking pot. It was better to kill an innocent person, the Khmer Rouge said, than to leave an enemy alive. It was nothing like the methodical, scientific German Genocide. They were tearing apart little children like fresh bread in front of their mothers, gouging out eyes, cutting open pregnant women. And this went on for four years. Two million people were either killed outright or starved to death. And to this day no one knows exactly what happened, what caused this kind of mad auto-genocide to come into being. Oh sure, it's easy to research what happened in Germany because we can speak German, and Hitler's dead or living in Argentina. But Pol Pot is recognized by the United States government. And he's still out there, waiting.

We don't know what happened because the Vietnamese invaded Cambodia in 1979 and *they* say it was a liberation. Others say it was a piece of cake, a xenophobic piece of cake. They invaded in '79 and now they're writing their own revisionist history. We don't know what went on. Maybe a cloud of evil did land and the people simply went mad.

But whatever was going on, Pol Pot is still alive and up there and waiting to return. He's protected by the United States and the United Nations, and the Red Cross brings him food. And he's fighting the Vietnamese up there, the people who originally taught *him* to fight. Roland Joffe said to me, 'My God, Spalding, morality is not a moveable feast.' But I keep seeing it moving, all the time.

My last big scene was with Sam Waterston in Waheen, Gulf of Siam. Not at the Pleasure Prison, where we were sleeping, but at this beautiful Victorian hotel in Waheen that they had emptied out for the film because it looked like the Hotel Phnom Penh. The only thing that made it inauthentic was that it didn't have a swimming pool or a tennis court. So the film built a swimming pool and a tennis court.

Now what I haven't told you is that the American Air Force had what it called 'homing beacons' on the ground. And when the planes flew over, six miles up, they could take a radar coordinate off those homing beacons and then the navigator threw a switch and all the bombs were dropped over the target by computer. So no one really dropped a bomb from six miles up; it was done on automatic. The beacons were everywhere. There was one on the American embassy. There was also one in Neak Luong, and on August 7, 1973, a navigator made a mistake. He threw his switch at the wrong time and dropped an entire load of bombs on this strategic ferry town, Neak Luong. The navigator was fined $700 for the mistake.

Sidney Schanberg told me that he heard about it and went up to cover it for *The New York Times*. But the American embassy had put an absolute press lock on the whole area; no one was allowed in. Sidney bribed his way in, snuck his way in with Dith Pran, and they paid people to get them there. He told me that he reached Neak Luong about two days after the accident, and that all the dead had been removed, but he saw blood and hair all over the bushes and speculated that more than 200 people had been killed. He told me the Cambodians put him under 'polite house arrest', so he couldn't break his story to the *Times*.

During the time he was under guard, the American embassy flew in officials to give out hundred-dollar bills to people who had lost family in the bombing, fifties to people who had lost arms or legs. And the Cambodians were grateful.

Sidney told me that he had the feeling he could just walk out if he wanted to; the Cambodians wouldn't shoot him in front of American embassy officials, he was pretty sure. As he started to walk, he heard the safeties on their guns click and men start screaming, 'Stop.' He said, 'This may sound strange, but I'd never felt more alive in my life than when I was right on the edge of death. I never felt more alive!'

Elizabeth Becker told me the same thing. She was reporting for the *Washington Post* and a colleague of hers was killed by the Khmer Rouge in the house they lived in. She felt remorse for her colleague but also an enormous sense of being alive. She told me about it as we sat on the steps of her Washington house drinking white wine, eating pâté with white bread. And I was listening but I wasn't looking at her. Instead I was watching some black ants crawl across the brick walk to eat his small piece of pâté that had fallen there. And into my frame of vision came Elizabeth's hand, holding a white linen napkin. She just reached down and wiped out the entire trail of ants with one sweep of her hand. I appeared to be listening to her but inside I was weeping, *oh my God, all those ants, all those innocent ants dead for no reason at all.*

Now what I had to say in my scene with Sam was simple – it was a little technical, but simple: 'A computer malfunction put out the wrong set of coordinates. Seems a single B-52 opened up over Neak Luong. There's a homing beacon right in the middle of town. Check it out, Sid.'

All right. Simple enough . . . for some actors. But *this* actor needs images for technical words like that. I have to build my own internal film, you see, or I can't remember the words.

By the way, I played one of those American officials who flew into Neak Luong. We were at an old garbage dump that they had made into Neak Luong, right outside Bangkok. The assistant director said, 'Would the artists please get on the choppers.' Now there is no way I would ordinarily get on a helicopter, but he called me an artist and hop, hop, I was right on that chopper like Pavlov's dog. They said it was only going to go up ten feet and then just land. All they needed was a shot of the embassy officials jumping off the choppers.

So I got on the helicopter and it went BRRRRRRRRR – straight up. Straight up above this incredible jungle. I felt like I was in a movie, like I was in *Apocalypse Now*, and then I realized that I *was* in a movie! They were filming me, and I had no fear, even though the door was wide open and I was looking down. Craig T. Nelson was practically falling out the door – we had no safety belts – but I suddenly had no fear because the camera eroticizes the space! It protects you like Colgate Guard-All. Even if the chopper crashed, at least there would be rushes, right? My friends could show them on New Year's Eve at the Performing Garage.

We went up six times and the feeling was triumphant. I was looking up the Chao Phraya River and I saw, my God, how much area the film controlled! Twenty square miles of Thai jungle, all the way up the river, there were Thai peasants throwing more rubber tires on the fire to make black smoke, to make it look like war, and I thought, of course! WAR THERAPY. Every country should make a major war movie every year. It would put a lot of people to work, help them get their rocks off. And when you land in that jungle you don't have to Method-act. When those helicopter blades are whirring overhead, you shout to be heard. You don't have to Method-act when you look down and see a Thai peasant covered with chicken giblets and fake blood in 110-degree weather for fifteen hours a day for five dollars a day. (If they're real amputees they get seven-fifty.) It's just like the real event!

So, 'a computer malfunctioned.' I had an image of a computer in my mind, spaghetti coming out of it – a malfunction. 'Put out the wrong coordinates . . . ,' for coordinates I had an image of an oscillator from a seventh-grade science project. I don't remember who had one, but it was a grid-work oscillator. 'It seems a single B-52 . . . ,' I remembered B-52s from many drunken dinners in front of the TV during That War. 'Opened up over Neak Luong . . . ,' I was having trouble with Neak Luong. It was a night shoot and I was a little hung over. At times I was calling it Luong Neak. I was a little shaky from that heavy party the night before, and the dose of marijuana and booze. But I didn't feel too bad about it because Roland told me that my character would be drinking a lot because he was very guilty. So I thought, to some extent, I was in character.

You would be amazed at what some people went through to get in character for this film. For instance, John Malkovich seemed to be in character all the time. He was the same on camera as off, and I couldn't figure it out. So I went to him and asked him, 'John, are you one of those actors who are in character all the time?' And he just said, 'No, Spalding, not at all.' I was a little confused but I finally figured out that John Malkovich's character was the kind of character who would say he wasn't in character when he really was.

'Okay, boys and girls, let's go. Take sixty-four.'

It was a night shoot and we were up to take sixty-four. And it was just the first scene of the night. I thought I had it down. 'A computer malfunction put out the wrong set of coordinates. It seems a single B-52 opened up over Neak Luong. There's a . . . ' and I couldn't get the image of the homing beacon. I said, 'There's a *housing device* right in the middle of town.'

'CUT. Okay, let's go back. Keep it together now.'

I don't know why I was feeling under so much pressure. I had already done my worst scene. It was one that was cut from the film, in which 888 Thai marching troops passed in front of what was supposed to be Lon Nol's reviewing stand. They were real Thai army troops playing Cambodians, and when the drummer got to my shoulder I was to be seen leaking information to Sam Waterston. When the drummer got to my shoulder I missed my cue. In 110 degrees, 888 troops had to march all the way back. It took about twenty minutes. Then Sam missed a cue. Then something went wrong with the camera. It took six takes, and by the sixth take, far into the day, I saw these troops coming at me and an insidious voice inside me was whispering, 'You're going to miss it, you're going to miss it, you're going to miss it.' Now who is that voice? And what is that voice? That's all I want to know.

'Okay, boys and girls, let's go. Take sixty-five.'

'A computer malfunction put out the wrong set of coordinates. It seems a single B-52 opened up over Luong . . . over Neak . . . sorry.'

'All right, Spalding. Take sixty-six.'

At last I had the image for homing beacon. I saw a pigeon, a homing pigeon, flying toward a lighthouse beacon in a children's storybook. Got it.

'Let's go. Take sixty-six.'

'A computer malfunction put out the wrong set of coordinates. It seems a single B-52 opened up over Neak Luong. There's a . . . ' and I knew it would work. It didn't matter what I was thinking, so long as I was thinking something. Because everyone looking at the film would be thinking their own thoughts and projecting them on me.

'There's a homing beacon right in the middle of town. Check it out, Sid.'

The entire crew burst into applause. Sixty-six takes later and five hours into the night we had finished the first scene of the evening. And I was told that it would cost $30,000 to process it, including the cost of the film and crew. Then, when I got back to New York, I was called in to redub the entire scene anyway, because of the sound of crickets. So what you hear in the film is my voice in New York City, reacting to some black-and-white footage shot one hot summer night on the Gulf of Siam.

A private car was waiting for us and Renée and I were driven back to the Pleasure Prison. As we rode along I was thinking, 'Why do I feel so inflated, so pumped up, so on edge? I have been here eight weeks and worked only eight days.' I mean, talk about mad dogs and Englishmen, the British were incredible. A sixty-year-old makeup man stood for hours each day in the burning sun, just to press ice packs on our necks so we wouldn't faint, and *I* was complaining? I was feeling ravaged, all spoiled and puffed up. But, oh, how I was going to miss it. How I was going to miss it.

Riding in the car, I said a silent farewell. Farewell to the fantastic breakfasts, the pineapple like I'd never tasted and probably never will taste again. Farewell to the fresh mango and papaya, farewell to the Thai maid and the fresh, clean, cotton sheets on the king-size bed every night. Farewell to the incredible free lunches under the circus tent with fresh meat flown in from America every day. Roast lamb, roast potatoes and green beans at 110 degrees, in accordance with British Equity. Farewell to the cakes and teas and ices at four. Farewell to the Thai driver with the tinted glasses and the Mercedes with the one-way windows. Farewell to the single fresh rose in the glass on my bureau every morning.

And just as I was dozing off in the Pleasure Prison, I had a flash. An inkling. I suddenly thought I knew what it was that killed Marilyn Monroe.

PART TWO

So I told Renée that I would be back by the eighth of July or as soon as I had a Perfect Moment, whichever occurred first.

Now, I thought it would be all right, I thought I would be able to make it back, but . . . all of a sudden I realized I had an open ticket on the airplane, and the last time I had an open ticket was in 1976 when I was in India, and I was almost hospitalized for not being able to make up my mind.

I thought I had grown up since then, I thought I had developed my choice-maker, but the same thing happened again and I thought, now I'm in this part of the world, I'm in Thailand, and how many times will I ever be here again? What should I do? Well, maybe I *should* go to China, was the first thing that came to mind. And I pictured myself hitchhiking through China. Then I thought, no, I'd maybe get stuck on some tour of the cities and it would be hot and it would be crowded – maybe Nepal. I would get up there in the mountains – then I thought, too landlocked, down to Bali, maybe. So I had a kind of China-Nepal-Bali triangle going in my mind, and I would keep taking my ticket to the woman who was in charge of transportation on the film, and I would say, 'Barbara, I think I'm going to be going to China.'

'Well, Spalding,' she'd say, 'I think you've got to go get a visa, and – why don't you just take the ticket? If you have trouble making up your mind, you deal with it. You've come to us enough.'

Around about that time, while I was going through the different triangles, I went to the Art Department video viewing room in the hotel (where we could do all of our homework, see *Cambodia Year Zero* or any other videotapes about Cambodia we wanted to see), and watched a videotape called *Going Back*. It's about four veterans who go back to Hanoi on Christmas of 1981. They had been over originally to kill people, and now they were going back to make friends . . . This was a fascinating tape. Tom Bird was one of the veterans in it, and he was also acting in *The Killing Fields*.

Now, I was really taken by the tape, not so much by the Amerasian children in the streets, although they were beautiful, or the people who were suffering in the hospitals from the effects of Agent Orange, but I was taken by the fact that Hanoi was filled with bicycles. I had never seen a city like it. The only sound to be heard was the sound of wind through bicycle spokes. And I thought, now there's where I'd like to go for my vacation. At least I wouldn't be a tourist there.

And I was beginning to feel more and more like 'The Little Drummer Girl'. I really wanted to be a *real* foreign correspondent, not someone *playing* one.

So I went to Tom Bird and asked, 'What are our chances of going to Vietnam?' And he said, 'We could will it. We could do it! We could do it if we put our minds to it. The best thing, Spalding, is to start off by going down to the Vietnamese embassy.'

Now, I had been to the American embassy and I was very intimidated by it, because the air conditioning was so central that I couldn't tell where the cooling was coming from. There was no draft, it was just like sitting in this big cool glass block with beautiful flame trees outside the window. The Vietnamese embassy was not so modern. It was just down the road, but in contrast to the American embassy it was a lot like a very clean Polish men's room. It was very sparse and very simple – there was no furniture. Well, the only piece of furniture was in the main room and it was this beautiful teak table that we all sat around to talk with the embassy official. This table was exquisite. They must have rescued it from the bombing. On the surface there was a hand-carved, three-dimensional relief of elephants tearing down teak trees with their trunks in order to make the table – so, you see, it was a reflective table – it told a story about itself. In fact, it was doubly reflective, even *reflexive*, because it had a piece of glass over it and every so often I would catch a reflection of myself in the glass. I was wearing a blue cotton Thai peasant outfit from the Thai cottage industries, and the embassy official said, 'They will like you very much in Hanoi with that outfit on.'

The Vietnamese official really listened to us, whereas the American ambassador had kind of pontificated. This Vietnamese official was really curious about what Tom Bird and I wanted to do in Vietnam, and he asked us to write a letter to Hanoi laying out our proposal. He said, 'First, before we begin our talk, could you please tell me – I've heard now that America has Vietnam on "back burner". Could you translate what means this "back burner", hm? Are we burning up?'

Tom, who is very politic, answered, 'No – no. Look at it this way. Now, say you have some rice and you have some coffee. You guys are the rice and Central America is the coffee. And what we're doing is we're talking about putting the rice on the back burner to keep it warm because we want to heat up the coffee on the front.'

'Ah, I see. Well, thank you very much. That explains that.'

Then Tom said, 'Now I would like you to meet America's number one Autobiographic Storyteller, Mr Spalding Gray.'

'Ah. Very pleased to meet you. Have you been on TV?'

I didn't know which way to go with this one. I didn't want to tell him right off that I didn't even *own* a television, particularly since I'd heard that NBC, CBS and ABC were going to be reporting from the streets of Hanoi come spring (providing that they'd agree to leave all their satellite equipment behind for the Vietnamese). And I was sure the Vietnamese wanted the American public at large to know certain things about Vietnam. So I thought, well, maybe I'd better go with it. I said, 'I'm not on TV yet, but I've got it on the back burner, actually.'

The David Letterman Show is interested. Every so often Jerry Mulligan, one of David's reps (and the son of an Irish cop from Cranston, Rhode Island), calls me up to find out how I'm doing: 'David wants to know what's going on with that funny guy behind the table downtown. And he wants to know, Spalding, if you could *say something funny to me over the phone.*'

'What was that?'

'David wants you to *say something funny over the phone to me right now*, so I can tell it to him.'

So I've got it on the back burner.

So, we decided that if it worked out, we would go to Vietnam. And I was able to reassure Renée, through Tom (Tom did it actually).

He just went to Renée and said in his deep, confident, assertive voice, 'Renée, Spalding and I are going to Hanoi together and I will have him back in Krummville by July 8.' And Renée said to me, 'Why can't you talk like that? Take a lesson from Tom. Even if you don't mean it, at least you could say it and put me at ease. I mean, I've got a twenty-four hour flight ahead of me. It would be nice to go home with some sense of when I'll see you again. Write me a letter later but give me a break now, please.'

Renée and I made up and we said a fond farewell outside the gates of the Pleasure Prison. I'd made up my mind to stay with Tom. After all, maybe Thailand would be the right place to have a Perfect Moment. I had heard that the next location was in Phuket, where they had a lot of magic mushrooms, so if I didn't have an *organic* Perfect Moment, I could always induce one. Why not? And I would use Tom Bird as my Magic Will Carpet. I would leave as soon as he left, and we would either go to Vietnam or fly home together. He had a few more scenes in the film but I was finished. I had finished my last big scene of sixty-six takes, and now I was going to hang on until Tom finished his last scene. So I asked if I could travel with the company down to Phuket, which is this beautiful island in the Indian Ocean, off the southern coast of Thailand. They were going to film location shots at a Coca-Cola factory there, where Sidney Schanberg was supposed to have first seen the Khmer Rouge. (Actually, he first saw them at a Pepsi factory on the outskirts of Phnom Penh, but they couldn't find a Pepsi factory in Phuket, so they settled for Coke.)

Transportation told me that I could come along, but that I couldn't have my own driver anymore; I could go on the 'Artists' Bus'.

I got on the bus early in the morning. It was supposed to be a fifteen-hour trip, and we were told that *maybe* we would be stopped by bandits or Thai police. It would be more likely that the Thai army would rob us. The only road to Phuket was a dirt road, a *dirt road* through this jungle.

When I got on the bus I didn't see any Artists, so I wasn't really sure whether I was on the right bus or not. But there was an interesting bunch of people I'd never been with before. Uberto Pasolini of the Pasolini film-and-banking family from Rome: twenty-eight years old and had dropped out of the family business to carry orangeade for the film. He wanted to work his way up from the bottom and eventually become a film producer. He was sitting in the very front seat of this kind of old, '50s Greyhound bus; sitting in the very front seat, looking out, pretending his head was a camera and doing pans with his eyes of this meaningless jungle. He was happy.

Next to him were the Cambodian refugees from Long Beach. They had been hired to come along to be authentic reference points. If there were any questions to be asked about the authenticity of the film's locations, they could be asked. And since Pol Pot had killed all Cambodian actors, they had to play some of the roles, too, although they weren't actors; they weren't trained in any way. They were refugee social workers from Long Beach.

Then there was Neevy Pal, a Cambodian who was related to Prince Sihanouk and a student at Whittier College. Neevy was sitting in front of me and trying to organize all of the Cambodians in the bus because she felt *The Killing Fields* was a neo-colonialist film, that the British were looking right through the Cambodians. They were polite to the Americans and to each other, but they looked right through the Cambodians and treated them like refugees. So she was pissed, and she was trying to organize all the Cambodians into a sort of Consciousness-Raising Group.

Just to my right was this guy who was, I believe, an electrician – a Spark – or one of the cooks, and he was saying, 'Spalding, what are you doing on this bus? Where's your driver? I would complain to British Equity if I were you.' Meanwhile, there was a battle going on over the air conditioner. One minute it was up and the next it was down, and it was cold up front and warm in the back. He kept saying, 'I would complain to British Equity if I were you. Where's your driver, boy? Where's your driver?'

And I said, 'I'll tell you the truth, I'm not in the film anymore—'

'Oh, along for a freebee, are you? Oh, that's good work if you can get it. Well, that's good work then, isn't it?'

So, I was there feeling a little bit like I was in – Vermont, because the air conditioner was on so high. I had my raincoat on and my scarf wrapped around my neck. It was 110 degrees out, monsoon whipping down through those meaningless palms, and about seven hours into the trip we stopped for lunch.

I think it must have been the only restaurant on that entire road to Phuket and by the time we arrived all the actors, who had come in their private cars, had filled up the main dining room so I sat outside with all the Cambodian refugees from Long Beach. I ordered baked fish and just as it arrived a monsoon came up so fast that it just swamped my fish before I could get it under cover. I just left it and ran inside where I tried to order a fish to go.

After the monsoon passed I found myself standing, slightly soggy, by the Artists' Bus and there was Ivan (Devil in My Ear) in the parking lot, and he came up, looking a little Mephistophelean (he had a gray beard, handsome man), and he said, 'Spalding. I'll be damned if I'm going to ride the rest of this next seven hours without being stoned. Will you join me in some Thai stick?'

I said, 'Umm, all right, you know, I'll give it a try, um, since I haven't been drinking or arguing with Renée, all right, I'll do it.'

So we took (puff-puff) just a couple of (puff) tokes and I had this mild paranoia come over me, just *mild*. I said, 'Ivan, by the way, what are you doing on the Artists' Bus? I notice that you're on it, too.'

'I don't know how I got on it,' he said. 'I didn't even know they were calling it the Artists' Bus.'

And I suddenly had a paranoid flash that there was *another* bus that we were supposed to be on, a much better bus, a perfectly air-conditioned Trailways bus gliding over a smooth macadam highway, filled with every kind of artist: Philip Glass, Laurie Anderson, John Lurie, Bill Irwin, Eric Bogosian, David Byrne, *Whoopi Goldberg*.

They were all there – with hookahs – talking interesting talk and lounging on these very comfortable mattresses and – worst of all – they were laughing! But then I just let all that go. I knew that it was just fantasy, just silly-billy paranoia and I thought, come on Spalding, either you're on the bus or you're off the bus. Be Here Now. And I found that I was on the bus and it was the right bus, the only bus and it was timeless, and I could have been in Thailand or Vermont. Inside, because of the air conditioner, it was like Vermont, and I put on my raincoat and wrapped my scarf around my neck and got out my little flask of Irish whiskey. Outside, it was like Thailand. In fact, it was Thailand. It was hot and the monsoon whipped down through meaningless palms like no travel poster I'd seen anywhere and it all looked like a Wallace Stevens poem:

A gold-feathered bird
Sings in the palm, without human meaning,
Without human feeling, a foreign song.

Inside the bus, Ivan had loaned me his stereo Walkman and I was finally catching up with Beethoven's String Quartets in Thailand. And looking out the window, monsoon pouring down, all of a sudden – in some timeless moment in the middle of the trip – we rounded this corner and there it was, this incredible vista of the Indian Ocean. I was totally not expecting it, I didn't expect it so soon or so late or so . . . I just didn't expect it.

It was like an oriental Hudson River School painting. The ocean was crashing in, this great white surf, the largest waves I had ever seen, under great, black monsoon skies, white birds blowing sideways, rainbows arching, palm trees ripping, Oh My God! – almost. About a number nine on my scale of ten for Perfect Moments. Had I been out there in my ocean briefs, I would have had to go home that afternoon.

Shortly after that we arrived at the Phuket Merlin, and it was so tacky, the rattiest hotel we'd been in. It wasn't near the water at all. I came into the hotel – we had been traveling for about fourteen hours – and out came this guy working on the film crew, a Thai, and he had this bucket filled with what looked like a mound of phosphorescent fungus glowing blue. And he said, 'I've got them. I've got them. I've got all the magic mushrooms, all anyone needs.'

Just *blooming* blue, they were *glowing* blue, these incredible magic mushrooms just giving off an aura of blue. I thought, there's no way I will take any substance from a man who smiles so much. He made me paranoid, he was so happy. It should be against the law, all that happiness – it was shocking. I was afraid that if I ate those mushrooms I'd never come back. That I'd end up staying on as a happy schoolteacher in Thailand.

The next day was a day off. I was staying with Tom Bird because I was trying to save all my money. I had $600 in Thai *bhat* saved up and I figured that if I didn't have a Perfect Moment, I would buy one. So I was staying in Tom's room, we were sharing a room, and on our day off some of us went down to what we had heard was Shangri-La – this most incredible beach.

Now I had thought this was just tourist hype. Every time I've traveled to foreign lands, I've always heard that Shangri-La was just around the corner. So we rented a car and we wound down through the water buffalo and the rice paddies and we came out on this *exquisite* beach. Ooh. No tourists. No flotsam. No jetsam. No cans. No plastic bags. Just water buffalo posing like statues in the mist at the far end of the beach. They were just standing there like they were stuffed. They looked like the Thai entry in the Robert Wilson Olympic Arts event. No ships out there in the Indian Ocean, huge surf – perfect Kodachrome day. The sun hadn't quite broken out and it was bright but not too sunny.

In the distance were some thatched huts where you could go have a little brunch and everyone went over there to order their fresh fish and pineapple and beer, and Ivan and I – like two kids – charged right down into the water. I couldn't believe it, it was body temperature, not too warm, just perfect. You could stay in it all day if you wanted to. I was charging in and out. Ivan went right out, right into the big stuff, but I stayed close to shore.

I was a little nervous about sharks. I have a lot of fears, phobias, and sharks and bears are at the top of the list. In fact, I'm the kind of guy who even checks out swimming pools before I go in. I often think some joker has put a shark in the pool as a practical joke. Also, I still had all my money tucked in my ocean briefs and I couldn't think of a good place to stash it. So I asked Ivan where I should put it and he said, 'Oh, just leave it up on the beach where my cameras are.'

He was a bit of a sadist playing into my masochism, and just as I was about to go into the water he said, 'You know, in Africa when I put my cameras on the beach, the natives would just run right out of the jungle and take them. What are you going to do? Chase them into the jungle. Noooooo.'

I was looking back at my money and coming and going, and then he said, 'Well Spalding, Spalding, listen man. On our next day off I'm going to teach you how to scuba dive. You'll see fish you've never seen before, you'll have Rapture of the Deep, man, and it will be incredible.'

And I said, 'Oh my God, at last. It's like an initiation. I'll become a man.' I've always wanted to overcome my fears with another guy, you know, skin diving and all that. I've always wanted to try scuba diving but I was afraid of sharks coming up from behind. And now Ivan would help me through my fears and become my scuba-guru.

Ivan said, 'We'll go. And Spalding, you will see fish of all colors – you have never seen anything like it . . . but there are these *Stone Fish* . . . and you don't want to step on one of them Spalding, because you'll be dead in seven seconds. There's no remedy, so wear your sneakers.'

He reminded me of when I was a kid with Kenny Mason. Once when

I was sledding in Barrington, Rhode Island, Kenny said, 'There's lions in those woods.' I was seven years old and I believed him. In Barrington, Rhode Island, lions in winter. I ran all the way home, crying.

So I was feeling like that seven-year-old again and I was running in and out of the water like this excited kid because I couldn't believe that I was there in Paradise with Ivan. I didn't think I deserved to be in such a beautiful spot and I'd run out of the water and down the beach to try to get an overview. I'd run down the beach and look back to try to see us there in the surf and each time I'd miss myself and then run back and down the beach and back and the third time back . . . Ivan was gone. He had been out in the big surf and he was *gone*, and I thought, oh no, holy shit. He's drowned. Ivan has drowned.

I mean, these things do happen, people do drown. I've read about it, and I read this warning issued by the film which said, 'Don't swim in Phuket'. There had been a number of drownings in recent years from the strong undertow, and the very first thing that went through my head – and it went very fast, the whole thing went very fast – was, of course. He's drowned. Making a film about this much death, some real person actually has to go.

The next thing that went through my head was, it's not my fault! He was suicidal!

And the next thing was, quickly! Find the most responsible man you can. There was no way I was going to swim out in that water, I couldn't get out into that big surf. The first person that came to mind was John Swain, the Paris correspondent for *The London Times*. He had been there when the Khmer Rouge invaded Phnom Penh. He was perhaps the most narcissistic of the reporters, because he had come to Thailand to watch himself be played by Julian Sands. And so I just did it. I just screamed, 'JOHN! JOHN SWAIN! COME QUICKLY, I CAN'T SEE IVAN!'

And everyone dropped their chopsticks and began to run. Some came across the swamp, some ran over the wooden bridge, and the first person to reach the beach was Judy Arthur, the publicist. Judy had been a lifeguard so she had the good sense to run along the high part of the beach. I was down by the dip of the lip of the sea and couldn't see out, and the others were trying to calm me down. My knees were shaking and I was on the verge of throwing up and people were saying, 'Listen, Spalding. Take it easy. Take it easy. He won't drown, he's from South Africa.' I was walking up and down the beach trying to interpret this, trying to figure it out, when Judy Arthur spotted Ivan way out. He had drifted down. Judy saw his head way out there and she called him in.

And I said, 'My God, Ivan! Ivan, listen man, I thought you'd drowned. I really did.'

He said, 'Spalding, I'm really sorry, man. Listen, don't worry about me, I won't drown. I'm from South Africa.'

Then everyone went back to brunch and I said, 'Ivan, don't do that again, please.' After promising he wouldn't, he turned to me and said, 'By the way Spalding, when you called, how many came? Did Judy Freeman come?'

And I said, 'Yes, Judy Freeman came, Judy Arthur came, all the Judies came. Let's go get something to eat.'

So we walked over to brunch and suddenly I realized that I was with all these Real People, and I was feeling more and more like 'The Little Drummer Girl'. I was with these real foreign correspondents. Up until then I'd been hanging out with actors – they're no one. They're conduits. They're not as threatening as Real People. It's one thing to build a role from a text, just build it and develop it. It's another to be playing someone – you know – playing Mark Twain or Harry Truman all the way across the United States, and never *being* them.

But Mark Twain and Harry Truman are dead. And I was playing a guy who was alive. He works for the American embassy in Bangkok and he's a Princeton graduate and speaks six languages including Khmer. I graduated from Emerson College and am still wrestling with American. And these people are all like foreign correspondents, people who can just get on a plane and *go* with no sense of loss. One minute they're in Beirut, the next they're in a nuclear submarine off the coast of southern France, now they're here, eating and talking about their experiences. They see the whole world as their stage.

John Swain, for instance, was arguing with people about whether or not there's any cocaine in the Khyber Pass. They were having an enormous discussion over that. Then Judy Arthur started talking about her sixth trip to China. Chris Menges, the cinematographer, was talking about his film, a trilogy he'd made tracing opium from Burma to Harlem. And he said there was a price on his head in Burma; the opium warlords who run the place wanted to kill him because he was with the good guys, and he had eighteen months of rushes on the back of a donkey that he couldn't get out of Burma. He was talking about that. Then there was Ivan, talking about how primitive the Amazon is. He was down there making a film about cocaine.

'Spalding, man! You should just go down there. It's unbelievable. It's truly wild. No Buddhist inhibitions, like here in Thailand.'

Then there was Roland Neveu, who had just flown in after photographing Beirut. He had been in Phnom Penh when the Khmer Rouge came in, and now he was here testing out his new underwater camera – just dropped in to say, 'Hi ho mates,' and have a beer before heading for a nuclear submarine off the coast of southern France.

And there was Minty Clinch, a publicist, who was talking about hitchhiking through Patagonia. Skip the hitchhiking; I couldn't even visualize Patagonia. And there was this beautiful woman who was on a forty-day fast. She was half Thai and half Scottish. What a mix. Oh, la-la.

Her mother had come over from Scotland to marry a Thai man – just the opposite of the way it usually is. They were both doctors, and they had this baby who turned into this fasting woman. She had these almond eyes, these Thai eyes and this Thai complexion, but this WASPish-Anglican bone structure and freckles, and she was very beautiful.

She was there fasting for forty days. She had first learned to fast at a Texas fast farm, and now she was here in Thailand doing it on her own, while watching us eat.

And then there was me, who was looking at this incredible bee that looked like a cartoon of a bee because it was so big and fluffy, and its stripes were so wide, and I was saying, 'Wow! Look at that bee.'

And everyone said, 'It's just a bee, Spalding.'

Soon, lunch was over and it was time to go back in swimming. Ivan and I rushed down to the beach like the two kids who couldn't wait an hour after eating.

And Ivan said, 'Hey, let's toke up.'

I said, 'All right. God knows I can let my Kundalini out on this beach.' It used to get stuck in my lower Chakra, but I knew I could just run it off on the beach.

I took two tokes and had a mildly paranoid episode about my money and where to hide it. At first I started digging holes in the sand, but then I changed my mind and went to hide it under the rubber mat in the van. Then I thought that this focus of all my concentration on hiding the money was setting up mind waves that could be read by the Thais and that they would find the money. And God knows they needed it more than I did. So, at last I just took it and left it, fully exposed, on the beach.

I could see Ivan way out in the big surf calling, 'Spalding! Spalding! I see you like the little waves. You don't know what living is until you get out here into this big stuff!' I really wanted to get out there.

I kept going out a little further and, each time, I would think of my money being stolen and I was less afraid of sharks. It just sort of happened naturally. I realized I was out a little further and a little further until all of a sudden I was out further than I had ever been in any ocean, in any world, anywhere. I was beyond Ivan even. I was so far out – I could tell that I had never been in this situation before because of the view of the shoreline. I had never seen the shore from that point of view before. It was so far away that I felt this enormous disconnection from Mother Earth.

Suddenly, there was no time and there was no fear and there was no body to bite. There were no longer any outlines. It was just one big ocean. My body had blended with the ocean. And there was just this round, smiling-ear-to-ear pumpkin-head perceiver on top, bobbing up and down. And up the perceiver would go with the waves, then down it would go, and the waves would come up around the perceiver, and it could have been in the middle of the Indian Ocean, because it could see no land. And then the waves would take the perceiver up to where it could look down this great wall of water, to where Judy Arthur and John Swain were body surfing – like on a Hawaiian travel poster – far below, and then – 'Whoop!' The perceiver would go up again. I don't know how long this went on. It was all very out of time until it was brought back into time by Ivan's voice calling, 'Spalding! Spalding, come back, man! I haven't tested those waters yet!'

I believed him and I thought that I was in trouble. And I fell back into time and back into my body and I swam in to Ivan. We treaded water together. I was panicked, always expecting to feel 'Chomp!' – you know, just 'Chomp!' – the whole lower part of my body gone from a big shark bite. Because now I was back in fearful time. I was also sad because I knew I'd had a Perfect Moment and I would now

have to go home. And Ivan swam out to test my waters and he came
back in choking . . .

'Oh-ahkkkhhh!'

. . . water pouring out of his nose and mouth and he said,
'Spalding, man, now I know what it's like to drown. I almost
drowned out there.'

And I thought, oh, shit. Now *I'm* going to have to go out and
'almost drown'. No, No, I won't fall into this male competitive trap.
I *know* what Ivan's idea of a Perfect Moment is. It's Death!

So I swam in and joined up with Penny Eyles, the Continuity lady.
Just who I needed at that point.

I said, 'Penny, listen, I had a Perfect Moment but I have no words for
it. But I can tell you about my new theory of Displacement of
Anxiety. You see, if you ever want to do something Penny, and
you're afraid to do it and you lack the courage, just take a big pile of
money and leave it somewhere where it can be stolen. Then you'll be
able to do what has to be done. Just concentrate on your money.'

She said, 'Spalding, Spalding, you're a strange bloke. You know
what? You think too much. What are you doing testing your fears at
forty-two years old? Didn't you do it as a lad?'

'No,' I said. 'Was I supposed to? Oh lord, did I miss that, too? Oh
no, I know, my brother Rocky did it all for me. He tested all his fears
at an early age. One of his biggest fears was the basement in our
house. When our parents would go away he'd turn out the lights and
crawl on his belly from his bedroom down the front stairs, then
down the basement stairs and, with his eyes closed, he would feel the
basement walls, every crack, feeling his way around the entire room
until he either died or didn't die.'

So Penny said, 'I want you to walk with me down this beach
without looking back once at your money. We will walk to the far
end of the beach together. Let's go.'

And I walked all the way down the beach with Penny backwards,
never once losing sight of my money. Then, when I got down to the
far end of the beach I fell into a new cluster of energy. There were
these enormous water buffalo that came up to my shoulder and these
ratty, ragtag Thai kids with sticks talking to the buffalo in Thai and
ignoring me. I was floating in between this boy-buffalo energy like
Casper the Friendly Ghost. I was in their energy field, in my ocean

briefs and ready to go anywhere they went. I was being swept away,
just like the water. I was going with them and I was happy, and all of a
sudden a human voice woke me and I drowned as I heard, in the
distance, Judy Freeman called, 'Spalding! Spalding! Time to go.
Time to go back to the Phuket Merlin.'

So I went. I had to. These people had become my umbilical cord. I
was breathing through them.

I got back to the hotel and I went to the person who was fast
becoming my father-confessor, Athol Fugard. Now, Athol seemed
to like hearing my stories, and also, he had just given up drinking so
he was buying me drinks and kind of living vicariously through me.

'Spalding! I am going to have an orange and you will have yourself
some beer. Now. What's been going on? Tell me all about your day.'

And I told him. I told him about the Perfect Moment in the Indian
Ocean and he said, 'Spalding. The sea's a lovely lady.' (He's South
African, like Ivan.) 'The sea's a lovely lady when you play in her, but
if you play *with* her, she's a bitch. Don't ever play with the sea.
You're lucky to be here. You're lucky to be alive.'

I believed him, and we went to eat – Athol, Graham Kennedy,
Tom Bird and I. Afterwards Tom and I went window-shopping for
whores and then went to bed. I slept rocked in the arms of the sea,
like a kid again in Jerusalem, Rhode Island with sand in my bed. It
was a beautiful night, perfect sleep, the bed rocking gently.

The next day was June 24 and it was a back-to-work day for those
that were still working on the film. I wanted to hang out on the set
because it was supposed to be a very . . . explosive day, when the
first bombs went off at the Coca-Cola factory.

When I got down to the set everything was in perpetual flames, like
a little version of hell. All the buildings had flaming gas jets around
them so they could burn all day without burning down. Coke trucks
were burning as well, and I got to throw cases of Coke at the wall, to
smash the bottles, make it look like a bomb had blown up. And the
Thai extras were lined up, covered with chicken giblets, fake blood
and what looked like very real third-degree burns created by the art
department. They were all lined up and smiling. While we were
trashing the area I decided that I wanted to talk to certain people. I
had a sense that Tom might be through with his role in the film any
time and we'd have to leave, either for Hanoi or Krummville. So I

was going into that kind of state when you think you're about to die or leave a place forever, and you want to just get to know everyone before you go.

Keith, the costumier, was first. I hadn't talked with him. He'd always struck me as a little mad, and I was telling him about my theory of Displacement of Anxiety and he said, 'I know all about it. Oh, sure. I've got a witch up there, white one, up in Nottingham. Oh, she's a blessed one. Every time I fly she gets mildly ill, in a pub, you see? She gets sick. She takes on my anxiety and I have a lovely flight. I know all about it. I knew this actress. She hated a fellow actor and she wanted to get him out of the show. She stuck a note on the stairs, under the carpet on the stage. It said, "May you trip and break your leg". And he did. Oh, I know all about it.'

Then I went on from Keith to talk to Haing Ngor. Now I hadn't talked directly to Haing about his story, but I certainly had heard about it. I think I felt ashamed, or I didn't want to bother him, because people had asked him about his story so many times before. He was playing the role of Dith Pran. Now, Haing had also been tortured for years under the Pol Pot regime, so to some extent he was reenacting his own life story as well as Pran's. As the story goes, Haing was a Cambodian gynecologist and he had been performing an emergency operation on someone in Phnom Penh when the Khmer Rouge broke into the hospital and demanded to know where the doctor was. Haing just threw down his stuff and said, 'I'm not a doctor, I'm a taxicab driver. I drove the doctor here.' And he left the patient on the operating table and became a cab driver from that day on.

The other thing about Haing Ngor that interested me was his anger. Of all the Cambodians that I met, his anger was most on the surface, and I think that's why he was cast in the role.

The others were always smiling. It was hard to believe they could still be smiling, but they were always smiling about everything. I don't know what it came from, the Buddhism or that they'd seen too much to talk about, but they were always very gentle and smiling. But Haing's rage was right there, and I went up and asked him what had happened to him.

'They put! Plastic! Plastic bag. Over my head!'

'And then?'

'And then. They take me. They tie me to a cross. And burn my legs. And burn me right here.'

And he showed me the burn marks on his legs.

'They burned you? How did you get through this? What were you thinking about? What was going on?'

'I know. If I tell the truth. I'm one hundred percent dead. Now I'm only ninety-eight percent dead. The truth. Hundred percent dead.'

'How did you escape?'

'They take me. And Khmer Rouge put. Me in jail.'

'They put you in jail, yes, and . . . '

'They. Burn it down.'

The Khmer Rouge were really crazy. They put him in jail and then set fire to it and, of course, the prisoners ran out. Some got burned, yes. Some escaped. Haing escaped and ate his way across Cambodia on bark and bugs – the traditional diet – leaves and lizards. At last he made it to a Thai refugee camp and now he's living in LA.

Then I went over to visit with the crew, the electricians. I envied their sort of blissful ignorance the most. They were the ones who, as soon as they arrived in Thailand, went down and bought Thai wives. Now I think it's a class thing. None of the actors did it. The electricians could do it. I don't know if it has to do with electricity or what, but I know the actors didn't buy women out front. They were more secretive about it and would sneak around doing it at night. These guys went right out and got these women and they made a little laughing family. I used to listen at their hotel doors sometimes. They'd be in there speaking pidgin English to each other in the shower.

'Hey, beeg guy, ohkeekyouass I keeckassoh ho ho ho!' laughing. I mean the major English they knew came from the popular records there: 'Lies, Lies, Lies, Liar', and 'Do You Want to Funk?' During the day the Thai wives hung out by the pool together and talked, and at night the men came home from work and everyone went out to eat. The Thai women knew just what to order and everyone had a good time there, laughing. The women talked among themselves and the men talked among themselves – now, not a radical idea, granted, but a lot happier than most nuclear families that I've come across in any McDonald's or Howard Johnson's. A lot more laughter coming off the table. I don't know what laughter is indicative of, but it has something to do with joy and letting go.

I've been with prostitutes in Amsterdam and New York City, and they are very cool, business-as-usual. It's like going to a very cold doctor. You just wouldn't naturally fall in love with one. But I think that you could very easily fall in love with a Thai whore, very easily. They really seemed to be having a good time there, feeding coconut-flavoured rice to the Sparks as they lounged before them like gargantuan Gauguins. If, in fact, they were all acting, then a good many of them should have received Academy Awards along with Haing Ngor.

And yes, I've heard the other side of it and I know it exists the way the darker side of everything exists. Just recently, while driving in LA, I heard a very angry woman talking on KPFK Radio about an investigation she had made of child prostitution in Thailand. She said that evil people were kidnapping ten-year-old girls and bringing them to the city to be prostitutes, and they were chaining them to the beds like slaves. When one of the whorehouses burned down all they found were these charred ten-year-old skeletons, chained to beds. I didn't hear about this until after I got back from Thailand, but while I was there it all looked like fun. I wanted in on it all, but I couldn't get in because I was too conflicted.

Then, all of a sudden, the guns went off and the machine-gun fire started, and the bombs. Five hundred Coke cases were blown across the warehouse. John Swain was running off camera behind Julian Sands, who was playing him, and John was yelling. 'What a lovely war! What a great war! You know you're not going to get shot!' This confirmed my whole idea of War Therapy.

We were running through the machine-gun fire, the black smoke pouring off burning rubber tires, and all of a sudden it was lunchtime. We all sat down at a table with these Thai peasants who were completely covered with blood – it looked like their faces were falling off – and we were all eating together when a monsoon suddenly came up and one of the tents blew down and a real Thai woman got knocked out for real. They carried her in and put her in the middle of the table where the food was. So it was the monsoon versus the film. Then the monsoon passed and the film began again and there was so much black smoke you couldn't even see the sky. There were rockets and machine-gun fire, and Judy Freeman, who was on sound, said to me, 'Spalding, my God, what are you feeling guilty about? What are you doing in the middle of a war when you could be down on Paradise Beach? Chris and I have rented a house down there that we never use. You're free to use it. Go, go. Have fun.'

*

So I thought, ooh, why not? What am I feeling guilty about? After all, let's not waste time on that.

I walked out – it was incredible. What a beautiful day. The sun was out, I felt like I was in seventh grade and I was just walking out of school at ten in the morning. Just a free boy. And I went back to the hotel and got Billy Paterson and his girlfriend Hildegarde and some of the Cambodian refugees, and we hired a car and went back to Karon Beach. Now, it wasn't as beautiful this time, it never is the second time around, but it was beautiful. And I was walking down the beach – completely empty, beautiful day, big surf – with one of the Cambodian refugees, and I said, 'So, what are you doing here? I mean what have you been doing – aren't you getting bored?'

'No, I'm "fighting" every night. Last night I "fought" six times.'

'What do you mean, "fighting"?'

It turned out that this was a euphemism for fucking. For some reason the Cambodians had all these code words for their amorous escapades. If a Cambodian was going for a massage, he'd refer to it as 'going for an interview'. This particular code had grown out of the fact that one of the Cambodians was there with his wife, and every time he went out for a massage and she asked where he was going, he told her he was going to be interviewed about the movie. (He had a very small role.)

So, massage equaled 'interview' and fucking equaled 'fighting'.

'You "fought" six times last night?' I said. 'Aren't you afraid of that new Southeast Asian strain of gonorrhea that's supposed to be so strong that it's knocking down doors?'

'No, no. Haing is a Cambodian gynecologist. He told me what to do. He says after you "fight" you drink a lot of beer to wash out the germs and in the morning you eat a lot of penicillin.'

So he was on a beer/penicillin diet. And he believed in it. He claimed it was working. We walked on the beach and he picked three fresh coconuts for us. He cut the tops off and we were drinking fresh coconut milk when we came upon two tourists. Now, on a beach like that, if you come upon only two tourists, sure, you're going to stop and talk.

It was Jack and Mary from Saudi Arabia – Mary via Dublin and Jack via Washington State. Mary was a nurse in Saudi Arabia and Jack was a plastic surgeon. They were traveling companions. They'd come on a vacation but Jack was particularly interested in Thailand because he said there were challenges in the plastic surgery field like in no other country. Jack had heard about the jealous Thai wives who cut off men's cocks and feed them to the ducks. And he had heard about the special plastic surgery wings where doctors sewed them back on. He said there were more challenges in plastic surgery in Thailand and the Philippines than in any other country, so he was thinking of staying on.

'Come! Come join us for lunch,' I cried. 'Come sup with us – tell us of your travels of the world.' It was all like a big Hemingway novel. 'Come! Sit! Tell us about Saudi Arabia!'

Mary started: 'Well, Saudi Arabia, my God. Man, you would not believe how primitive it is. They still have public executions there, and if you're a foreigner you just get pushed right up to the front and when you see the head come off, plop, you faint dead away. Oh, and they cut off hands there. They cut off hands for thievery and they cauterize the stumps in boiling oil. Oh, also, they still do stoning, oh, do they ever. And it's modern. It's a more contemporary style – I was there. There was this woman, she was an adulteress and she got pregnant. They waited for the baby to be born, then they buried her in sand up to her neck and drove a big dump truck up filled with stones and just dumped them on her head. That's their modern stoning method. What do you think of that?'

I said, 'Good God! Thank God I live in America!'

So the conversation ran its course and spiraled down, as it often does at any dinner table, from sex, death and taxes to shit and money, depending on whether it's mixed company. In this case it was mixed company, so it all ended with money. Now I don't mind talking about money. When people ask me what I make, I tell them. But for many, money is a taboo subject. My father would never talk about it. He never told how much he made.

It all started when Billy Paterson said to me, 'So Spalding, what are you going to do with all the money you make?'

'What? What money?' This was a medium-budget film, about twenty million, and I had been told that everyone was making the same salary except Sam Waterston who was making a little more, and the Cambodians who were making a lot less.

And Billy said, 'Well, I'll tell you if you tell me.'

'All right. You go first.'

'Well, as far as I know all the Brits are making $3,000 a week plus $325 a week for expenses.'

'Ohuhoh. I thought I was doing very well, but I'm making $1,500 plus $325, and $3,000 is twice as much, isn't it?'

'Well, Spalding, you know, maybe that's because you don't have an agent.'

All of a sudden I saw white. Of course! An agent! What am I doing lying on the beach like an old hippie at forty-two years old, trying to have Perfect Moments in Thailand? What am I doing searching for Cosmic Consciousness? Cosmic Consciousness belongs to the independently wealthy in this day and age. Go! Get an agent! Yes! Do not go to Hanoi! Do not pass Go! Go directly to Hollywood and get an agent! After all, what is this film about? Survival! Whose survival? My survival. Go! Get an agent! Go do five Hollywood films you don't really like. Do them! Get a house out in the Hamptons where you can have your *own* Perfect Moments in your *own* backyard. Have your friends come over for an afternoon of Perfect Moments. Return to your own ocean. Go! Go! Go to Hollywood and get an agent!

Exhausted from this epiphany, I staggered down to the beach, and went into a semi-miasma sleep in which I thought I was back on Long Island, in the Hamptons, hearing the sound of my own ocean without ever having to travel twenty-four hours on Thai Air. And I was half asleep when I heard someone yelling, 'Boat People! Boatpeopleboatpeopleboatpeople *Boat People*!'

I woke to see the Thai waiter from the restaurant looking out to sea with binoculars and I got up and looked out. And, way out, I saw this ancient old craft like an old wooden cider tub, bobbing with all these little heads along the edge like Wynken, Blynken and Nod. They were *way* out there and some Thai fishermen were trying to lasso their boat, and they looked like real Vietnamese boat people. But was it the real thing? I couldn't believe it – just when I was beginning to forget about Vietnam and dream of the Hamptons, these wretched sea gypsies came into view.

And Jack – Jack from Saudi Arabia via Washington; Jack who was the kind of guy who was so in touch with his body he was out of touch with it; the kind of guy who would climb Mount Everest for the weekend just to ski down it and videotape himself doing it – Jack walked over, pulled down his goggles and proceeded to go into the water, like in a cartoon.

And like a buzz saw he cut right through my Perfect Moment area . . .

right through Ivan's chartered waters . . .

and disappeared into the Indian Ocean.

I was pacing up and down the beach. Twenty minutes later he strolled back out of the ocean and I said, 'What the fuck? Where were you? Where'd you go?'

And he said, in that casual, laid-back, almost indifferent way, 'Oh, I just wanted to swim out and see if they were real boat people, but they got towed away before I got out there.'

'Jack, how far out would you say that was?'

'Oh, a mile, mile-and-a-half.'

'Do you do that sort of thing often?'

'Well, I do like long distance swimming. Once, when I was swimming about two-and-a-half hours off the coast of Jersey . . . '

'Two-and-a-half hours? What if a thunderstorm had come up?'

A distant, whimsical smile passed as Jack said, 'Yeah . . . I ran into this big leviathan-type thing, I mean whatever it was, it should not have let me hit it, and I panicked and started to swim in.'

(If you can imagine the quality of a panicked swim two-and-a-half hours out.)

'I swam in and the next day a guy had his leg bitten off right to his knee, in knee-deep water, by a shark. So I just might have run into that shark but I was lucky and hit it in the nose.'

Jack and Mary wanted to ride into town with us. They said Shangri-La was not very interesting at night. In fact, it was a bore and all they did was 'fight'. They wanted to dine with us in town.

'Sure. C'mon in. There's always interesting configurations – there are 130 of us. Sometimes you eat meals with people you like, other times you just go along and discover new people.'

When I got back to the hotel I found that Tom Bird had finished his last scene and I thought, oh, God, time for the Last Supper. So I was really kind of down and I tried to talk Tom into staying on for a few days and going to Karon Beach.

'Tom, you've got to stay. You've really got to stay. We're going to have a beautiful, beautiful time at the beach, take the magic mushrooms. Just stay about three extra days?'

'Spalding, brush that sand off your legs before you come in here.'

So I knew something weird was going on. I really should have confronted him on it. If I have any major regrets about this trip, it was that I didn't confront Tom Bird about why he wouldn't go to that beach.

It was time for dinner and a bunch of us went to an outdoor restaurant right on the edge of the Indian Ocean. There were about twenty of us and it all looked and felt like a big Thanksgiving dinner, the Last Supper right at the edge of the world. The islands beyond, over which sweet, cooling trade winds blew, gave off no light or life. It was just us and the Thai waiters moving under multicoloured Japanese lanterns that swayed in the winds.

David Puttnam sat at the head of the table and I sat to his left with my back to the sea. David was holding up a picture of John Malkovich and saying, 'So, I hear John doesn't want to do any more films. He says he wants to return to the Steppenwolf Theatre Company in Chicago.' John was sitting at the far end of the table and I was a little drunk and saying, 'Yes, I think the lady doth protheth too much.' John was winking back at me and taking it all good-naturedly.

Now, I was feeling a little competitive, I admit it. I had been doing solo performance for so long that I had forgotten all that competitive stuff that comes up when you begin to mix and mingle with a lot of Talent. I had been down at the Performing Garage for so long that I'd lost touch with that scene. I know that not only is John a good actor, he's also a good storyteller. He could be sitting behind a table just like I do somewhere far away, let's say in Chicago or Alaska, telling stories not unlike these.

My question is, could I play Biff on Broadway? Are we interchangeable? John just gets work. It seems to just come to him because he's not needy. Also, he has a good manager. It's not just that he has an agent, he also has a *very good* manager. In fact, I don't know if you noticed, but when *The Killing Fields* was reviewed in *The New York Times*, there was also a small article in another part of the paper about the blackout on the Q.E.II, and who did they contact to interview by telephone satellite? John Malkovich. How did he get on the Q.E.II? His manager. And how did *The Times* know he was there? His manager. And how did the lights go out? His manager. (And how did Ronald Reagan become President?) They set it up like that to get the reverb. It's an echo – you see, the review isn't enough.

Now, I'm sitting at the table and it's not that John Malkovich reminds me of my brother, or that David Puttnam reminds me of my father, but there is some archetypal family scene going on there. I mean, like David Puttnam, my father sat at the head of the table, but he never talked as much as David Puttnam. The only two things my father ever said were, 'All things are relative' and 'Whatever you do, marry a wealthy woman.' Now I thought that was good advice. You had the physical and the metaphysical. And he was a good provider, like David Puttnam.

Every Sunday there was steak and every Monday there was a roast – roast beef, roast lamb. And I can remember on Monday, passing my plate up for more of that blood-rare roast beef. I wasn't hungry, you know, but I was going up for thirds. Now, I know to some extent I was trying to eat my father's body. I understand that. But I would pass it up anyway, and he would send it back and it would have to go by my brother Rocky – Rockwell Junior, who was kind of the autocrat of the table. He would take a big piece of beef off my plate and pop it into his mouth. And I would say, 'What was that about?' and he'd say, 'Toll.'

Also, Rocky had a game called 'Dime'. He had a paper route and so he often had a pocket full of dimes, and he would run around yelling 'Dime!' and if you touched him, you got a dime. But just before you touched him he'd say, 'Deal's off!' He also had a proclamation of 'Forbidden Names'. The names that rubbed him the wrong way all just happened to be my friends' names, and if I said them, I got hit. No big deal. The names were nothing special – I mean, I look both ways before I say them now, actually.

'Lucille Bisbano . . . ' (Pow!)
'Steve Sea . . . ' (Punch! Punch!)
'Heather Henry . . . ' (Chop! Chop!)

Then my little brother Channing was born. When Chan was born I knew what jealousy was, because Rocky fell in love with Chan. And one warm summer day when he was four years old, I led Chan naked into the middle of Rumstick Road and stood him on the white line and told him to stay there. My mother rushed out just in time to save him from the speeding cars.

Now, I'm not saying that Chan is John Malkovich, or that David Puttnam is my father – but there we were, and something of that family order was going down, and I was hoping David Puttnam would pay for the meal. (He didn't.) It was my Last Supper and I really wanted him to know. I wanted him to love me so much that he could read my mind. After all, he had paid for Craig T. Nelson's last meal. They had a huge party when Craig T. left, but Craig was a Professional Actor, and he left as soon as his last scene was over. If Craig didn't have another job to go to, at least he acted like he did, and I was beginning to feel like this poor relative.

The reason I know that John Malkovich is a good storyteller is that we had to tell dirty jokes. The film was a 'buddy' movie, it was about *male bonding*. I'd never been with men in a situation like this in my life. I was never in a fraternity. I was never in any kind of male bonding situations. And we'd all get together for lunch, or cocktails at six, and we'd all just sit around and *bond*, talking about what happened that day.

And at one particular luncheon, a Cambodian refugee who wanted to bring back dirty jokes for his friends in Long Beach asked us to tell some for his collection. He asked people to go around in a circle and tell dirty jokes. I didn't know any dirty jokes – I couldn't think of any – but I wanted to be one of the guys so when my turn came I said, 'All right, all right. There was this couple . . .' (I remembered one) 'a generic couple, we'll call them Dick and Jane. It was back in the fifties. It was their first date and they were both very uptight. Dick was very nervous about his appearance there in Jane's living room, and there was a dog, too, Spot. Jane's dog, Spot, a collie asleep on the floor. So Dick had done everything to prepare himself: 5-Day Stay-Dry Deodorant Pads, Aqua-Velva, Listerine. Jane was the same, all scrubbed down with Lysol and properly dressed. They were just, you know, petting in the living room – except Dick was very nervous and he had gone off his diet. Just before coming over, he had eaten a big bowl of baked beans with red cabbage on top. And for dessert, he'd had two green pears and some figs and raisins. So he was letting out those Silent But Deadly, unbelievable steamy hot burners. You wouldn't hear them come but when they filled the room you *knew* it. He would just ease them out as he leaned over to kiss Jane on the cheek, and then as he leaned back, he'd say, "Oh, Spot! Good God! Jane, where'd you get this dog? Did you say it was a thoroughbred collie?" And then Dick would ease out another one and say, "Oh, Spot! Oh! One more like that and we'll take you to the pound to have you gassed on your own gas." Then, just as Dick let loose with the last hot burner, Jane leapt up and yelled, "C'mon Spot, let's get out of here before he shits on us both!" '

That was all I could think of. Oh, no, wait. There was one other. 'This traveling salesman who is desperate to find a room stops at this hotel in the South and the owner says there aren't any more rooms. "There's one upstairs but you can't have it."

"Why?"

"Well, the screens are ripped, there are flies. You wouldn't sleep. There's every kind of fly. There's bottle flies, green flies, deer flies, black flies and house flies, and you wouldn't sleep, I'm telling you. Horse flies, even."

"I'll take it."

And the next morning, he comes down completely rested and the manager says, "You look like you slept. What'd you do?"

"Just a little 'bunching'. I had to bunch the flies."

"What do you mean, you 'bunched' the flies?"

"Well, I took a shit in the corner and I went to bed!" '

So then it was John Malkovich's turn. And, by the way, the Cambodian was laughing at every line. I don't know if it had to do with the translation, the Buddhist Tolerance, the Polymorphous perverse quality of the Cambodian culture or what. But the Cambodians, at least this one, didn't seem to have any concept of 'punch line'. The whole joke seemed to be funny to him, and he'd laugh at every line.

Anyway, it was John's turn and he said, 'There was this elephant . . . '

'Hhha-ha-ha,' the Cambodian is already laughing.

' . . . and a mouse. And the mouse was in love with the elephant. And there was a monkey up in a tree throwing down coconuts, screaming monkey invectives. The elephant was a gal and the mouse was a guy, and the mouse was trying to mount the elephant. It was erotic love. And the mouse would take these little running jumps and bounce off the back of the elephant. At last, the mouse took a long run and made it up and just as it mounted the elephant, the monkey hit the elephant on the head with a coconut and the elephant fell to its knees, totally stunned. And the mouse cried out, "Yeah! Suffer, bitch!" '

So I turned to the Cambodian and asked, 'Which joke did you like?'

'Malkovich! The Malkovich joke!'

'All right, tell it back, 'cause I want to hear if you got the punch line.'

'There was an elephant. Ahh-hah-hah. And a mouse, and the mouse was in love with the elephant. Eh-heh. And there was a monkey up in the tree. And the monkey yells down, "HEY ELEPHANT! YOU MAKE GOOD LOVE!" '

So I was feeling a little on edge. It was my last night there and Mary, the nurse from Saudi Arabia via Dublin, was next to me and she was driving me nuts. She kept calling me 'Baldwin' – 'Baldwin' this, 'Baldwin' that. I kept correcting her and she'd say, 'Baldwin, you would not *believe* – you think the Saudis are stupid? Oh, my God man, the Pakistanis are even worse. I tell you, I was a nurse there and I had to get a urine sample from this Pakistani bloke. I gave him a little jar and he went behind a curtain and an emergency came up and I forgot about him. Two hours later he came out and handed me the bottle and it had a half-inch of sperm in it. And he said, "That's all I could get in two hours." '

Back at the hotel I fell asleep and I dreamt that I was taking care of some pet fish and I put them in the oven with some wild fish and forgot all about them, and then I thought, oh, my God, they're burning up. And I went and opened the oven and the fish were looking back at me with these intelligent, human eyes. And one of them turned into John Malkovich, who seemed completely indifferent to being saved.

The next day was my last, and I felt as if I were going to the gallows. I wanted to say goodbye like a man, and if I couldn't be one, I was going to imitate one. I had seen enough of them, been on the film, watched how everyone behaved. And I went around to each person and acted as though I'd made up my mind.

'Goodbye, mate.'

'Yep, take it easy. I'll work with you again. You look out for those whores, now.'

'Oh, yeah.'

'Hey, big guy. It's been good workin' with you.'

'Goodbye.'

'Yeah.'

'It's a beautiful film.'

'Yeah, I really believe in it.'

'Right, bye.'

'Yeah.'

'Hey, guys, it doesn't get much better than this.'

And when I got to Athol Fugard, he turned to me and said, 'So, Spalding. You're leaving Paradise?'

'Athol (oh!) Athol (I!) uh, Athol (uh!), I – I was thinking that maybe I should (oh!) eh, uh, wait a minute, Athol, you really think I, uh . . . '

'Return to Renée. She's a lovely lady. Go back, Spalding! Take what you've learned here and go back. It's all the same, you know.'

I wanted to believe him.

And Tom and I got on the plane back to Bangkok. As soon as we arrived, Tom went right to the Vietnamese embassy and I went right to John Malkovich's tailor over on Silom Road and said, 'You know that suit that John Malkovich had made here? The one that looked sort of sloppy and sort of neat all at once? The one that looked something like a cross between a suit and a parachute?'

'Oh, yes. He designed it himself.'

'Make me one just like it.'

'Surely Mr Gray can afford two suits at such a price.'

'All right, two – one brown and one gray – and three of the shirts, the Malkovich shirts. The ones he had copied from that Paris design.'

I went back to the hotel, where Tom told me that we might have to wait three or four more days before we could get into Vietnam.

I said, 'Well, what do you think?'

'No. I have to get back to Sis.'

Tom's girlfriend's name was Sis and they had rented a house with some other people in Bridgehampton, Long Island for the summer. I realized then that I was riding on his Love/Libido Carpet. It was no longer the Magic Will Carpet. And I said, 'Tom, couldn't you go with me tonight to Pat Pong and at least work out the sexual part of it? You know, we'll pick up some Thai gals and let off some of the pressure from the old pressure cooker?'

'No. I've got to get back. I went to those whores during the war and got gonorrhea twice. I'm not interested.'

'Well, would you come down with me then so I can say goodbye to Joy?' Joy was my Pat Pong girlfriend.

Going down to the Captain's Table where Joy worked seemed like a kind of strange homecoming. Her whole face lit up when she saw me and she really seemed happy. We did what we'd always done the three or four times I'd visited her before. We sat in a corner of the bar and I put my arm around her and we watched the other girls dance until closing time. There was nothing to say. She didn't speak English and I didn't speak Thai. She sat there almost naked in her two-piece bathing suit. I had no idea how old she was. Maybe nineteen.

She had a perfectly exquisite body. It was very small and childlike but at the same time ripe and fully developed like that of a mature woman. She was a splendid, dark miniature and what I loved most was the texture of her skin. Joy was a joy to touch and knowing that I could, for a little extra money, go home with her at any time, I preferred that kind of suspended waiting and almost innocent touching.

She did her best to keep smiling whenever I looked at her, but there were times when I was able to steal a secret glance and then I would see another side of Joy. I would catch her in a slightly drained and more reflective melancholy state, and I realized how much was always going on behind the scenes and how little I knew or wanted to know. Most of all I realized that I could never get to it without language.

It was then that I realized that I was just like all the others, a lonely displaced man in Thailand, and like all the others I couldn't live long without the simple touch of women. At first I'd seen them all around me on the streets and I was satisfied to live only in my eyes. To gaze on their flesh was enough. But after awhile I needed to touch and it was not unlike the way in which I needed to take my shoes off in order to dig my toes into Karon Beach.

You see, when you see that river of flesh coming at you in the streets, it's very hard not to want to touch. It's very hard not to see one flesh as all flesh. You get taken over like a curious child. At first Joy seemed happy to see me and we could ride on that novelty. The softness of her skin was like a kind of heaven on earth and I wanted to keep it that way and not think. But when I sat long enough with Joy I could see the joy drain out and a kind of melancholy despondency creep into her face. And when the stage lights went out and the house lights came up at quarter to one, I could see everyone scatter like cockroaches under fluorescent light. And I could see the bruises like rotten fruit on the girls' legs.

When we got back to the hotel I realized something was wrong – because two basic intentions in making love are pleasurable relief through sex, and some recognizable change in 'the other'. I could never really see the change in this particular other. And why should I expect change? After all, I was paying her. And I figured whatever she said or did was just an act. Also I think it had a lot to do with language. Eighty percent of erotic love for me is the language in and around the event. But she spoke very little English. All she could (or would) say, over and over, was 'Joy like you.' I figured she said that to all the guys, but she was so convincing. I really wanted to believe her.

In the morning I'd try to feed her from a big bowl of fresh fruit that the hotel supplied. I'd say, 'Joy want banana?' And she'd always giggle, shake her head 'no' and disappear under the pillow. She could fit under the pillow.

This time I said, 'No, no, no, Joy. It's time to go, Joy. I'm going back to New York City.' And as I took her down to the cab, she looked like a little Minnie Mouse in high heels. And instead of getting into the cab she pushed me into it and ran back to the hotel. And the sliding electric glass doors opened and closed and she stood there waving goodbye as though she lived in the hotel and I was going home in the cab. All I could say was, 'No, no, Joy.'

Tom and I gobbled some tranquilizers. In Thailand you can buy valium right over the counter like candy. We gobbled some valium and called our driver for the last trip to the plane. And on that plane I was spoiled for the last time. We got to ride in business class, high up in those big chairs at the top of the spiral staircase. High up above the sound of the engines. It was like flying in a big, silent, magic motel, an airborne Holiday Inn. We pulled down our sleep masks and all I remembered was Karachi by night, a three-dollar cup of coffee in the Frankfurt airport, trying to buy a bottle of Russian vodka at Heathrow. (The lady was trying to sell me Smirnoff's and I said, 'Listen lady, this is made in New Jersey.' She said, 'No, it's Russian. It's real Russian vodka.')

'At last, America! New York City!' And then, 'Oh, my God, are we ugly!' I wasn't ready for it. New York City was bad enough but Krummville was worse. And I had had this idea that as soon as I got back I would catch up on everything – I would be a changed man. I'd adopt a Cambodian family, I'd have my teeth taken care of, pay my taxes, clean my loft – try to put it at perfect white, right angles – wash the windows, get out all the old sweaters I never wear and take them to the Cambodian refugees in Far Rockaway. I'd heard that the

Cambodians march from Far Rockaway to Chinatown on the Beltway every day to buy rice because they are so confused by the subway system that they prefer walking. I saw myself as their new brother, hiking and chanting along at their sides. They'd be wearing all the old mothball-reeking V-neck sweaters that Gram Gray made for me so many years ago, that now lie at the bottom of that black trunk. At last I would do something for them. At last I'd be of service.

But instead I ended up in Krummville with Renée and it was horrid. Horrid because I didn't want to be there and I saw all the hardwoods as palm trees. At night I dreamed of taking the magic mushrooms and scuba diving with Ivan on a perfect enchanted isle somewhere in the Indian Ocean. I treated Renée like a Thai whore and I refused to go food shopping and I didn't want to cook and I was a wha-wha-wha little two-year-old. Just wha-wha-wha all over the place.

And Renée said, 'Spald, calm down. Get it together. You're going to lose it. Remember how you came back to get a Hollywood agent, how you came back to make contacts and try to land another feature film? Well, we're not making any contacts here in Krummville, so I think we should go down to Bridgehampton to visit Sis and Tom. They've been nice enough to extend an invitation and you could swim in your ocean and make some contacts as well. I mean, really, I'm beginning to feel like poor white trash up here.'

So we went to Bridgehampton. I had never been to the Hamptons in summer, but it was not all that unfamiliar. When I got there I recognized it from all the Michelob ads I'd seen on TV. There was this big, beautiful white house on a quarter-acre of green lawn. It was one of those beautiful turn-of-century houses that used to have a family in it back in the days of families, and now it was filled with beautiful couples all on the verge of breaking up, and lonely singles who had just broken up and didn't feel ready to re-commit just yet. They were all playing volleyball on the front lawn and toking up in between games, and I couldn't believe the ball just didn't turn into a seagull and swoop out over the horizon.

Next to the volleyball net was a convenient red cooler filled with Michelob, Lowenbrau, Diet Pepsi, Tab and 7-Up. And I was in charge of the bluefish – I was sure I knew about bluefish: how to buy it, how to cook it. But I wasn't in sync with the guy in charge of the coals. He had let those Briquets burn too long, so I was spraying more napalm on the coals to try and get a flame, and at the same time I made the mistake of toking off of a very strong joint and suddenly everything went prehistoric. The next thing I remember is that a group of us were all sitting around this formal table with a big white linen tablecloth and a candelabra in the center, and someone was saying, 'Would you please pass the bluefish sushi?'

But I wasn't hungry. I was looking down at my hand, which was in the middle of a white plate, and it was peeling, looking like a piece of chicken with the tan peeling off like some sort of time-lapse situation in Walt Disney's *Painted Desert*. And I said, 'No, thank you. I've got all I can eat right here.'

And – Ahruuuuuuuuuuuuuh! – I went down on my hand, and the next thing I knew my head was in Renée's lap and I was saying, 'Ahhhhhh, my God! Something awful has happened! I'm supposed to be in *Thailand!* Nothing is ever going to go right in my life again! I've ruined it!'

I fled from the table with my hand across my forehead like I had a bad case of Dostoyevskian brain fever, like Konstantin Gavrilovich in *The Seagull*. I ran out onto the porch where I threw myself into the hammock as, in the background, I heard the people at the table talking about 'the gasoline-flavored bluefish sushi.'

Renée rushed out to comfort me and I said, 'Renée, Renée, it was a mission, a mission! I was on a mission. I'm not supposed to be back here. It wasn't just about making a film. I was about to have something revealed to me on that beach. I was supposed to be in Hanoi, I was supposed to be in Thailand. It was a mission. God wanted to speak to me through those magic mushrooms. I was on the verge of overcoming my fears, on the verge of making friends with Vietnam. It was a *mission*.'

And I looked up from the hammock to see Tom Bird, this mighty Vietnam veteran, standing over me saying in a deep strong voice, 'SPALDING! BE HERE NOW!'

And I flew back in the hammock, my face turning into a ninety-year-old man's face with a dry, twisted mouth and no teeth, and it felt like my face was falling off and the face cried, 'Tom, Tom, what are you guilty about? Why couldn't you go to Paradise Beach and take the mushrooms? I know you're guilty because you killed people. You killed the Vietnamese. But why am I guilty? Why? Why?'

And Tom bellowed again, 'SPALDING! BE HERE NOW!

Do you think I want to be here?'

And suddenly I realized that this strong, silent man was also suffering. He just knew how to shut up about it.

Okay, get it together, Spalding, get it together. The next day, a little shaky and hung over, I met a couple that had just come in from sailing off Block Island. I thought, my God, that's my territory. They were sailing my seas. I was born in Rhode Island with a silver spoon in my mouth. I was born with the name Spalding Gray. Why didn't I have a big boat? What was I doing living up in Krummville at forty-two years old, when *Esquire* says I should be making my age in money?

And I came to the shocking realization that it was now too late to become a banker, a doctor, a lawyer or a psychiatrist. It was too late. But I could go to Hollywood and *play* one, and make twice as much. So I thought, 'Time to get it together. Time to make some decisions,' and in order to strengthen my decision-making muscles, I went to Barnes & Noble and bought a hypnotist's cassette, 'How to Make Decisions – Success Series Unlimited.'

Every night Renée and I would listen on the stereo earphones, and the voice would hypnotize us and put us right out. And in the morning we were supposed to drink a large glass of water to wash all the subliminal suggestions down into the subconscious. It seemed to work. I was indeed feeling more decisive.

Just around that time, I was asked to interview people under the Brooklyn Bridge, as a performance piece to commemorate the Bridge Centennial. I was to try to get them to tell personal stories about the Bridge, under the Bridge. Well, not exactly a great career choice, but at least it was a sane, simple way back into show business. And then, because of these interviews and my role in *The Killing Fields*, I was asked to come in and be interviewed by Hope Newly on WMCA Talk Radio, on a show called 'For Singles Only'.

Hope called me and said that she remembered me from college and would love to see me again. I couldn't quite place her but I looked forward to the interview. I was beginning to feel that I was getting back on my feet.

When I went to the Hope Newly Show, the first thing I heard was Hope interviewing a woman about her new 'consciousness-raising' group for older women who are in love with younger men. The next person who came on was a woman discussing a cure for baldness – and I perked up. She was saying that we don't inherit baldness, we inherit the tendency toward oil in the pores. And for $2,000 (money back guaranteed), you can get a special shampoo to remove that oil, because what's under that oil are these fully-grown hairs, like little pig's tails, like little pubies. They're all scrunched up in there, fully grown just waiting to pop out. And as soon as you wash out that oil, up they pop like cork screws. You've seen them on balding men, all combed across the bald spot like wavy fields of Shredded Wheat. Those are the new hairs.

Then it was my turn to come on. Hope said, 'Hi, everyone out there. This is Hope Newly, "For Singles Only". And I want everyone out there to hug yourself and say, "Hi, me. I'm happy to be single." All right? I want you to welcome Spalding Gray, star of stage, screen and television.'

I don't know where she got my résumé but she said, 'Spalding, I will never forget the first day that we met, in Boston.'

'Uuuum . . .'

Now this is why I don't have a house in the Hamptons, I'm convinced now. I don't know how to play along and make myself up as I go. I said, 'You're going to have to refresh my memory, Hope. I don't remember. I've never seen you before in my life, I swear!'

Well, she let that go and we started talking about the film, and I could tell by the way she was reacting to me that talking about *The Killing Fields* was like talking about cancer before there's a cure. And I figured that her audience felt the same way, so we shifted the subject. She said, 'Well, why don't you tell our audience something about the difference between television acting and film acting. No, better still, why don't you tell them what films they may have seen you in besides *The Killing Fields*. We'll take it from there.'

I took a pause and thought, well, here I go, time for fiction. Time to make myself up.

'Well, I don't know if they've seen my latest, *Leftover Life to Kill*. It's the story of the demise of Dylan Thomas, and his wife's struggle to go on after his death. I play a lesser American poet who comes to her Welsh boathouse to console her. Your audience probably hasn't seen it – it's a cult film that plays in Welsh theatres at midnight. Then there's, oh, *Time of the Assassins*. We did that in southern France and it's about Rimbaud – what a fascinating guy, what a scallywag! Do you know he gave up writing poetry at nineteen to become a gunrunner? I play a lesser American poet who visits him on his deathbed. Strange man. He had all his money hidden in his hernia truss. That one hasn't been released yet, but it's due to come out this fall.'

'Well, we look forward to it. Yes.'

Then I went out on a limb a little further and said, 'Oh, I played a romantic lead in a ski film. I was a ski instructor in *Canadian Sunset*.'

'Really?' Hope said. 'How wonderful. Where was it filmed?'

Suddenly I drew a blank on all the cities in Canada . . . and then Toronto came to mind, so I just said, 'Toronto.'

And Hope just went and pushed me right off the limb by saying, 'Toronto? I didn't know there was any skiing up there. I thought that it was all flat country.'

'Oh, yes, it's very flat. Really. Actually, the film built a mountain. Fascinating to watch that. The building of the mountain was a whole film in itself and they made a separate documentary about the building of the mountain called *Too Steep to Fall*. But basically, that's the difference between film acting and TV acting. In TV, they go to the mountain and in film, they bring the mountain to them.'

Now everything was going fine. I was making myself up. I've seen people make themselves up in an afternoon, become instant holy men, just make themselves up. I saw Richard Schechner do it in Central Park. It was on a lovely May day, back in the days when the Hare Krishnas used to chant from the Bowery up to Central Park, and they'd be so high by the time they reached the park that they'd look as if they were floating six inches off the pavement. They'd all come floating down the steps of Bethesda Fountain and a crowd of about two hundred people would gather around. Well, on one beautiful May Sunday, this spectacle stirred Richard's competitive juices and he took off all his clothes except for his Jockey underwear and asked me to hold them for him while he took out his Indian prayer rug, laid it by the fountain and stood on his head. This outrageous new spectacle immediately drew the crowds away from the Hares to him. I got a little panicked. It looked very much like a *Suddenly Last Summer* situation. All I could see were the soles of Richard's feet sticking up through the crowd, and I could see some of the people dropping little chunks of Italian Ices down through the holes in his underwear.

After about twenty minutes of this, Richard came down and ran over to me and said, 'Quickly, give me my clothes. Let's get out of here.' And as he was getting dressed I looked over to see that he had about twenty-five new converts ready to follow him anywhere.

Some of them were asking, 'When will you return?' As Richard answered over his shoulder, 'I shall return,' others asked, 'Where are you going?' And Richard said, 'I am walking east.'

I think they would have followed him right into the East River without a doubt in their heads.

Now, to some extent, Sri Rama Krishna also made himself up. He was an actor of sorts. He was the last great Indian saint who didn't have twenty-nine Rolls Royces – the last great *poor* Indian guru.

Sri Rama Krishna went through a number of dynamic character transformations in which he became the people he worshipped. Although he was a Hindu, he was in no way hung up on one religion. He embraced them all. When he worshipped Christ, he became Christ; when he worshipped Buddha, he became him. He even performed his tantric practices with a woman and when he worshipped Mother Kali he *became* a woman and people in the Kali temple would mistake him for one. He had no sense of self. He was an actor, a conduit, a man without an identity. And because he lived in India, he didn't have to go to a psychiatrist. He was seen as a holy man and not as a psychotic. At last, a naked sadhu ran out of the jungle, stuck a sharp stone between Sri Rama's eyes and he saw Nothing.

Now, who are the holy people in the West? Actors and actresses. They are the only people who can say they don't know who they are and not be put away in an insane asylum for it. Peter Sellers, the actor, was not unlike Sri Rama Krishna to the extent that he made himself up and acted as a conduit through which he allowed many voices to pass. Sellers insisted that he never knew who he was. In the West that was a problem, so he had to go to a psychiatrist, but in my mind, he was a kind of holy man. And in our utilitarian, materialistic world, where is Mecca for these holy people of the West? It's the furthest west they can go without going east. It's Hollywood. And where does their immortality have its being? On film. The image set forever in celluloid. And who is God? The camera. The ever-present, omniscient third eye. And what is the Holy Eucharist? Money!

So I said, 'I'm going!' And I put on the magic John Malkovich suit, the brown one, I took my Thai *bhat* and converted it into $600, got a ticket on TWA and headed out to Hollywood to select an agent.

After the plane took off without crashing, I was opening one of those fucking little salad dressing packets and – 'Oh, *shit*! Oh, Lord, why does this always happen the one time I put a suit on? Chewing gum flies to me on the subway and sticks. Salad dressing eats through my new pants.'

This traveling salesman next to me said, 'Don't worry about it, take it right in to the cleaners as soon as you get there. Hope it's colorfast. Where'd you have it made?'

'Bangkok.'

'Oh. Well I don't know about that. You never know how those guys will put something together.'

So as soon as I arrived in Venice I took my suit to the cleaners and rushed right down to see the boardwalk. I was so excited to be in a large city that was so close to a major ocean – I couldn't wait to see and breathe that ocean. I couldn't wait to see and walk on that boardwalk I'd heard so much about. I thought, the agent can wait for a day. I'm going to see that Pacific Ocean.

When I got down to the boardwalk I was a little disappointed to find that there were no boards. It turned out to be an asphalt walk. But still, I was excited to be by the ocean, and as I was walking along that asphalt boardwalk with a bounce, breathing deep, an unmarked car pulled up behind me and two unmarked guys jumped out. Holding chrome-plated forty-fives with both hands, they braced themselves on the top of the open car doors and almost blew away two winos. I thought I was in a movie or at least on *Hill Street Blues*, and I ducked behind a pizza counter. I watched these two unmarked men run up and press the barrels of their guns right to the winos' heads, handcuff their arms behind them, knee them in the back and then throw them into the unmarked car. I thought, Lordy, Lordy, this is dangerous territory. I better go get my magic John Malkovich suit on. But the suit wasn't ready yet, and soon cocktail hour rolled around.

I decided to ride out on my borrowed ten-speed bike in search of beer. I found a little beer store on a side road and went in and bought a king-size can of Rainier Ale, and I just couldn't wait to get home – I opened it right outside the store. I was brown-bagging and chug-a-lugging just like I would in New York, when this L.A.P.D. cruiser came full speed down the little sidestreet and did a U-turn. And something about the way the car turned made me think that maybe they were after me. Like they had beer radar. And I wondered, can it be that they would take time out of their busy schedule to bust me for drinking one king-size can of Rainier Ale?

Not wanting to take any chances, I chucked it into a cardboard box beside me which was filled with empty beer cans. The police pulled up and shined the spotlight attached to the side of their car right on that box, and the two of them got out of the car and went over and pulled out the very can from which I'd been drinking. Somehow they were able to pick that can out from all the others. And they pushed me up against the wall of the beer store and made me put my hands over my head while they searched me with a club.

'What's your name? Where's your ID?'

'I don't have my wallet. I left it back at the house where I'm staying – and my name is Spalding Gray.'

'Oh, yeah? What do they call you?'

'They call me Spalding Gray. I swear it.'

And one of the cops said, 'Okay, get in the car,' while the other one put my bike in the trunk. And just as I was getting into the cruiser the cop who was handling my bike demanded to search me.

'Okay, I know my partner's searched you but we like to do double searches around here just to make sure.'

So I got searched again and then they put me in the back of the cruiser and said, 'What's the address of the house you're staying at?' And for a moment I blanked out. Then I remembered six days in a Las Vegas jail in 1977 for refusing to give my name to an officer when first asked, and I remembered 9227 Boccaccio. It just came to me like that – and I thought, oh my God, I'm getting good. I'm getting healthier. I'm on my way to success.

They drove me there. It was a very short trip and when we got there one cop stayed in the car to guard me while the other went into 9227 Boccaccio to find out if anyone knew one Spalding Gray. And luckily, someone there knew me that day and the cop came right back out and said, 'Okay, get your bike out of the trunk and consider yourself lucky for getting a free ride home.

I would rather have ridden my bike home, I thought, but I didn't tell them that. What I did say was, 'Look, I don't want to sound ungrateful or testy, but I just flew in from New York City and people brown-bag all the time in New York, so I didn't know.'

The cop replied in a very stern voice, like a voice I remembered from boarding school, 'I think if you check your New York City laws you'll find that it's against the law to drink in the streets. We just happen to enforce our laws here in LA.'

*

Right, to bed! The next day I got up bright and early, feeling like a new man, and I went and got my suit out of the cleaners and got my friends to drive me to Ugly Duckling Car Rental, which was the cheapest I could find. I rented an Ugly Duckling Toyota. The only problem with the car that I could see was that the seat was broken so that it was at the angle of a lounge chair, and I could barely see over the windshield.

By that time I had boiled it all down to two agencies. If both were interested I would have to make the choice between them. One was Writers and Artists and the other was Smith Freedman Associates. First, I visited Writers and Artists and they were very nice – I think they wanted to sign me. The only problem, as I saw it, was that they were not 'other' enough. They were too much like My People. They were very WASPy and I could see them all wearing topsiders and vacationing on Martha's Vineyard. Also, I wasn't sure if it would be such a good idea to be represented under the title 'Writers and Artists' in this day and age if, in fact, I wanted to make enough money to buy a house in the Hamptons.

So I decided to drive over and see Susan Smith at Smith Freedman Associates, and if she wanted to sign me I'd do it. As soon as I walked into her office she said, 'We want you. We want to sign you right now.'

Well, I was kind of sober about all this because it was all so smiley, all going so fast. I responded in my very serious and rather ponderous East Coast way, 'Well, that's nice, isn't it? Now let me think about it.'

And Susan said, 'Would you have smiled if we said we didn't want you?' Then she said, 'Let's go, we don't have time for this. You've got one day left out here and we want to send you out to all the casting agents in town just to say, "Hi. I'm a new face in town and I'm with Smith Freedman." '

They gave me a map of all the studios and I headed out to the first stop, Warner Brothers, to audition for *The Karate Kid*. They had me read for the role of the tough guy, the kind of karate killer who teaches all the neighborhood kids his aggressive, evil ways. Well, you can imagine how that went.

The next stop was *Hill Street Blues*, which went a little better. Gerri Windsor, the casting director, was very nice and she told me that if I moved out there she could almost guarantee me some work on the show. I asked her how she could say that when she hadn't even auditioned me, and she said, 'New faces. We're always looking for new faces and you're a new face. With a good agent. So I think we're pretty safe in saying that if you move out here we can get you work – but you have to live out here because we really can't afford to fly you out.'

So I left *Hill Street* and continued to follow my little map to ABC, NBC and CBS. All was going fine, but by noon I understood why all actors out there have air-conditioned cars. My Ugly Duckling wasn't air-conditioned and I was beginning to leak through my shirt. Also, that hot, dry air was turning my hair into an insane frizzball. I was coming unglued. And by the time I reached Twentieth Century-Fox I looked like a madman.

I parked the Ugly Duckling, being careful not to park it within eye-view of the casting director's office because I'd heard that they look out to see what you're driving, and the Ugly Duckling was not looking good in comparison to the other cars in that lot. I went into the office and was happy and surprised to find that the receptionist recognized me from my monologues – and she was excited to see me.

'Oh, Spalding Gray, what are you doing here looking for work? You should be working all the time. You could play a lawyer, you could play a doctor, you could play a psychiatrist . . . '

I went inside the casting director's office and quickly realized that she had no idea who I was, beyond being a 'new face'. There was something both comforting and discomforting about being there. The comforting part was the physical office itself, the fantastic white couch and the way in which it received me as I sank in and slowly gave up all thoughts of ever moving again. Also, the clean view out the window of lush palms and pines, coupled with the secure feeling of being in that oh-so-clean, solid room. And most of all, the way the corners of the ceiling and walls came together at perfect, solid white, right angles. But the discomforting part of the experience came when she told me that she just called me in to see me, 'have a look', I think she meant. But she said, 'We've heard all about you and now we'd like to see you.'

And we made small talk while she looked and I could feel my imperfect jawline sagging, my face puffing and my bald spot shining. I could see all those things and I suddenly and clearly realized what it feels like to be a woman scrutinized by a man. I've hardly ever had that feeling before. Only in Morocco.

But the big, soft couch had made me feel secure, and I found that I had made it on time, without getting lost or arrested, to all my interviews and I felt a kind of Triumph of the Will as I sped along the freeways in my little Ugly Duckling.

The only problem was that the front seat had fallen all the way back and was now resting on the back seat. I was using this as a positive experience by holding myself erect by the wheel and giving my stomach muscles a good isometric workout. It was wonderful to be out on the open freeway again and feeling that I had willed it all, and also feeling, isn't it funny that after you've willed something you wonder why you wanted to will it in the first place? But it felt good anyway.

Think of it, I considered, way back on the beaches of Thailand I wanted an agent and now I've got one. I've willed it and I got it and isn't that what everyone out here wants?

An agent. Even my friends the Cambodian refugees from Long Beach wanted to know how they could get an agent. They had suddenly found that they were in a very good feature film and were sure that the next logical step in the progression was to get a Hollywood agent. When I went to visit them they asked me if I could help them get one. An agent. An agent. 'Can you help us get an agent?' I wanted to help but I couldn't imagine where Cambodians would find steady work in the Industry. Then a very perverse idea occurred to me. Norman Lear had just produced a sitcom called *A.K.A. Pablo* that had given a lot of Chicanos steady work. Perhaps the new sitcom of the eighties could be *A.K.A. Pol Pot* – which would give all my Cambodian friends a lot of work.

It wasn't all that far-fetched. I got the idea from a very poignant film I had seen at the Margaret Mead Festival a few years earlier. The film was about the relocation of the Laotian Hmong tribes. After the CIA lost the war in Laos all the Hmongs had to get out fast because they sided with 'the American military effort in Laos'. The film was about their relocation from Thai refugee camps to immigrant condos in Washington State.

They all arrived at these furnitureless condominiums that had wall-to-wall shag carpeting as long as your fingers. I guess they saw the shag as a kind of organic growth so they began by washing it down with a garden hose and then sweeping the water into a heating duct, thinking it was a drain. After that they tried to cook chicken breasts in the toaster. It was all very sad and very funny at the same time.

The supermarket confused them totally. Thinking it was a bar of soap, they bought a big, yellow block of Velveeta cheese. This is how I picture the opening shot of the sitcom: a Cambodian singing 'Do You Want to Funk?' in the shower as he washes under his arms with a large yellow block of Velveeta, which is breaking into chunks from the hot water and washing down the drain in yellow streams.

So I had gotten an agent by willing it and I was home-free on the freeway, and didn't it feel oh-so-good to put the pedal to the metal and spin. Turn up the radio and blast. And, yes, I could do it, we could do it. Renée and I could move out here and have a little house in a canyon. A little bungalow which all came together in solid, clean, white, right angles. We could do it. I could get some work on *Hill Street*, *St. Elsewhere* or *Knots Landing* and we could do it.

I would come home exhausted after a day's work at the studio and instead of having cocktail hour, I'd go jogging around the reservoir while Renée arranged sun-dried tomatoes and smoked mozzarella and tossed a big bowl of sprouts and leafy greens. We could do it. And I'd come in all sinewy and tired, just wanted to eat and rest and be with, and sleep with, my little Renée. My little sweetie. And soon the beautiful children would come along and there'd be fun with them on weekends out in the high desert, or downwind, surfing off Venice. And we'd make it. The kids would grow up and we'd have enough money to send them to good schools. Renée and I would grow old together and we'd make it. We'd make it through.

Then the freeway would grind down into an impossible gridlock situation and clog with smog. And the Ugly Duckling would come almost to a dead stop, and the image of MX missiles flying low over pine trees would flash in my mind. I needed to get back. I had to get back to the East Coast to save the world and stop the war.

And wasn't life about service? Didn't I have enough pleasure in my life and wasn't it now time to help ease the pain of others? And the Bodhisatva's vow came to me: If all people can't reside in a state of pleasure in Southern California, then no one can until all can. And I could see the State of California collapsing, not from earthquakes, but from the weight of the world as all the wretched of the earth clamored toward the sun that broke through bare lemon trees and devoured fruit bushes. How could I think of my pleasure when the world still suffered so? How? How? How? Oh, the shame of it!

I needed to get back to give my old sweaters away to the Cambodian refugees in Far Rockaway. And the death image of Jean Donovan – chopped to death in El Salvador – came to me. And the *Cocktail Party* voice of Celia Coplestone from her anthill crucifixion played in my ears:

> But first I must tell
>   you
> That I should really LIKE to think there's something
>   wrong with me –
> Because, if there isn't then there's something wrong,
> Or at least, very different from what it seemed to
>   be,
> With the world itself – and that's much more
>   frightening!
> That would be terrible. So I'd rather believe
> There is something wrong with me, that could be
>   put right.

And I thought, I've got to get back where it all counts. I've got to get back.

Then the traffic would pick up and everything would feel clear, as the not-so-long-dead voice of Alan Watts floated up from his Sausalito houseboat saying, 'Relax, Spalding, relax. Enjoy. You're in California now. What is there to feel guilty about? Relax. Enjoy. Life's a party. So what if you came in at the end of it? Relax. Enjoy.'

I made it back to Venice and had a couple of good-sized shots of tequila and went to bed. And I had this dream.

I was babysitting for a boy in a cabin in the woods. There was this huge fireplace, and the boy kept playing a game with me where he would run into the fireplace and get partially consumed by the flames and then run out – just before he was completely consumed – and reconstitute himself. I was very nervous. I was watching him out of the corner of my eye and all of a sudden he ran in and I saw that he was completely in flames. There was no torso left and the flames were in the shape of legs, flame-legs. And I grabbed the fire-poker to try and pull him out and . . . nothing. It just went right through the flames; there was no substance. And the flames burned down and left this pile of gray ash on the hearth.

I turned to see, in the corner of the cabin, a straw boy, an effigy of the real boy. And I took the gray ash in my hands and went over and blew it into the straw boy's side. Slowly, the effigy came alive. And his face had this great, ear-to-ear, joyous, all-knowing, friendly smile as he shook his head. And I realized that he hadn't wanted to come back, that he had chosen to be consumed by the flames – and then the spirit went out of the straw boy and I was left holding this empty, straw effigy in my arms. I thought, how am I ever going to tell this story to his mother? No one will believe me. And I went searching for someone to tell the story to. I found that I was wandering through the streets of Hollywood.

The first person I came across was Ron Vawter, an actor friend from a theatre company called The Wooster Group, and I told Ron the story. He said, 'You should have called the police right away. You need a witness with authority. There's no way you're going to prove that this happened and there's no way you can re-enact it.'

I left Ron and continued my search for the straw boy's mother, and came upon Elizabeth LeCompte, the director of The Wooster Group. She was sitting, drinking orangeade with the boy's mother by a Hollywood pool. I started to tell them the story but I couldn't articulate it and instead of telling the Straw Boy Story, in a very loud, theatrical voice I said, 'THE REASON I'M UPSET IS THAT I WAS JUST IN A NEW PECKINPAH MOVIE OF CHEKHOV'S SEAGULL . . .'

And I had played the role of Konstantin Gavrilovich, the writer who shoots himself in the head at the end of the play . . .

'AND WHAT I'M UPSET ABOUT – IS THAT I SAW THE FILM, I LIKED IT, BUT I CAN'T REMEMBER DOING IT. I can't remember acting in it. All I saw was an image with no memory attached.'

And I knew all the time I was telling this story that it was a cover for the real story, the Straw Boy Story, which, for some reason, I found impossible to tell.

SEX AND DEATH TO
THE AGE 14

FOR
RENÉE
MY PARENTS
ROCKY & CHAN
AND THAT DELIGHTFUL PARADE OF OTHERS IN-BETWEEN,
SPECIAL THANKS TO THE JOHN SIMON GUGGENHEIM FOUNDATION

I can remember riding beside the Barrington River on the back of my mother's bicycle and she was shouting out and celebrating because we had just dropped the bomb on the Japs in Hiroshima, and that meant that her two brothers were coming home. A lot of people died in World War II. I didn't know any.

The first death which occurred in *our* family was a cocker spaniel. Jill. Jealous Jill. We called her that because she was very jealous when my little brother was born. Jill died of distemper, which I thought meant bad temper because she was always jealous. But before she died, she bit me. Not *just* before she died, but some time before. I was harrassing her with a rubber submarine, as I often did in the pantry of our house in Barrington, Rhode Island, and she turned on me and took a chunk out of my wrist; it looked like a bite out of an apple from my point of view. I guess it wasn't because I don't have a scar. I ran to my mother and she said, 'You had it coming to you, dear, for harassing the dog with a rubber submarine.'

When we were 14, a group of us used to try to knock ourselves out. Organically. By taking 20 deep breaths, head held between our legs, and then coming up real fast and blowing on our thumbs without letting out any air. Then all the blood would rush up or down, I don't know which, but it would rush somewhere, fast. And we would hope to pass out, but it never worked. Then we'd spin in circles until we all got so dizzy that we fell down. Then we went home.

So one day I was in the bathtub taking a very hot bath. It was a cold day and the radiator was going full blast. I got out of the tub and thought, well, this is a good time to knock myself out, I'm so dizzy, I'm halfway there. So I took 20 deep breaths and went right out, and on my way out I hit my head on the sink, which was kind of a double knockout. When I landed my arm fell against the radiator. I must have been out quite a long time because when I came to, I lifted my arm up and it was like this dripping-rare-red roast beef, third-degree burn. Actually it didn't hurt at all because I was in shock, a steam burn on my finger would have hurt more. I ran downstairs and showed it to my mother and she said, 'Put some soap on it dear, and wrap it in gauze.' She was a Christian Scientist, so she had a distance on those things.

The next day when I got to school, the burn began to drip through the gauze. I went down to the infirmary, and when the nurse saw it she screamed. 'What, you haven't been to a doctor with this? That's a third-degree burn. You've got to get to a doctor right away.' So I went back home and told my mother what the nurse had said, and my mother said, 'Well, it's your choice, dear. It's your choice.'

Anyway, Jill died of distemper and I can remember I was wearing a tee shirt with a little red heart on it, and after the dog died I remember seeing the heart – my heart, the dog's heart, a heart – float up against a very clear blue sky. There was no pollution then in Barrington, Rhode Island. My mother told me that I stopped talking for a long time after that. She said they were thinking of taking me to a psychiatrist, but I don't know where they were going to find a psychiatrist in Barrington, Rhode Island, in 1946. Maybe they were thinking of Providence.

After Jill died, we got another dog, a beagle. We named the beagle Bugle because he made a sound like a bugle when he followed a scent. And Bugle would often get a scent in the fields behind our house where we used to play. We had a particular little grassy area we called 'Hitler's hideout', inspired by World War II, where we would play Korean war games on weekends. My mother forbade them on Sundays and discouraged them on weekdays, so Saturdays were usually pretty intense.

We had toy rifles and used a galvanized metal garden bug sprayer for a flame thrower, which one of us would wear on his back. It was attached to a long hose which led to a little pump handle, and instead of DDT we would shoot water out of it. Also, Ralston Russell's father had brought back a German luger from the war, as well as a German helmet, complete with swastikas. The luger had had its firing pin removed, but it was very real. The helmet seemed even more real. You could almost smell the dead German's sweat on the leather band inside. I assumed someone had taken this helmet right off a dead soldier, but I couldn't imagine Mr Russell doing that. He was a Christian Science practitioner during the war and I didn't think he'd seen much combat. I had always thought of him as a gray flannel mystic in his little office off their basement rec room where he went every day, dressed in a three-piece suit, to pray for sick people. They didn't even have to be there. He just sat and concentrated real hard on knowing 'the truth' and sent out all his thoughts to wherever his patients were lying, waiting to get better. But maybe Mr Russell did see action. Maybe he was in the field trying to bring dead GIs back to life. But the gun and helmet were very real. I was sure I could smell the enemy on them.

Judy Griggs was the only girl in the neighbourhood and she lived next door to us. Her father was my father's boss at the screw-machine plant, and I remember that they had a very big yard with an apple orchard at the end of it. Judy played a game with us in her yard called 'Ice Lady'. The Griggses had a clothesline shaped like the Pentagon, and Mrs Griggs would hang her sheets out to dry on it. Judy, who was the Ice Lady, would chase us through the rows of clean sheets until she touched one of us, and we had to freeze and stand still like a statue. Judy was queen of her backyard, but she wanted more. She wanted to be a member of our gang, which had only four of us in it, all boys. Judy tried to prove to us that she was a boy by putting a garden hose between her legs while her sister, Bethany, turned on the water. Once she used a turkey baster, but that still wasn't enough to convince us. We forced her to go into the fields with us and pull down her pants to show us that she really was a boy. Instead of a tinkler we saw her, well, I don't think we had a name for it actually, but I remember it as this very small, fleshy slit where her tinkler might have been if she had one. Then we took her into our chicken coop and tortured her mildly by tying her to a post and stirring up all the dust from the dirt floor with a broom. We'd leave her there until the dust settled, and she seemed to like it. At least she gave every sign of liking it.

The Griggses had hired an Italian yard man named Tony Pazzulo. Tony was lots of fun – he used to pick us up and swing us around and bury us under piles of raked leaves. The most fun was being thrown around by him. Our fathers, Dad and Mr Griggs, never touched us in that rough, playful way, and we all loved it. One day Tony took the cover off the cesspool for some reason and we all looked down into it.

It was a great dark pool of 'grunts' and 'doots' (we called the big ones 'grunts' and the small ones 'doots'), and suddenly the Griggses' yard took on a new dimension, even after Tony put the cesspool cover back on.

Shortly after Tony uncovered the cesspool, Mr Griggs bought a whole bunch of chickens. One Saturday he cut off all their heads while we watched. He used the stump of a big tree for a chopping block and held the chickens' heads down on it while he cut them off with an ax. Then the chickens ran headless around the yard with blood spurting from their necks until they flopped down on the ground and died.

Soon after Judy Griggs pulled her pants down, houses began to grow in the back fields. We played in the foundations and among the electrical wires and saw wallboards go on and the houses get finished and the new neighbors move in. I can remember once being up on some scaffolding and seeing some boards lying against a house, and I just decided to push them down on my friend Tim Morton. I didn't think about it. I just pushed and they fell and crushed him. I thought I had killed him, not only because of the way he was lying down there, but also because of the way his father ran, jumping over the hedge, to pick up Tim's limp body in his arms. I was terrified. I ducked back in through the window of the unfinished house to hide, and my older brother, Rocky, who stayed out on the scaffolding, had to take the blame. Tony Morton just stood there with his son's broken body in his arms, yelling up at Rocky, 'I'll be back to deal with you, my friend.' I felt scared for Rocky. I felt scared for all of us.

Not long after that, Tim died of lung cancer. He was very young and no one seemed able to diagnose it. They thought it was what they called a lung fungus that had been brought back by American soldiers from the Korean War. Tim's death was a strange kind of relief because we'd always heard that one in four would have to die of something – cancer, tuberculosis, polio, whatever – so I always wondered who would be the *one* of the four of us who hung out together. That was often on my mind.

We lost Bugle the beagle in the back fields during hunting season. My mother told me not to worry about it, this was something that happened. Hunters often stole dogs during the hunting season, so probably some nice, loving hunter had given Bugle a good warm home.

Shortly after Bugle disappeared we got a cocker spaniel that chased cars. I don't remember its name, but I do remember it chased cars and Harvey Flynt said we could cure this if we filled a squirt gun with vinegar and shot the spaniel in the eye with it every time it chased our car. But before we could try this, the dog was run over by a truck bringing cement to one of the new houses in the back fields.

Then we got another dog which we called Roughy because it was so rough with us. Soon after we got it, Dad said, 'I'm sorry boys, but we're going to have to give Roughy away because he's too rough.' By then my brother Rocky had become very attached to Roughy and didn't want to see him go. He wanted to save some memory of the dog, so he took one of Roughy's fresh 'doots' and put it in a jelly jar with a tight cap and kept it by his bed next to the little radio that had a Bob Hope decal on it and a white plastic dial that looked like a poached egg when it was lit.

Some time after that my mother took us out into the yard. It was summer and we sat in the shade of a big elm while she read to us from a book about the reproduction of cows.

We gave up at last on dogs and switched to cats. Our first cat's name was Kitzel. All I remember about Kitzel was that she was a calico who lived a long time and liked to eat corn-on-the-cob. After Kitzel grew up, I wanted a kitten, so I got a kitten from the Griggses that I called Mittens. I named her Mittens because she had little white markings on her front paws. And I had this relationship with Mittens: I would make a sound, kind of a half-blow, half-whistle (we called it a *wumple*), and Mittens would come running. Then one weekend she didn't come and I looked everywhere for her. The only place I did not look was the cellar of our barn. My brother Rocky told me that he had seen footprints of the Blain brothers down there. The Blain brothers were ten-foot-tall hairy men who roamed the Rhode Island countryside and were known to jump over eight-foot-high hurricane fences with a deer under each arm, or a child, because they were running out of deer in Rhode Island. Rocky told me the brothers had last been seen at the Boy Scout camp, Camp Yiago, not too far from where we lived.

At the end of the weekend, my mother said that she had seen the trash truck pick up Mittens's little body on Friday by the side of Rumstick Road, and she hadn't had the heart to tell me. Mom cheered me up by telling me that I could get another kitten.

And I did. I got another kitten and I named it Mittens, Mittens the Second. That Mittens was killed on Rumstick Road by Mrs Jessup driving a large black Chrysler at dusk. I saw it happen and began to run away, and Mrs Jessup ran after me to try to apologize and comfort me, but I ran ahead of her because I didn't want to see her. I ran into my house and up to my bedroom. I couldn't catch my breath and felt like I was suffocating.

This reminded me of the time when I woke up in the middle of the night and saw my brother Rocky standing on his bed, blue in the face and gasping for air, crying out that he was dying. My mother and father were standing beside the bed trying to quiet him, and Mom said, 'Calm down dear, it's all in your mind.' And after he calmed down, my father went back to bed, and my mother turned out the light and sat on the edge of Rocky's bed in the dark. The only illumination in the room was a cluster of fluorescent decals on the ceiling, of the Big Dipper, the Little Dipper, Saturn, and the Moon. We were all very quiet, in the dark, and then Rocky would start in, 'Mom, when I die, is it forever?' and Mom said, 'Yes.' And then Rocky said, 'Mom, when I die is it forever and ever?' And she said, 'Yes, dear.' And then he said, 'Mom, when I die is it forever and ever and ever?' And she said, 'Uh-huh, dear.' And he said, 'Mom, when I die is it forever and ever and ever and ever . . . ' I just went right off to this.

Rocky used to take me into the bottom of his bed – he called it Noss Hall, a foreign land under the blankets – and tell me that he loved me over and over again. I can remember the smell of his feet and how his sweat made a yellow ring around his collar – *yellow sweat*. Shortly after that, he left me for my Gram Gray, who lived with us. On Sundays I was allowed to go into their room and get into bed with my gramma, just to listen to Jack Benny and 'Allen's Alley'. I can remember the smell of my gramma – the smell of her flesh and the way it hung so soft and old – and the feel of her silk nightgown. I can remember that better than any contact with my mother.

My mother and I had two physical rituals that I clearly recall. One was the cleaning of my tinkler. We called it a tinkler then. Since I'm not circumcised, she would clean it every Saturday with cotton and baby oil and she would turn me quite firmly over her knee and go at it like a cleaning woman with a Chore Girl. She would do it very hard and it would hurt and I'd squirm in her arms.

The other ritual was 'making a path' – she'd sit at the edge of my bed and I'd stick out my arm and she'd make a path with her finger up the inside of my arm. She'd do this until I was almost hypnotized and went right out. Sometimes, my friend Ralston Russell would stay overnight, and my mother would sit in between our twin beds and we'd both stick out our arms and she'd make double paths.

After Mittens the Second died I got a third kitten that I named Mittens, which I think might have been a mistake. I found this Mittens's body one cold February day during double sessions. In the seventh grade we had double sessions because there weren't enough teachers to go around, so I went to school in the afternoons and got the mornings off to play. I'd go out and play and leave my math homework for my gramma to do, and then I'd come in and copy it over. I never learned how to add as a result. Gram smoked Viceroys and blew the smoke in my face. It went in blue and came out gray, and I liked the smell.

I would play outside with Patrick Scully and Scott Tarbox. Patrick Scully's father had a very good collection of pornographic pictures. He was in real estate and often had reason to go to Tijuana on business, and he would send back these picture postcards of matadors and bulls to his wife saying, 'Hi, having a lovely time at the bullfights in Tijuana.' And we thought, bullfights, yeah I bet. His entire bureau drawer was overflowing with these pornographic pictures, which he made no attempt to hide. Patrick and I would take out our favorite pictures, roll them up, put them in a jar, and bury them in Patrick's backyard. Then when we wanted to look at them again we'd just go dig them up. They were old and kind of yellowed, like tintypes. I used to imagine that the naked people in the pictures were very old or dead by the time I was looking at them, and somehow that added some spice to it.

Our favorite picture was an odd one, and that's why it was our favorite, I'm sure. We couldn't figure out what was going on in it. It was a picture of a man standing naked with this huge semi-erection (anything was huge to us, at 11 years old), and this semi-erection was just sort of lobbing down into a glass of water, which made it look even bigger because the glass magnified it. Then there was this naked woman kneeling in front of the glass, who was either about to drink out of it or had just finished drinking, I don't know which, but we found this photo fascinating because we couldn't imagine our parents doing this to have us. (Was that what sex was all about?) So we'd just look at it and then roll it up again, put it back in the jar, and bury it.

We didn't talk about this because we didn't have much of a vocabulary then. A penis was a tinkler, a dick, or a boner if it was hard, and my mother's breasts we called pontoons. That was about it, at 11 years old. Then one day Mrs Tarbox caught us changing into our bathing suits to go for a swim. We were all naked, Patrick, Scott, and me, and we clutched our suits over our tinklers and Mrs Tarbox said, 'What, are you modest?' And we didn't know what *that* meant and we weren't the kind to go look it up. But all of us were stamp collectors, and we each had something called 'The Modern Stamp Album'. So we equated the word *modest* with *modern*. It became the key sexy phrase – kind of a catchall – that we used whenever we wanted to talk about something dirty. We'd giggle and ask, 'Is that a Modern Stamp Album picture?' 'Is that a Modern Stamp Album house?' 'Is that a Modern Stamp Album movie?' Then we'd burst into hysterics and laugh until we fell down.

So it was during double sessions that I found Mittens the Third frozen in the backyard, just frozen solid like a package of green beans. My mother said the cat must have gotten into some rat poison. She had an explanation for every death. It was never mysterious.

I never knew what happened to the bodies. Someone took care of them. I don't remember any funerals; in the Christian Science Church there are no funerals at all. But, come to think of it, we did have a little graveyard with popsicle-stick crosses out behind the outhouse. That was the graveyard where we buried the little wild animals like mice and sparrows. Once I found a mouse near our back step and it was *alive* with maggots, so many maggots that its whole body was moving as though it were alive. We didn't bury that one. It was gone in three days.

As for domestic animals, most of them were buried out by the currant bushes in the apple orchard behind the house.

Shortly after we made the popsicle-stick graveyard, the polio epidemic came to town. I was terrified of ending up in an iron lung. We'd see pictures of them on TV. Paul Winchell and Jerry Mahoney were always trying to raise money for the March of Dimes, and we'd see them standing by an iron lung with huge rearview mirrors, and I'd think, God, how hideous. It would be like being buried alive.

Mrs Brinch, our fifth-grade science teacher, didn't help. She was obsessed with polio. At the end of the year she showed us pictures of polio victims she was taking care of and said, 'Now get plenty of rest this summer, drink a lot of water, be careful where you swim, don't go into any crowded movie theaters and remember, you can contact polio at any time.'

In the Christian Science Church you had to go to Sunday School until you were 20. There were a number of Sunday School teachers but the one I remember best is Chad Oswald. He always had a number of wonderful healings to tell about.

Each week we were asked to bring in a healing story of our own. This meant that each week something bad had to happen to us so we could be healed. For instance, I would say, 'I came down our back steps, tripped and fell and hit my head on the cement, and I knew the Truth and I was healed.' Then Ralston Russell, who was also in that class, would say, 'Oh, *that* cement, that's cheap cement. It's not hard – it's like rubber.' And I knew that was a class thing because the Russells had more money and could afford a firmer cement.

When I stayed over at Ralston's we talked to each other in the dark from the twin beds. We pulled down our pajama bottoms and talked about how it felt to be naked against the cotton sheets. One time, Mrs Russell, who was listening at the door, burst in and said, 'You both pull up your pants right now!'

Once I had this little piece of flesh growing off my nose. It was like a little stalactite, and it wouldn't go away. It was very embarrassing because it looked like a piece of snot and all my friends kept telling me to wipe my nose. My mother asked the Christian Science practitioner to pray for the stalactite to drop off. I got impatient and wanted to have a doctor burn it off, but Mom said, 'Please give it one more day, dear,' so I agreed. On that last day I was being tutored in math (since my gramma had done all my math homework for me, I couldn't add without doing it on my fingers), and my tutor said, 'It looks like you need to wipe your nose. Let me get you some Kleenex.' And I thought, oh, no, here we go again. So I pretended to be wiping my nose and the little stalactite just dropped right off.

Being Christian Scientists we had to work very hard in order to keep a hot line to God. If we let this hot line down, there was a chance that the polio germs might get in, so I was working overtime. When we got tired of working we could call the practitioner who would take over and pray for us while we rested up. We thought the polio germs were everywhere. Once Chan, my little brother, came home from kindergarten with his rest blanket, and on it were some little red threads. He said, 'Look, these are polio germs; they're so big you can see them,' and I believed him. Ralston Russell told me that he knew someone who stuck out his tongue and got polio instantly – the tongue just stayed out there, paralysed. So I was getting fearful. I was washing my hands with rubbing alcohol and staying out of crowded movie theaters in August and swimming with my head very high above the water. And I made it through the polio epidemic.

After I found the third Mittens dead, I sort of gave up on cats and started to get involved with birds. Eddie Potter and I both bought ducks for Easter. He named his Carl Duck, after our seventh-grade teacher Carl Caputo. I don't remember what I named mine. Eddie and I were close friends. Eddie was the kind of guy who would laugh at anything. He would buy an orange popsicle, eat half of it, and then instead of offering it to me or another friend, he'd throw the other half in the sand and stamp on it and laugh. Another thing he laughed at was cars that got stuck in the sand, particularly those old double-ended Studebakers. He would stand there, screaming with laughter, pointing at the back tires spinning in the sand.

Eddie and I used to play strip poker together; I would usually win, so Eddie would end up naked. The rule was that the loser would have to go through some mild ordeal, some little punishment, nothing very big. One of my punishments was to make Eddie crawl down between his twin beds. Most of Barrington, Rhode Island, was made up of twin beds. I don't think I saw a double bed until I got to Boston. My parents had twin beds that were very close together. When I was feeling anxious and no one was home I would go into my mother's walk-in closet, look at all her dresses, look at the line of shoes, and look at myself in her full-length mirror on the door. I liked that very much. Then, dressed only in my underwear, I would crawl between my parents' beds and hang there, just hang there until I felt all right.

My mother's parents, who lived down the street, had twin beds also, but theirs were wider apart because they had a larger bedroom. They fell in love at Hope High School and got married right after graduation. They had a good marriage and three children. My gramma's two sisters were not so lucky in love. There was Aunt Tud, who was jilted early on by a coffee plantation owner and never got involved with men after that. She became very plump. She'd always cook the meal bread and mince pies at Christmas and Thanksgiving. And then there was my Aunt Belle, who married Bob Budlong. They never had any children, but Bob made up for that because he was kind of like a half-child, half-man who ran a little grocery store in Scituate, Rhode Island. He could never stand collecting money from his customers, the poor people of Scituate, so he finally gave the whole store away and they ended up living in a trailer. It was very cold in that trailer, so when my grandparents went down to Florida for the winter, they'd invite Bob and Belle to stay in their home. This house was immaculate, like a joyful funeral parlor, with wall-to-wall carpeting.

At Christmas and Thanksgiving, Bob would blow up great long balloons that he brought from his store. He'd let them loose in my gramma's house and we'd all laugh as they sputtered around the room spraying juice over my grampa's bald head until at last they withered and dove into the after-dinner mints. Then Bob would fall asleep with his hands clasped over his belly and his stubby cigar stuck between his lips.

Bob would often take me for driving lessons. We'd drive all around Barrington waving at friends. I could barely see over the wheel or reach the clutch, never mind the brakes, and I loved it. After my driving lesson we'd come back to the house to watch 'Queen for a Day'. I don't know where Aunt Belle was all this time, maybe upstairs reading *Science and Health*. 'Queen for a Day' was Uncle Bob's favorite TV show. We'd watch it together and he would weep and clap to try to make the applause meter go up for his favorite contestant. Then, exhausted from all his clapping, he would fall asleep, leaving his cigar balanced on my gramma's coffee table, flaking ashes on her rug. Next 'The Mickey Mouse Club' would come on, and I'd stay very awake because I had a crush on Annette Funicello at the time. Sometime during the final song, Bob would wake up and say, 'When is "Queen for a Day" going to be on?' And I'd say, 'Uh, Bob. We just saw "Queen for a Day".' And he'd say, 'Well tell me all about it, tell me who won.' Then we'd go down to the Barrington shopping center, and he'd stick little hard candies down the backs of children. But I don't remember whether Bob and Belle had twin beds or a double bed in their trailer.

So Eddie's little punishment for losing at strip poker was to slip down between the twin beds and crawl naked over the little dust-balls, fuzzies we called them. Then he'd come up the other side of the bed smiling, covered with fuzzies and looking for more. I couldn't think of any more punishments, it wasn't my specialty, so he'd begin making up his own. I would be the witness. He'd take a little cocktail dish, the kind you'd use for pigs-in-the-blanket or smoked clams, and he would put his dick on it – still connected of course. Then he'd go downstairs and display it to Rita Darezzo, the cleaning woman, as though it were a rare hors d'oeuvre, calling, 'Rita, it's cocktail time!'

Anyway, the ducks were growing up; they were reaching puberty and my duck's quack was getting deeper. Winter was coming, and I was keeping the duck in the playroom so that it wouldn't mess up the house and would go on the linoleum. I put a little game board, a Karom board, in the doorway of the playroom to keep it in there. One Sunday I went up to get ready for Sunday School. I had to wear this woolen suit, which I hated, and to keep it from itching I'd put on my pajamas first. I was very thick. When I came downstairs, the board had fallen down and the duck was gone. I searched the house, but I couldn't find it anywhere. Then I walked over and lifted up the board and there it was, flat, like pressed duck, like Daffy Duck after the steamroller has run over him. It didn't look real. It didn't look like any duck I'd known. I couldn't figure out how a board that thin could have done something like that. I thought my father must have stepped on it, by accident. I thought he must have come into the playroom and stepped on the board, but I didn't want to think that. I don't know who took care of the little body, but I went off to Sunday School.

After the duck, I continued with the birds and got a parakeet that I called Budgy. This parakeet was one of the blue ones – there were two kinds, blue and green – and it cost $7.50. I had a wonderful relationship with Budgy for about a year. I would whistle from my room and he would whistle back from downstairs. Then I would run down, feed him, change his water and clean the bottom of his cage. About a year went by and one day I whistled and whistled and . . . you know the rest. I went downstairs and there he was, on his back on the bottom of the cage with his little claws curled up. I thought he must have died of a heart attack or pneumonia because I was told these tropical birds were not used to the New England climate.

*

After a short break with no pets, or maybe just a random turtle or two in between, a next-door neighbor offered me an empty 50-gallon fish tank. I thought, why not, they're 90 percent water and I won't give them names. I bought every kind of tropical fish. I had the black mollies, the zebra fish, the neons, the swordtails, the guppies, the catfish, the angel fish and the Siamese fighters, who bit the tails off the angel fish. And they died. They died often. The proliferation of death made me more indifferent to it, I think. I would take the little white net and scoop them up and ride them down on my bike to one of the lots in the neighborhood that hadn't been developed yet. I'd give them an outdoor burial by flicking them out of the net and into the grass.

About a mile down the road from that vacant lot lived the Lillows, who had the first television in the neighborhood, and we would go there to watch 'Howdy Doody'. One day a group of us were coming out of the house and we looked up and saw Stokes Lillow hanging from a pine tree, showing us his asshole. We were standing there looking up and he was just hanging there like a little koala bear, spreading his cheeks. I had never seen anything like that before. I don't think I had even seen my own.

Shortly after Stokes Lillow showed us his asshole, that vacant lot was developed and a German family with a strange name moved in – the Lindbergers. Now this seemed odd to us, like they were from some other side of some other tracks. We hadn't seen any Germans, we hadn't seen any blacks, we hadn't seen any Jews, we hadn't seen anything but Rhode Island WASPs. So in came the Lindbergers, and they were a strange family. First of all, there were more than three children in the family, that was the first odd thing. The second odd thing was that Mr Lindberger was having an affair with his secretary. Mrs Lindberger told my mother this, and my mother told me. (My mother and I were very close – actually we dated all the way through college – and so she'd tell me these intimate things.) I didn't know anything about affairs. I thought they only happened in New Hampshire because my grandmother had lent me her copy of *Peyton Place*. It was the first real novel I ever read, and it got me started. After that I went on to Jack Kerouac and Thomas Wolfe. My mother said to me, 'Mr Lindberger is having an affair with his secretary because every time Mr Lindberger touches Mrs Lindberger she gets an electric shock.' So they were having these electric shock treatments, but they weren't having any kind of love life. But he was a good provider. He would always come home late at night in his Lincoln Continental, a big black Lincoln Continental with the spare tire built into the trunk. He took very good care of his children – he had five of them – and he was a good father. He'd see his secretary at night and come home late.

I made friends with Larry Lindberger, who was a couple of years older and had a parakeet. But he had a completely different relationship with his parakeet than I did. He would let it out of the cage, let it fly around the dining room, then take a wet towel, twist it up and snap the bird right out of the air. And the bird would go like a feather bullet, ricochet off the window, and then flutter around with its tail dragging like an overloaded B-49 trying to take off. He'd snap it maybe one more time and then he'd put it back in its cage so it could rest up for the next day. When I saw this, I knew Larry and I had a different aesthetic. But I didn't stop him from hitting the bird, I just watched and took it in.

So the fish died out and the tank got emptied and I gave up on animals and started to get interested in people. I had been putting this off as long as possible. But before I got involved with people I went on what you might call a shooting spree. I got a pellet pistol, went outside and started shooting everything in sight. All the songbirds on telephone wires, frogs, and one squirrel, which we ate – it tasted like a rat. The frog legs we ate too. They were very skinny, not like you'd get in a French restaurant, but tasty.

I wanted to buy a shotgun so I could go duck hunting, but my father said no. And I knew by then that when my father said no it meant yes, so I kept at him. At last I got a single-barrel Winchester 20 gauge and began to hunt for black ducks. I wasn't a very good shot and would often only wound them and have to finish them off with my switchblade. I'd hold them down and slit their throats. It was awful.

Then one day when I was out on my paper route down near Potter's Cove I heard mallard ducks quacking and got very excited because I'd never shot a mallard before. So I got up real early the next morning and went down to Potter's Cove. Just when I got there a huge flock of mallards took off in this spectacular V-formation, and I just stood there and watched. I don't know why I didn't pull the trigger. I wanted to think it was against the law to shoot ducks before dawn.

Shortly after that I sold my gun to my father and he put it away in a closet.

Then I started going to dancing school on Friday nights. That meant Friday-night baths, after which I put on my pajamas and my blue wool suit over them, and my white gloves – then I went downstairs to wait for the car pool to pick me up. While I was waiting I would look for sexy pictures in any magazine I could find. We didn't have any *National Geographics*. The only sexy pictures in our house besides the underwear ads in the Sears Roebuck catalog were to be found in *Life* magazine, which arrived every Friday, just in time.

I found two erotic pictures in *Life* magazine that I kept going back to. One was of Prince Charles jumping over hurdles as a young boy, which I kept under the bed and used to look at every time I was anxious. The other was of the collapse of Rome, with everyone crawling around in the streets half naked. Maybe they had the plague. I thought, this is really sexy: anything goes now because there are no more rules. Everyone can just do what they want sexually.

I'd be looking at this picture when the car pool would come and take me away to dancing school and I'd have to snap into the box step. I would dance with Sue Wheelock, my partner, and they would play 'Sweet Sue' on the piano. I had a recording of 'Sweet Sue' on a Paul Whiteman record. It was one of those painted records with a picture of the whole Paul Whiteman band that spun into a blur of color when I turned the record player on. I loved that song; it went, 'Every star above, reminds me of the one I love, Sweet Sue, it's you' in one of those high, 1920s crooner voices. And I would say to Sue Wheelock, 'Isn't it a coincidence that they're playing "Sweet Sue"?' as though it implied that we were meant for each other. That chance and destiny had smiled down from above. But she thought I was just trying to put the make on her at an early age, so that didn't get me very far.

I had a relationship on another dancefloor with Sally Funk. We were in every jitterbug contest in the canteen in seventh grade. We were real good jitterbuggers, but it never went beyond the dancefloor. Then I fell in love with Julie Brooks, and Julie Brooks I can only describe as an angel – very full lips, olive skin, long brown hair. Julie and I and a bunch of us who were hanging out together would have kissing contests. We would all get together and see how long two people could hold a kiss. Someone would time it while the rest of us stood around watching, smoking Lucky Strike Regulars. Julie and I used to kiss for about 20 minutes, just holding our lips pressed tight with no movement at all. I was very uncomfortable because it was hard to breathe. The other thing we'd do is have make-out sessions in Julie's house when her mother wasn't there, playing 'Sha-Boom, Sha-Boom' on her little automatic 45-record player. Then we got into dry humping in the field behind Julie's house in September in the sun. I always liked it in the sun. Six of us would go out there, three boys and three girls, and we'd make different spots in the grass and make out. Julie was always wearing those madras Bermuda shorts that were so popular in the late fifties, and I would get my hand up on her right thigh, and that was enough. I'd never go any further, in my mind the rest was a jungle. Once I did touch the jungle, briefly, and I told my friend Ryan Ryder about it. He said, 'What, you touched the place she pees out of?' That brought me down and fast. I think he was jealous, but I didn't know about jealousy then. I didn't know about jealousy until two weeks later. So I went back to keeping my hand on her thigh, dry humping until I would come. I would come in my jeans and then we'd go have vanilla Cokes. I was happy and I thought she was happy, too; things were going fine until one of the girls, Linda Chipperfield, asked her mother if she could get pregnant through her clothes, and we never saw Linda again. I think her mother kept her in forever. So that broke up our club.

Around that time I told Julie that I was going to fuck her; we had just gotten up the courage to say 'fuck' in public. It was probably more exciting than the actual act, although none of us in the neighborhood had even done it yet. Ryan always warned us to be careful about saying it on the streets. He said that we could be brought up on a morals charge and we'd get our driver's licenses revoked. But none of us had our driver's licenses yet.

Telling Julie I was going to fuck her was kind of like a threat and a promise, a threat to me and a promise to her. I thought it was time. I gave her two weeks, I don't know why it was two, but it was going to be the second Saturday in October. I didn't know how I was going to do it.

The Saturday before the Saturday that I was going after Julie my father said that we should go play golf. This was odd to me, we had never played golf before. Later I found out from my gramma that my father's father, Grampa Gray, told him the facts of life out on a golf course. But we didn't even belong to a country club. In Barrington, Rhode Island, there were two classes of people, those who belonged to the Rhode Island Country Club and those who didn't. We didn't. So my father and I had to play golf at the Wampanaug public course, just over the border in Seekonk, Massachusetts. It was a little nine-hole course that we called Swampanaug because when it rained it was mostly under water. When we got to about the fourth hole, my father said, 'You know, there was a gal at our plant . . .' he meant his factory (he worked at a very conservative factory that made screw machines and they didn't even allow Coca-Cola until the old boss retired) '. . . there was this gal at our office who had a turkey in the oven, and she wouldn't admit it because she wasn't married. Everyone knew she had a turkey in the oven, it was as plain as the nose on her face. Everyone was looking at it. It was disgusting. She stayed around until she had this turkey, and then she left.'

After a long silence, he said, 'You know, there are diseases that make you blind.' Now I knew that sex and blindness somehow went together because Ray Strite told me that if you got sperm in your eyes, you could go temporarily blind and that men on Devil's Island would rub sperm in their eyes in the morning to get out of a particularly difficult work shift. So I did have that equation in my head.

Then I began to get paranoid. I suspected that there might be a plot afoot, that Mrs Brooks had called my father and said, 'You know, your son is going to fuck my daughter and you better take him out on a golf course and tell him he's going to go blind if he does that.' Also Reverend Quigley's wife had seen Julie and me wrestling in the backyard and had come out and slapped a part of Julie's anatomy and said that people our age do not wrestle, boys and girls do not wrestle together, this was a rule in our neighborhood. I thought that maybe Mrs Quigley had told Mrs Brooks. I saw that my father was as nervous as I was, or more so, so I tried to relieve him by saying, 'I won't do it, I won't do whatever it is that you're talking about. I won't do it.'

That Saturday I went to see Julie. And I found out that Julie had played Spin the Bottle with Billy Patterson the night before, and that they had ended up exchanging shirts. That meant that he had seen Julie in her bra and she had seen his skinny bare chest. So that was it with Julie. That was pretty much it until I was 25, it was a heavy rejection. I went off with Ryan, the one who told me not to touch the place she pees out of, to see *Heaven Knows, Mr Allison* in Providence.

Some weeks later I tried to get Julie back. I began to force myself on her. I would hold her down and try to kiss her, and she would push me away. And no one was around to tell me that this was not the way to win someone back. No one was giving me any information. They were telling me about turkeys and going blind, but they were not telling me how to get Julie Brooks back, which was the advice I was looking for.

Shortly after that masturbation took hand. I'm not saying that it was Julie's fault – actually I had discovered it while I was going out with her. Thurston Beckingham had told me that if you took a piece of animal fur and rubbed your dick real fast it would feel good. That's all, just rub it and it would feel good. I didn't have any animal fur around the house and I wasn't the type of kid to go out and buy some just to do that. But there were a lot of Davy Crockett hats in the neighbourhood. Then one night I just began doing it with my right hand (we called it Madam Palm and her five lovely daughters), just instinctively, like a monkey. I didn't expect anything to come of it, but after about half an hour I had an ejaculation. That was a surprise, no one had told me that I could do it on my own. I think I kept at it just because it felt good. Then it became a kind of . . . I wouldn't call it a habit exactly, but it was something that I practiced often at night. I would read *Sexology* magazine to try to find out if I was going to grow hair on my palms or go crazy.

Eventually, the masturbation became more elaborate, the way those things do. There was a big mansion across the street from our house that the president of Blackstone Valley Gas and Electric owned, and I would run around in his backyard, naked under a full moon, swinging from pine trees like a monkey, over marble statues of women in the nude. That was one of the excitements. The other was mirrors.

I began to like to masturbate in front of mirrors. The mirror was very important because, being a Christian Scientist, I kind of lost track of my body; for many years it was denied me. So it became important for me to look at what was there, to get a good sense of it. Also, my father had a deck of playing cards with naked women on them, airbrush jobs, like the photo of Marilyn Monroe naked on that red velvet spread. When my parents weren't home I would go into their room and take these cards out of his bureau drawer and look at them. Just look at them. This would get me excited and then I would cross the room to my mother's full-length mirror. On the way I would have to pass her bureau, on top of which were pictures of all my relatives: my grampa in his business suit, my aunt in her wedding dress, and my two uncles in their navy uniforms. They all had incredibly serious looks and their eyes seemed to follow me as I passed. I was young enough to maintain an erection past that, get to the mirror, and masturbate in front of it, catching glimpses over my shoulder of my uncles, my grampa, and my aunt.

There were no real private places to masturbate in the neighborhood, and no one had locks on their bedroom doors. Friends would sometimes report getting caught by their mothers, which I could not imagine. There was a bathhouse at the yacht club with private stalls, but my father would always rush me, calling out, 'Hurry up! What's taking you so long to change?' There was a hole in the wall where you could look through to the girls' side, which I did only once and no one was there. Then we'd have group masturbation, in Gill Leach's attic. It wasn't exactly a circle jerk, it was just to see who would come first. I don't think we kept score.

But once again something happened to make me paranoid. My parents decided to send me away to a religious camp for the summer, Camp Genesis on Cape Cod. I don't know why. The camp had nothing to do with Christian Science, it was more of a Holy-Roller-type fire-and-brimstone camp. It was coeducational. The boys and girls were divided by a cold, cold lake: the boys on the north shore, the girls on the south. It was there at Camp Genesis that I fell in love with Timmy Cox. Timmy was as pretty as Julie Brooks, only he was a boy, which was very confusing. I decided to keep a safe distance. I just looked at Timmy, endlessly. Then one day he hit me in the head with his shoe. He must have sensed something, he just threw the shoe across the tent and hit me, knocked me out. They took me to the infirmary, and I guess they gave me some sort of sleeping pill to make me relax. I started to go out, but never having had sleeping pills before I thought the nurse might have given me an overdose, and I began to fight to stay awake. After I got back to the tent, Timmy apologized, and I realized I had to do something else with my attraction to him.

   That's when the spitting began. At night, after lights out, I would spit into my right hand and then fling it across the tent until someone cried out, 'Hey, who spit?' And I knew it had hit someone. They would always blame the person in the bed over them. I did this almost every night. I did this for a long time until my friend Ryan Ryder sent me a letter in which he asked how the spitting was going. Someone in the tent got ahold of the letter and threatened to tell our counselor. I was afraid of being punished by him. He was an ex-stockcar driver and a recent born-again Christian, and I had never been beaten before. I knew the guy who had read the letter was stealing live ammunition from Edwards Air Force Base, which was next to our camp. I threatened to tell on him if he told on me. We had a good blackmail relationship going and he never turned me in.

   At the end of July, my mother came to camp to pick me up. The whole family was going to a reunion for my Grampa Gray, who lived in Holland, Michigan. Now Grampa Gray was an odd man. He was married three times, first to my Gram Gray. They got divorced shortly after my father was born. Gram Gray told me that she had stayed with Curtis for as long as she did because the sex life was so good. For 10 years. And she never got involved with another man after that.

   I had been out to Holland, Michigan, to visit Grampa Gray once before, when I was much younger, and I can remember only one thing about it: One morning I was sitting downstairs at the breakfast table and he came down wearing a Harpo Marx wig and said, 'Come here, boy, come here and sit on my lap.' I sat on his lap and he said, 'You be a good boy or I'll pour this whiskey down your neck.' I said, 'Oh, you wouldn't dare.' And he did, he poured the whole glass down the back of my neck, and I started to cry.

   But this time, as we were driving away from Camp Genesis, my mother said to me, 'Spalding dear, I have some bad news. Grampa Gray has passed away. He died of a heart attack. Lois called up and said to come out anyway for a party. Curtis would have loved it.' Lois was Grampa Gray's third wife. Dad called her a real card, a hell of a gal, and Mom said she was the life of the party. Once when she came to visit us she got drunk and put on a rubber Mortimer Snerd mask. We all laughed and went to the Fore 'n Aft steak house, and on the way Grampa Gray tried to feel up Gram Gray, his first wife, while Lois sat in the back.

   When we got out to Michigan, we had a big party. I played

boogie-woogie on the piano while Dad danced into the night with a tall blonde relative I'd never seen before. Mom went to bed early because she didn't drink. I remember masturbating in an upstairs closet and reading about a sex slaying in *True Detective* magazine in which the naked bodies of two 11-year-old boys were found in the trunk of a car not far from Grampa Gray's farm.

As soon as I got home from Michigan, my friend Spike Claxton came over to see me. He had just gotten his driver's license and had bought a '49 Ford coupe. He asked me if I wanted to go over to Dirty Dick Dixon's to have my tubes cleaned. I didn't know what he was talking about, but I wanted to get out of the house and I was curious. We drove over to Dirty Dick's, which was on the other side of town where all the tract houses with lawns like golf greens were. Dirty Dick Dixon's was right in the middle of this little development, surrounded by trees and overgrown hedges to prevent people from looking in. We pulled into the clamshell driveway and went through the side door into the kitchen, where there was a table with whiskey bottles on it. Dirty Dick was there and some guys from Bay Springs – Tony De Luca, Izzie de Rosa, Mickey de Silva – all in their dungaree jackets. There were some porn pictures spread out on the table. Not very good ones – mostly close-ups, mostly hair. And in the corner by the refrigerator stood Chad Oswald, my old Sunday School teacher. I could only see this as a coincidence. Here we were face-to-face and I thought he should leave. But instead of leaving he just went into the living room and sat down. Then Spike turned to me and said, 'Hey, you see that guy who just went into the living room? I saw him here last night, he had his schlong out on the table and it was *huge*. It was like a piece of Polish sausage.' And I said, 'Oh, really?'

So we all went into the living room to wait to get our tubes cleaned in the tube-cleaning room, or whatever it was, the guest bedroom. And Dirty Dick kept coming out to take us in one at a time. At that point I'd given up on the idea of having my tubes cleaned, in fact, I didn't even feel like I had any tubes to be cleaned. I just sat there looking across at the Sunday School teacher, when suddenly a fight broke out. Spike Claxton hit Tony De Luca. Over went a chair. Over went a lamp. And the Sunday School teacher raced for the front door and we ran back. Spike and I jumped into his car, spun rubber, spun clamshells, got out of there, got home. I didn't tell anyone about it. I decided to keep it a secret.

The next day Spike called up and said, 'Hey, Dirty Dick called me this morning and told me never to bring that Gray boy over again. What's the problem? What did you say to him? What's up?' I just said, 'I don't know, Spike, I don't know.' Then a week later my mother said to me, 'Oh, I saw Chad Oswald at a concert with his mother. He'd make some gal a real good husband. Why do you think he doesn't get married?' And I just said, 'I don't know, Mom, I don't know.'

At the time I was getting straight E's in school. E was for failure, and they wrote it in red. So I was failing everything. I really wanted to transfer into the automobile mechanics course, but they only let Italians take that. I ended up in the business course, but I didn't do very well there either, since my gramma had always done all my math homework. So instead of adding and subtracting I began to systematically destroy the school.

I would get rotten eggs from in back of the supermarket. I'd bring them to school with me in the morning, and when the halls were crowded, I'd lob them into the Latin teacher's room. Other times I'd break off the lead from a pencil in the lock of Mrs Brumage's door so we wouldn't have to go into her all-boys English class to stand and recite Portia's speech, 'The quality of mercy is not strained . . .'

At last I began building bombs. I'd take a birthday candle and stick it in a wad of clay, lay a big cherry bomb firecracker at the bottom of the candle, and put it behind a toilet in the boys' room. It's not as though I never thought someone might sit on that toilet – I did think about it, I did think that would be bad. Then I'd light the candle and head for English class from where, exactly 15 minutes later, I'd hear this enormous explosion and all the teachers would run out to try to catch the mad bomber. They'd round up all the boys, whose ears were still ringing from the blast, and take them down to be interrogated in the principal's office, but no one ever knew anything. Finally, Mr Balducci, the science teacher, offered a $5 reward for any information leading to the identity of this mad bomber. No one turned me in.

My older brother, Rocky, also tried to wreck the high school. At last, he was suspended for jumping up and down on the roof during a band concert. He really wanted to be a Maine guide, and once he tried to run away to Maine. But he did it the hard way, by crawling out his bedroom window, inching along the gutter, and climbing down a pine tree. He only got as far as Pawtucket. When he got back, he couldn't stand living in the big house anymore, so he stole some lumber and built a shack in our backyard.

Rocky used to have this problem. When he was out on his paper route, he would see trucks dumping dirt into the new foundations of the big houses and he'd hallucinate a child being covered over by the dirt. He would come home and tell my mother, 'I just saw someone being buried alive.' My mother would say, 'It's only your imagination, dear. Sit down.' Then she'd read to him from the Bible or from *Science and Health* to ground his imagination. In the winter when he was out on his paper route riding alongside the Barrington River, he'd see a hole in the ice and imagine that a child was falling through it. He'd come back and tell my mother, 'I saw a child falling through the ice, it's drowning! We've got to call the police.' And she'd say, 'Sit down, dear, let me read to you from the Bible.' Finally, my parents thought Rocky should go away to school to straighten out and buckle down. They sent him to Fitchton Academy in New Hampshire, and he hated it there. He would call my father up and say, 'You've got to get me out of this school, I'm very unhappy.' Then my father would go up and get him and when they'd get as far as the Howard Johnson's at the Portsmouth rotary my father would say, 'Let's stop here and get a clam roll.' But Rocky was paralysed. He couldn't go in. He was convinced that he was going to kill someone in the restaurant. They drove all the way back to Barrington on empty stomachs.

So my father said to me, 'We're thinking of sending you to Fitchton Academy. It's time to buckle down or you'll end up in the navy. It's shape up or ship out for you, my friend.'

Fitchton was run by a rabble-rouser, Colton W. Cartwright. He would have 'squirm sessions' on Sundays with the students, at which he made these Cotton Mather speeches. He would start by holding up a water glass saying, 'Eighty percent of the Coca-Cola glasses in America have active syphilis germs on the edge.' That was just the opener. He'd go on from there for an hour. He'd say, 'Today it is the jungles of Laos. Tomorrow it will be the cornfields of Fitchton!' This was the school that they were thinking of sending me to, and I had to go up there for an interview.

My mother drove. It was about a four-, five-hour trip up to Fitchton, New Hampshire. I might have been thinking about Susan Tice, the first girl in our neighborhood to get a two-piece, leopard-skin bathing suit. I was constantly dreaming of being on a desert island with Susan, just the two of us. I would dream of her in school and I'd get an erection. Then I'd have to go up to the board to do some math, and I'd have to kind of force it down and then walk bent over like a cripple. So, I guess I was thinking of Susan Tice all the way up to Fitchton.

We got up there, walked in, and C. W. Cartwright in his three-piece suit looked at us from under his bushy eyebrows and said, 'Well, my friend, what's going on with you? Look at this report card. Straight E's. Why aren't you buckling down? What's the problem?' Now, no one had asked me anything like this before, just straight out. He just took me aside, a stranger. It was kind of sobering. I wasn't ready for it.

Out of nowhere, I said, 'Well, since *they* have invented the hydrogen bomb, there is no future. Not only does it negate my consciousness, it negates that of Beethoven's.' There was a long pause. He looked back at me and said, 'That's what *they* said when *they* invented the crossbow.' Now I knew there was a difference between the hydrogen bomb and the crossbow, but I didn't know how to tell him because I was too intimidated by his three-piece suit and his bushy eyebrows. I just looked back at him, and Mom and I drove back in a kind of funk.

Later we got a letter from Fitchton Academy, and my father said, 'This is awful. They are not going to accept you because of your attitude. You're going to end up in the navy.' Which frightened me. I believed him this time. So my father said, 'I'm going to write C. W. Cartwright a letter and request that he give you a second interview. Do you think you can promise me that you'll cooperate with him this time?' So I said, 'All right, yes, I'll give it a try.' And my mother drove me all the way up again. I walked into C. W. Cartwright's office, and he said, 'Well, my friend, can you promise us that you'll buckle down?' And I said, 'Yes, yes. I'll buckle down. I'll buckle down. I'll do it, I'll buckle down.'

BOOZE, CARS, AND
COLLEGE GIRLS

BOOZE

My mother was a Christian Scientist, so she didn't drink. But she drank a lot before she became one. She used to date Jed Hanley, whose father owned the Narragansett Brewery and whose grandfather owned the Mount Hope Bridge. My mother, Jed, and the whole gang would go down to Prudence Island for keg parties. Patience and Prudence were two islands in Narragansett Bay, just under the Mount Hope Bridge. They chose Prudence Island for their parties and drained the kegs dry. Mom told me that she remembered lying under the dripping spigot to catch the last drops, and then she'd stagger home. And her mother, my Gram Horton, would ask, 'What's wrong, honey?' And she'd answer, 'Oh, nothing. I guess I had too many sandwiches.' And Gramp Horton would believe her.

My father was a drinking man. He drank 'tall ones', bourbon and water on ice. No short ones for him, and no wine. We never saw wine in our house. We did see beer. Boh Beer. Boh was short for Bohemian and cost about $2.85 a case. My father always drank it at basement temperature. When I was very young, he let me have little sips. He'd give it to me in a little one-ounce beer mug with a little cork in the bottom.

The first time I saw wine was when my Uncle Tinky brought two bottles of Great Western sparkling burgundy to Gram and Gramp Horton's for Thanksgiving. I sat next to Gram Gray, who didn't like sparkling burgundy all that much, so she took only a few sips and left the rest for me. That meant I had almost two glasses, and that sparkling burgundy made me so happy I wanted more.

I went to my friend Pete which was short for Meatman Pete, which was an alias for Lowell Prout. Lowell changed his name right after he heard the song 'Meatman Pete' on an album called 'Songs Your

Mother Never Knew.' I actually have the album, given to me by the owner of a record store in Warren. The store was right next to a Catholic church, and the owner was afraid of offending the priest who often came in to browse. One day I was in the store looking for the 45 of 'WPLJ' (White Port Lemon Juice) by the Four Deuces, and the owner quite suddenly just took the album 'Songs Your Mother Never Knew' and said, 'Here, do me a favor, get this filth out of here.' I grabbed the album and went back to Lowell's to play it. There were some great songs, but the ones I remember best were 'Where Can I Find a Cherry for My Banana Split?' and 'Meatman Pete'. So I went to my friend Pete and said, 'Wine is good. Wine is a good thing,' and we set out on a quest to find the sparkling burgundy.

We had a plan. We'd drive to the beginning of Mount Hope Bridge, then turn around so we wouldn't have to pay the toll, and head back toward Providence to pick up sailors hitchhiking up to Newport – older sailors, career men, guys who were over 21 and wouldn't mind buying us booze in exchange for a ride.

When we got to the package store – in Rhode Island they always call liquor stores package stores, I guess because the liquor had to be wrapped in brown paper – we wanted to ask the sailors to buy us sparkling burgundy, but I was too embarrassed. Sparkling burgundy seemed like an unmanly request. So I just told the sailor to get wine, red wine.

He came out with a bottle of Petri port, and that's when Pete and I found out about other kinds of wine. Petri port was sweet ruby red, and had twice the amount of alcohol as the sparkling burgundy. I missed the bubbles. But it felt thick and warm in my belly as we guzzled it down, late at night, parked in Pete's '49 Ford at the far end of a deserted gravel pit. It made us laugh a lot and feel so good that we wanted more.

It wasn't long before we developed a code language over the phone in which we could discuss our runs for sailors without giving ourselves away to our parents. We referred to our booze runs as 'going bowling' and our drunken daytime drinking sessions – getting drunk in the day had become the thing to do – as 'luncheons'. Our conversation went something like this: 'Hi Pete. Let's go bowling tonight and plan on a luncheon two days from now.' Our code word for sparkling burgundy, which had become the eternal quest, was

'Scabaskiblio'. It was a crazy word that came out of the bubbly feeling produced by that wine.

By the time we'd thought up that word we'd gotten up the courage to ask the sailors for sparkling burgundy, but most of the stores along the Newport–Providence route didn't stock the stuff. Also, most of the sailors seemed stubbornly attached to buying only Petri port, as though they were on some sort of sales commission. I guess they just went for the first red wine they saw, and Petri port was well displayed.

Most of the luncheons were held at Pete's house because both his parents worked in the day. Pete would put on a record of Sidney Bechet, or Fats Waller playing 'Your Feets Too Big', and then we'd start drinking until we'd get so rambunctiously drunk we had to let off steam. We'd do that by jumping out his second-storey window, landing on the lawn and then running around back upstairs and jumping out again.

Soon Ryan Ryder joined our luncheon club, but Ryan liked vodka. He liked vodka because he said it had no smell and the authorities couldn't detect it on your breath. He liked Mr Boston Vodka, maybe because we lived close to Boston or maybe because of the Cold War (Ryan was the conservative among us). We liked Mr Boston, too, and we liked it cold. Real cold.

Sometimes we'd make 'Russian oranges' to take down and suck on in the Barrington shopping center. We'd just cut the top off an orange and slowly pour the vodka in. Then stand around and get real high sucking on oranges.

Once when my parents were away and I was staying with my grandparents, Ryan and I planned a big luncheon at my house. It was summer and hot. Three days before the luncheon we'd buried a pint of Mr Boston deep in our freezer under all my father's meat. My father loved meat and would wrap it himself in freezer paper, so the freezer was filled with what looked like frozen generic Christmas presents. We dug down deep and buried the vodka under a pork roast and some frozen venison. When we pulled it out, it was real cold and viscous, as though it was right on the edge of freezing.

This luncheon, Ryan and I drank the cold vodka straight. After we finished the pint, Ryan wanted to take a swim in the Barrington River, which was right at the bottom of our road.

So we went staggering down Chapin Road on that August afternoon, and I noticed that Ryan was falling down on all these suburban lawns. At first I thought he was doing it as a joke, but soon I realized he was really drunk. Not far from the end of the road was one of those immaculate tract houses with a manicured lawn that looked like a putting green, a rooster weather vane, an American bald eagle over the two-car garage, permanent metal awnings over all the windows and a small air conditioner in the bedroom window. It was one of those houses that seemed to have eyes. It always looked like no one was home, but you felt like the whole house was watching your every move. I don't know why Ryan chose that lawn to fall down on so many times, but he did, and he did it over and over. He stood up and fell down, then he stood up again and fell down again.

When we got to the bottom of Chapin Road, a police cruiser was waiting for us. The cop just sat there like he was in full control of the whole situation, and when he saw us, he got out. He stood right in front of us and said, 'Okay boys, get in the car.' And Ryan said, 'What do you mean, why?' And the cop just goes, 'You're drunk, that's why.' And Ryan said, 'Drunk? What do you mean, drunk? You can't smell vodka.'

I didn't know what real drinking was until I met Felix Quinn. I met Felix at Fitchton Academy in New Hampshire, where my parents sent me when my grades were so bad I almost had to join the navy. Felix was the first worldly drinker I'd met. His father was a composer and had sent Felix to an American school in Germany where Felix had had the opportunity to attend some real German brewfests. It was there that he learned the good old German drinking expression, 'Beer on wine, das is fine, wine on beer, das is fear'. Felix knew everything about drinking and also how to hold his booze well; he was no thimble-belly.

We didn't drink at all at Fitchton Academy. It was absolutely forbidden. If you were caught drinking you'd be immediately expelled. But we made stabs at it on weekends. We'd drink orange extract and brew our own hard cider in the dorm rooms.

It was not easy to brew a gallon jug of hard cider without being discovered. In order to speed up the fermentation process we added raisins. We built a water seal from a piece of clear plastic tubing, which ran into a glass of water and let the gas out without letting in destructive bacteria from the air. If air got in, the cider turned into a vinegary solution that smelled like skunk cabbage. We called it 'skunk-o'. We'd say, 'Your brew's gone skunk-o, man. Dump it.'

It was also not easy to hide a gallon jug with a water seal in those little dorm rooms. In the autumn, the height of the cider season, teachers would check for illegal brew almost every day. I had mine hidden in the inside of a large wooden hi-fi speaker cabinet that my roommate had built. We played a lot of Fats Waller to make the cider brew faster.

Before I thought of the speaker cabinet (which was eventually found out), I kept the cider jug on its side in an old, black doctor's satchel I'd bought for $2 at the Fitchton fair. This was also before I had a water seal, and every day I'd slowly remove the cap to ease the fermenting gas. Once I forgot to do this and the gas was building so fast that when I got back from soccer practice I found that the jug had exploded. Glass was embedded in the side of the satchel. Thousands of fruit flies swarmed around a sticky, brown liquid puddle which oozed from the bottom of the bag.

If we couldn't drink at Fitchton Academy, we could at least plan how and when we would drink away from school. Felix and I planned two big luncheons, which were becoming more like lost weekends. The first was to take place over Christmas vacation at Felix's place in New York City. I was excited. I had never been to New York City before, and Felix had told me it was easy to get served there. They often didn't ask for ID. Besides, his father would take us out to all the clubs.

What I wasn't prepared for were his parents and the way they lived. I'd never seen anything like it before. They lived in a hotel and drank an awful lot. They claimed to be looking for an apartment but never got around to finding one, so they were paying some huge daily fee to live in the Henry Hudson Hotel. I mean, it wasn't even a residential hotel. They'd stay in their rooms, watch TV, and order from room service. Felix's father was on some crazy diet where he'd order steak from room service, chew it 40 times till he got all the flavor out of it, then throw the pulp out the twenty-second-storey window. Felix's mother was a beer alcoholic, and it didn't take much to get her off. She'd hide bottles of Miller High Life all over the three-room suite.

The place was a nuthouse. When I arrived his father was standing in a scattered pile of sheet music, dressed only in his boxer shorts. He had run out of inspiration and was just standing there waiting to be inspired. He acted like W. C. Fields and kept muttering little phrases like, 'My wife, poor wretch' and 'Sucking mule!'

Felix's parents had both grown up in Iowa, where his father had studied music. He won a thousand-dollar prize for an original composition for bassoon and with that money he and his wife moved to New York City. It looked to me like New York had been their undoing. They both hated cities and didn't like to go out of the hotel. They seemed like each other's albatross. There were no clocks in their hotel rooms, but Felix's mother said she could tell time by the flow of traffic on Eighth Avenue.

When I arrived, they carried on as though I'd been living there for months. For Christmas Felix had given his mother a copy of *Mrs 'Arris Goes to Paris* by Paul Gallico, and she seemed to like the title of the book better than the book itself. After a few beers, she'd begin chanting the title like an incantation. Over and over, drawing it out long and full in her Iowa accent, she'd say, 'Felix, honey, I just love that book you gave me for Christmas. *Mrs 'Arris Goes to Paris*, by Paul Gee-allico,' giving special drunken emphasis to the name. She repeated this over and over, like a two-year-old, until the phrase evolved into, 'Felix, honey, I'd shoot myself, but I don't have any ammo . . . yeeammo . . . yammo!' And then she'd pass out and Felix would fall upon her like a beast of prey, searching her pockets and shoes for money to go drinking.

Because there wasn't room at the Henry Hudson, Felix's father put us in our own room at the Hotel Chelsea on 23rd Street. From there we were able to rendezvous to go drinking with him. We'd start drinking in our room around noon and were pretty ripped by the time the traditional cocktail hour came around. By dinner time we'd end up at one of the restaurants with his father. We tried them all. Keene's Chophouse, The Round Table, and Eddie Condon's, which Felix said was the most important spot, because Eddie drank so much. The Top of the Sixes wouldn't let us in because we didn't have ties and jackets, and not even Felix's father's reputation helped. We even ended up at the White Horse Tavern on New Year's Eve. I remember that well because it was 1960, and a big fat man raised his glass and said, 'Here's to the sexy sixties.'

Once, close to dawn, Felix and I were returning to our hotel in a cab on the way back from Chinatown. We were quite drunk and couldn't find a place open to get another drink. Felix began to grind his teeth and I couldn't stand the sound. It was like bone crushing bone. I told him to stop it, but he wouldn't. I couldn't stand it anymore, so I hit him in the mouth. I couldn't believe I had done that. I'd never done anything like that before.

We had a good time in New York City, but soon vacation was over and it was time to take the train back to Fitchton, New Hampshire. Felix said that the only way to travel by train was to pack a pint of Hennessy Five-Star brandy in our underwear. It had to be Hennessy Five-Star. He seemed to know how to do it all, and I let him instruct me.

We both bought pints of Hennessy and a couple of pieces of clear plastic tubing at a tropical fish store. We buried the Hennessy deep in our jockey shorts and ran the tubes up and out the top of our shorts so we could sip discreetly the whole way from New York to Boston.

We planned to meet Owen Parker in Boston. Owen went to school with us at Fitchton and had spent Christmas at his grandmother's in Cleveland. We intended to drink some more before we caught the Budliner out of North Station to Conway, New Hampshire.

We met Owen and went to Harvard Square, where we talked some over-age Harvard student into buying us a quart of Petri port. After that we were lucky enough to find an open, heated basement somewhere down a Cambridge side street, and we got totally ripped. Somehow we made it to North Station, with time to spare.

Just before we went into North Station I told Owen and Felix to wait for me while I went into an Irish bar to try to get served. For me it was a real sign of maturity to be served under age, and I'd had no trouble doing it in New York. Now I wanted to try Boston. I went in and ordered a 15-cent draft of Schaefer and got served with no problem. I was very proud. As I sat there downing my draft among those big Irish hurly-burlies, Felix ran in crying, 'Come quick! Owen is in trouble!' I said, 'I'll be right there, just let me finish my beer.'

When I got outside, Owen was lying unconscious in the gutter. He was still wearing his London Fog raincoat, but both his black penny loafers were lying on the sidewalk. At first it looked like he had been hit by a car. There was an emergency ambulance and a big Irish cop was standing over him bellowing. 'Does anyone know this boy?' Felix and I just stood there, stunned. We didn't know what to do. We just stood there and watched Owen being loaded into the emergency van on a stretcher and taken away. He looked dead.

The trip north on the Budliner was somber and depressing. The booze began to wear off as the sun was going down and we rolled through slushy back lots into the night. We spent most of the trip looking at our drunken faces reflected in the windows until, at last, the conductor cried, 'This stop Conway.' From there we had to either hitch or take a cab.

Just as I got up to get off, Felix reached up and grabbed the stainless steel handle on the corner of the seat. His hand wrapped around it like a vise-grip, and he wouldn't let go. He began to grind his teeth. I tried to talk him into letting go, but he wouldn't respond. The conductor kept saying, 'Conway, everybody off for Conway.' I began to pull Felix's arm, but couldn't break his grip. The conductor joined in and began to pull, but it didn't help. We tried new positions. I wrapped my arms around Felix's waist and pulled, and the conductor put his arms around my waist and pulled. At last Felix let go, and we almost flew out the open door at the end of the car.

Outside, the winter wind quickly sobered me, but it didn't seem to affect Felix. I pleaded with him as we slipped and slid over the ice-crusted snow. 'Felix, Felix, Felix, what's going on?' At last, he staggered onto someone's lawn and collapsed, like a broken puppet, over a Century 21 FOR SALE sign. Three windows in the big house lit up as I dragged him back to the sidewalk.

Eventually the cold air sobered Felix up and we were able to hitchhike to Fitchton from the outskirts of town. The driver didn't say a word the whole way. After we reached Fitchton, I found that I still had a pint of Petri port in my bag, and I decided to hide it in the snow out behind the dormitory. For weeks afterward, a bunch of us would stand in the glaring sun in our shirtsleeves at lunch hour, looking down at the melting snow as it gradually revealed the bright ruby of the Petri port bottle. No one dared touch it. I just stood there, disowning it in my mind. I think one of the janitors finally found it and drank it in one gulp.

After Owen didn't return on schedule, it quickly became known through the grapevine that Felix and I had left him in the streets of Boston. Someone at Mass. General had found Owen's wallet and called the school. An emergency meeting of six male teachers was called, and C. W. Cartwright summoned Felix and me in to be interrogated. Felix told them everything, to the point of bragging. He told them about the brandy and the plastic tube. He told about the Petri port in Boston. He even told about how much we drank in New York and how his father paid for drinks in the bars at night.

I think the teachers were a little stunned, but it was difficult to tell from their traditional New England poker faces. Mr Larson was the first to respond. Mr Larson was gray all over; his hair was gray, his face was gray, and he wore a gray suit with a gray tie. He taught English and talked real slow, with a heavy Maine accent. I had taken a class with him, and he taught as though he was in a kind of trance. We spent the entire semester dissecting one book, *The Virginian*. Mr Larson coached the baseball team, and his claim to fame was that he'd once played left field for the Boston Red Sox.

Mr Larson started in on Felix. 'You know, Felix, when I was with the Boston Red Sox there was a fella, another ballplayer, who liked to drink an awful lot. It wasn't long before he was spending so much money on drink that he had none left for food, so he gave up eatin' in favor of drink. And it sounds pretty much like you're headed in the same direction.' And that was it. That was all Mr Larson had to say.

No one else did much talking. No one seemed very concerned about why we left Owen there in the streets of Boston. At last, after reviewing the case, C. W. Cartwright asked if we had any Fitchton Academy stickers on our luggage. Well, Felix and I were not the kind to put school stickers on our bags – or anywhere else for that matter. So we were lucky, I guess. I think it was because we didn't have Fitchton stickers on our bag that we weren't thrown out of school.

Owen was back the next day, after a wild night at Mass. General. He'd always been real skinny and done all he could to gain weight. He even ate yeast tablets, but nothing seemed to work. When the yeast didn't work he began to wear three or four layers of sweaters and sweatshirts under his London Fog raincoat. Anyway, they didn't waste any time getting him undressed at Mass. General. They just took a big scissors and cut the sweaters and sweatshirts right up the middle, and when he got back and people came to visit him in his room, he proudly displayed his new style of vest. Then he told us about having his stomach pumped. He was very popular for about two weeks.

The next lost weekend was to be more properly planned so that we wouldn't fall victim to outside circumstances. We wanted to find the perfect private place to drink, and we thought we had. Boyd Sutton's parents owned a real island off the coast of Maine. It had a stone house as well as spruce trees and sheep. Boyd said the sheep were left alone all winter to graze and feed on the trees. In the summer the whole family sheared them and slaughtered a few to eat. He told us that their diet of spruce gave the meat a wonderful pungent flavor and that the queen of England often dined on spruce-fed lamb. I was raring to go. We planned the big trip for our spring break in April. It would still be cold but, most likely, really beautiful.

The plan was to contact Pete and Ryan down in Barrington. They would load Pete's car with a big supply of booze and then drive up to Fitchton Academy to pick up Felix, Owen, Boyd, and me, and then we would all try to make it to the coast before night. It was important that we get there by dark so that we would see the island and not motor past it to England.

All went well except the timing. It turned out to be a long trip and by the time we got to Boyd's little dory in Martinville, it was dark. Boyd insisted that he could find the island blindfolded. We loaded the little boat with cases of Black Label beer, cheap rum, and Petri port. As we started the outboard motor, Boyd warned us not to move lest we capsize the boat and die of exposure within a matter of minutes. That water was very cold.

The island was not much more than a mile out, and we hit the landing beach square on, just as Boyd had promised. We carried our supplies into the stone house, which was built right on a little knoll in the middle of the island. It was very cold in the house so we all went to bed early to rest up for some hard drinking the next day.

In the morning we started with scrambled eggs, which we washed down with ice-cold quarts of Black Label. Minutes after that cold beer hit those eggs, we were all outside on the rocks throwing up like gushing fire hydrants. The day was ruined. No one felt like drinking anymore, and there was nothing else to talk about. Boyd took the boat out to look for lobsters but found nothing. Pete, who was horny, chased after some sheep. The rest of us wandered aimlessly around the island.

Soon it was summer and that meant the Newport Jazz Festival, where the object was to get as drunk as possible to the music of Dizzy Gillespie, Gerry Mulligan, the Jazz Messengers, and, of course, The Duke. We planned a big luncheon rendezvous at my parents' house on Narragansett Bay.

Felix came up early just to get out of the Manhattan summer. He was going to stay with me for the week before the festival. I had a summer job working on the Barrington trash truck, where I was learning about all kinds of new beers. Up until the trash truck we'd been content with Black Label or Narragansett.

Barrington was a dry town, but they had money and a little culture, so much of the population would drive to Providence to buy imported beers. It was in those wealthy trash cans that I first discovered Heineken's and Löwenbräu – when Löwenbräu was still a German beer – and got excited about the possibility of new highs to be had from sipping those exotic brews. I had no problem getting exactly what we wanted because I worked with Willy West and Crusher Henry on the back of the Barrington trash truck. They were both over-age and had no qualms about buying any kind of booze for me. I even tore a Heineken's ad from a magazine, so they could carry it into the package store and make no mistake about it.

When my parents were away, we'd have big stupid beer blasts in our basement rec room. We'd send out for pizza and get disgustingly drunk. Then Crusher Henry would stand in the corner of the rec room and we'd all charge at him, one at a time, and bounce off his 275-pound belly, while he farted and burped like a backfiring bumper car at Crescent Park.

One party night, I made the mistake of mixing Petri port with Ballantine ale from a big green quart bottle we called 'the Green Hornet'. I filled half my glass with port and the other half with Bally, and mixed them together with a steak knife. The next thing I remember was waking up in my bedroom to find the whole room spinning, and I knew I was going to be very sick. The sickness came on me so fast that I couldn't make it to the bathroom, so I grabbed the first container at hand. It was a black homburg hat I had bought at the Fitchton fair, and I went down on my knees and began to fill it up with a mixture of half-digested pizza, Petri port, and ale.

By then my father had been awakened by my retching and was standing over me, patiently waiting for the hat to be filled. I emptied out just before the hat overflowed, and then fell back into bed and passed out.

The next morning I wanted to find that hat. I was curious, and I was real hung over, and I didn't know what else to to but book for it. I looked in all the wastebaskets in the house. I looked in the trash can, I looked everywhere, but I didn't find that hat. Maybe Dad just threw it over the sea wall, I thought, but I never asked him. We didn't have that kind of relationship.

*

As soon as Felix arrived from New York City, my mother took one look at him and saw that he needed rehabilitation, so she put him right to work digging up crab grass on our front lawn. To stay cool in New York City, Felix had been hanging out in the air-conditioned 42nd Street movie theaters, drinking Rock and Rye, the rye with rock candy at the bottom of the bottle. Now he was happy to be out of the city and digging crab grass in Rhode Island. I'd never seen him happier. While he worked on the lawn in the day, I worked on the trash truck, and at night we'd hang out in the rec room listening to Art Blakey and the Jazz Messengers.

One Monday we planned a luncheon just for the two of us. We both took the day off, Felix from his crab grass and me from the trash truck. We started with orange blossoms in the late morning, which led into lots of beer accompanied by buckets of fresh clams by noon. After lunch we went for a drunken swim in the bay to sober up. We swam out to some rocks and back. All went well until Felix reached the little beach where he proceeded to impale himself on a six-inch rusty spike which protruded from a giant piece of driftwood. What was remarkable was that he kept his sense of humor about it all, hopping around on his left foot, half crying, half laughing, the blood spurting from the bottom of his right foot, which he held high in the air.

I helped him to the downstairs lavatory, where we put his injured foot into the sink to soak. While he was soaking it, I went to Mom and suggested that we get him over to Doctor Dawson for a tetanus shot. Mom, who had become an ardent Christian Scientist by then, said, 'I wouldn't worry about it, dear. That boy has enough alcohol in him to kill off anything, including himself.'

Felix didn't seem interested in going to the doctor either, so I went upstairs to take a shower, while Felix stayed in the downstairs bathroom soaking his foot. Just as I got in the shower my younger brother, Chan, started knocking on the door, crying out, 'Come quick, something weird has happened to Felix.' I wrapped a towel around myself and rushed downstairs to find Felix's body blocking the half-open lavatory door. I forced my way in and discovered him lying stunned on the floor. The room was a complete shambles. In his right hand Felix was holding a stainless steel rod which had been one of the legs to the sink. And now, with both legs missing, the sink was slowly tearing away from the wall just above his head. It looked like his good foot had slipped in a puddle of bay water, and he had gone down knocking both legs out from under the sink, hitting his head on the toilet as he went. So, there he was, lying dazed and dizzy, trying desperately to reconstruct the original look of the bathroom by forcing one of the stainless steel sink legs against the wall, as though it had once been a towel rack. Felix had completely trashed the bathroom in one slip.

The Newport Jazz Festival was upon us before we knew it. We barely had time to sober up before major preparations had to be made. The person who bought the booze for us this time was my father. I felt like I had graduated. Felix and I went with him to his favorite liquor store in Warren, Rhode Island, and we selected what we wanted. I bought a bottle of Gordon's gin all for myself. I think Felix bought a fifth of Jack Daniel's. We knew that the Jazz Festival police would frisk us at the gates, so we made intricate plans for hiding our liquor. I had bought a silver body flask that was contoured to slide down into my underwear. Felix had created an ingenious hot-water-bottle flask with a clear plastic tube running out the top so that he could sip Jack Daniel's once he had strapped the hot water bag around his waist. With his shirt pulled over it, it looked like a regular little organic paunch . . . a little beer belly filled with whiskey.

Boyd Sutton showed up on the opening day of the festival, and we all drove down to Newport in his Morris Minor to spend a drunken day on the beach as a pre-festival warm-up. We got ripped drinking beer in the hot sun and then took the scenic route to the jazz festival, the famous Five Mile Drive with all the mansions. 'Look at this one. Look at that. There's the Vanderbilt place,' I cried. By then I had started to drink gin, which was occasionally coming up as soon as it went down, and Boyd would have to stop his car to let me throw up under a hedge. Then I would get back in the car and continue as tour guide, until Felix got so fed up he said, 'Skip the real estate and get me to the bar.'

For miles around the festival, the streets were overflowing with cars and people. We found an obscure side street and parked the Morris Minor, then rushed to the outdoor ballpark where the festival was being held. The main entrance gate was filled with a manic, pushy, demanding crowd. Somebody had just thrown up near the gate, and it looked like their whole stomach had come up and landed on the sidewalk. The vomit looked like a big, throbbing pile of strawberry ice cream and someone, maybe the vomiter himself, was standing over it crying, 'Ice cream here. Ice cream here. Get your fresh strawberry ice cream here.'

We got past the gate with no problem. Behind the police, in a corner against the wall, we could see a pile of bottles they had confiscated. Enough to get them through an entire Newport winter.

After a hot warm-up session with the Eddie Condon All Stars my gin began to stay down and I was rapidly getting into that drunken state we all so desired. By the time Duke Ellington came on, we were dancing in the aisles and on our wooden chairs. We danced so hard our feet crashed through the slats. There seemed to be two kinds of people at the festival that year; those who got drunk and danced wildly, like us, and those who sat and smoked pipes filled with tobacco and listened to the music. Turning around to face us, one of the pipe smokers said, 'Where's your couth?' Dancing up a storm we screamed back, 'We left it at home!'

After the concert we got lost and couldn't find the car. We wandered in the rain, stupefied and wet. At last we decided to hitchhike home. We got as far as the Barrington shopping center and then there were no more cars. It must have been about three or four in the morning by then and I decided I had better call my father from a pay phone outside Al's Gulf station. When my father got there, we couldn't get Felix in the car. He just locked his arms tight around a fire hydrant and sat there, grinding his teeth. My father and I both pulled, me giving Felix judo chops, and at last we got him loose.

CARS

My father owned a '54 two-tone gray and royal blue Ford. It had an automatic transmission, which made it difficult to spin the wheel unless you could find a patch of sand. Then, if you put it in low and floored it, it would leave a small strip. I didn't have my driver's license, but I loved to drive and would often ask my mother if I could go park the car in the garage. I would go out and sit in the car, put on my sunglasses and just rev the engine until I felt like James Dean in *Giant*. Then I would drive all over the neighborhood waving to friends and neighbors, looking for patches of sand where I could spin the wheels.

My mother asked me if I wanted to go see *East of Eden* and I said, 'No. I don't want to see any more Bible stories.' Shortly after that, James Dean was killed when his Porsche Spyder hit a Ford sedan driven by a man named Turnupseed. My mother lamented the loss of the man. She said, 'We've lost a great actor.' I felt sorry for the car. The Porsche Spyder was my favorite. The picture of his mangled car was displayed in all the driver ed classes in California. I saw the photo in a magazine in the Rexall drugstore at the Barrington shopping center.

When I was 15 I wanted to become a driver for the Ferrari team. That's what I wanted to be when I grew up. I wanted to be like the Marquis de Portago, the Italian who raced for the Ferrari team. He was the one who put an end to the *millemeglia* when his car had a blowout at 130 miles an hour, killing seven people. I saw the picture of the bodies flying through the air in *Life* magazine. He was a very handsome man. There was also a picture of the marquis kissing his girlfriend, who was an American movie star. And under the picture was a caption, 'I make love every night and I'm not ashamed to admit it.' Every night, God, that was incredible to me then. I was a virgin at the time, and I just couldn't imagine it.

The Marquis de Portago was my distant hero, but at home it was Donny Renshaw. We called him Donny Duals because he had dual exhausts on his car. I'm not saying that was unusual – so did Olds-mobiles, Cadillacs, and Pontiacs at that time – but he had dual straight pipes. No muffler. Donny had a '40 Ford coupe with patches of primer on it, dual carburetors, and a radical cam that made the whole thing rough-idle like a John Deere tractor about to stall out.

When he geared down on Rumstick Road, I'd jump up and run to my window. It was like the call of the wild. Also, Donny had dropped out of school to become a steeplejack and the thought of him up there on that white, pointed Congregational Church steeple just hanging there, jacking, was too much. I mean, he was a saint to me, a poet. When he wasn't up there, he was just driving the car up and down Rumstick Road, and then at 10 o'clock in the morning, while we were in high school, he would pull in, pull a U-y in front of the Automobile Mechanics Course garage, lay a strip and roar back out. And I thought, that's what I want to do when I'm 16. The only problem was I had vertigo, so I didn't know about the steeplejack stuff, but I was definitely going to get one of those cars.

Now Donny Duals was the local hero; we couldn't get close to him. We never saw him outside of his car, except once when it was in the shop. He was walking up Rumstick Road and my brothers and I went across the street to get a closer look. My younger brother Chan had a cap gun that Donny grabbed out of his hand and my older brother Rocky said, 'Hey, come on. Give him a break, he's just a little kid. Have a heart.' And Donny goes like this, 'Yeah, sure, great. Ya got one?'

At the time I was learning how to drive without my driver's license. I was learning how to drive like an old woman with my Gram Gray in her '48 Chevy stick shift down on Half-Mile Road.

I was also learning how to drive on my own. I had always wanted a '40 Ford coupe. Other than the '32 Ford coupe, the '40 was one of the most sought-after cars around. Once when my parents were away on a ski trip in Vermont, Spike Claxton and I happened to be over in Bay Springs and spotted one just parked in a driveway. It didn't have a for sale sign on it, but I thought we should make an offer anyway. When we knocked on the door of the house an old man answered, and I just offered him $75 cash for the car. I had two paper routes at the time – a morning route and an evening one – and $75 was all I'd saved up from both of them. When the man said yes, I just rushed off to my bank, took out all my savings, and bought the car.

Then a strange thing happened, a strange thing that felt like a dream. The owner, perhaps because he was so happy to get all that money for such a piece of junk, just left his plates on the car and let me drive it away. Spike and I just took that car and drove it all over town. We even drove it up to Providence and around Blackstone Boulevard, then back to Barrington, and then up to Providence again. I parked it in my yard and just looked at it. It was so beautiful I couldn't stand it. I knew I had to find a place for it before the weekend was over because my parents were coming home. So at last I moved it, knocking down some of the rose bushes, along the edge of our garage and parked it next to the little shack my brother Rocky had built when he wanted to become a Maine guide.

My parents were very upset when they came home and saw all the squashed rose bushes and this '40 Ford, which looked like a piece of junk, sitting in their backyard. We had a big fight. 'What are you going to do with it?' they asked. I told them that I was going to fix it up, rebuild the engine, and convert it into a perfect street-rod. I think they wanted to believe me. They wanted to think that this would be a worthy endeavor, a wholesome activity to keep me off the streets.

So, with the help of some friends, I did get the engine out. I got it down into our basement and tore it apart. I got all the valves and pistons removed and then I got bored and just left it there. I couldn't stand the constant grease on my hands. I had seen the insides of that engine and that was enough. It was then that I knew I didn't want to be an automobile mechanic.

I don't remember what happened to that engine block, but I sold the body of the car to Jeff Howe for $35 and he had it towed back out over the rose bushes, dropped a four-barrel '57 Chevy engine in it, and made himself a fine street-rod. I looked the other way every time it passed. I was keeping in touch with my racecar driving at Seekonk Speedway, a quarter-mile stockcar track in Massachusetts, where all these incredibly fast and loud cars went around in circles. They had no mufflers at all and you could hear the sound and see the search-lights from the speedway 10 miles away. A bunch of us would go up there early, just as the sun was going down, build a ladder out of fallen trees and climb up over the fence to get in free so we could have money to buy beer.

I first practiced driving on the clamshell driveway out behind our house on Rumstick Road. That driveway was only about 40 feet long, so there was no chance of getting up much speed, and since I didn't have my driver's license I couldn't continue out onto the street. Because of this, most of the practice consisted of 'backing and filling', until one day a bunch of us got carried away and just had an orgy of spinning wheels. I made that family car spin and dig, while my friends looked on and cheered, until the clamshell driveway looked like Normandy Beach after the invasion. And in the middle of almost destroying the entire driveway, we were interrupted with a quasi citizen's arrest by Desmond Musgrove from next door. Desmond was slightly retarded and thought he was a cop. He had a big Schwinn bicycle and would ride around town talking into his hand like it was a CB radio. It was difficult to tell his age, but he was a big guy, not to be fooled with. Anyway, he came over and put a quick stop to it all. He even tried to fingerprint us with his official True Detective G-Man Fingerprint kit.

The other clamshell driveway where I practiced was at Craig Crane's in Bristol, Rhode Island, and that was more spectacular. His parents had this fantastic mile-long clamshell driveway at the end of Papasquash Point, and Ryan, Craig, and I used it as a race track. So that he wouldn't wreck their car, Craig's parents bought him a '49 Packard convertible with overdrive and also a little lever you could throw to convert it from hydraulic shift into standard. None of us had our driver's license yet, so we'd just drive Craig's Packard up and down that mile-long clamshell driveway. The only problem, as Ryan saw it, was that the Packard wasn't loud enough. Ryan was obsessed with what we called 'highway sounds'. So was I, in fact, and so was Scott Tarbox. We picked 'highway sounds' up from the Chuck Berry 45 single 'Maybelline.'

Ryan knew how to make fabulous highway sounds with his mouth. Ryan, Scott, and I would sit around drinking vanilla Cokes at the Rexall drugstore and Scott would say, 'Hey, Moe,' (he called Ryan 'Moe') 'I'll pay you a nickel to make a highway sound.' And Ryan, just sitting there on a stool, would put his mouth into gear and let out with these incredible rapping highway sounds. Saliva flying everywhere. Scott would go wild and say, 'Do it again, Moe, only this time don't use the clutch. Just slam shift through the gears!' Then Scott would up the fee and pay him a dime for slam-shifting this time, and Ryan would make the sound. After that we'd wander out and lean against the drugstore and talk about the cars driving in and out of the shopping center.

On rainy days we'd sit around and listen to recordings of road races. I had all the records with the best highway sounds. I had 'The Sounds of Seabring', 'Sounds from Watkins Glen', and best of all, a recording of Le Mans on which we could listen to a real Le Mans start, where the drivers would have to run from a starting line, jump in their cars, and start them up. Then there was this thunderous noise of all the cars pealing rubber as they took off.

Another favorite record was 'Pit Stop' – you could hear the drivers talk when they pulled in for repairs. You could hear the actual voices of Phil Hill, Juan Manuel Fangio, Porfirio Rubirosa, and Wolfgang von Tripps, who was eventually killed in a race. After that happened, my brother Rocky, who had just found out about existentialism, said that it wasn't really a meaningless death because Wolfgang was doing exactly what he wanted when he died. Not to have raced would have made him something else, something other than a racecar driver. I thought I understood.

Well, we'd sit around and listen to 'Sounds from Watkins Glen' and hear all the men talk so that we could pick up on the actual lingo:

'Well, what's going on here anyway? Well, what's going on, it looks like we're having some technical inspection.'

'Did you get my car through inspection?'

'Yeah, it's all done.'

'You mean you actually got it through this time? How many times did you have to go back?'

'Well, that's pretty good, that's par for the course.'

'What was wrong with it?'

'Uh, a toe rim on the rear wheel.'

'Toe rim on the rear wheel, okay, well I never heard of that either. Probably their machine.'

'Probably.'

'On the rear wheel alignment – there *is* no alignment on the rear wheels.'

'The only thing that could happen is if there's a bent axle or something of that nature.'

'A bent wheel might do it. Other than that there's no adjustment for it.'

'There's no toe in and no toe out.'

'We could have a bent bell housing as well, slightly bent over there.'

'That's unlikely though.'

'Hey, what do we have here? This is George Hansen, he's an old Jaguar driver. I think we might call George Mr Jaguar. One of the oldest Jaguar drivers, not in age, not in age, but in the length of time driving Jaguars. Recently George graduated from a production class. And now he runs a one-forty, excuse me, he *used* to run a one-twenty, he now has a . . . and he's gonna run that up here . . .'

But Craig's Packard did not make the kind of highway sounds Ryan wanted to hear, so whenever Craig was inside watching soap operas (which was often), Ryan would go under Craig's car with a little ax and chop some holes in his muffler, then he'd ask Craig to come out and do a test drive around the yard. And Craig would do it, he'd act dumb and say, 'Hey guys, what do you want me to do that for?' And Ryan would just say, 'Go on and do it. Just give it a try.' So Craig would drive it around the circle in front of his house and then go back in to watch TV. And Ryan would crawl under the car and give the muffler a few more whacks. This went on for a period of time, until Craig's Packard finally sounded like it needed a new muffler.

Craig was very possessive of his Packard and would rarely let us drive it. I really wanted my own car to race on his clamshell driveway, so I bought a '37 Plymouth for $35. I bought it in Barrington and drove it unregistered, without a license, down to Bristol. The windshield opened with a little crank and we let the fresh air blow in. Ryan rode shotgun and kept an eye out for cops. It was a very exciting trip. When we got to Bristol, we took the side route to Craig's along Colt's Drive, a semiprivate winding road that used to belong to the Colt estate along the edges of Narragansett Bay. It wound around like a racetrack road and we took those corners like we were in a Ferrari.

When we got to Craig's, the first thing Ryan did was to crawl under the Plymouth and rip off the entire exhaust system. Off came the muffler and off came the tail pipe. Then we bought a piece of flex-pipe at Western Auto and attached it, so it was running directly off the manifold and back out under the running board. And we were off. It was fantastic! It sounded like the whole of Seekonk Speedway on a Saturday night.

Craig's parents owned a hundred acres of land, so there was no one around to complain, and we'd just drive that Plymouth up and down the clamshell driveway, slam-shifting through the gears as flames shot out the straight pipe under the door. Then I'd let Ryan take it for a spin, and spin is what we'd do. Oh how we'd spin. We'd get it to the top of the driveway and then gun it, and drive it flat out until we reached the right-angle turn at the bottom, and we'd go into that turn at full-tilt boogie. The car would slide off the clamshell, spin almost full circle, bounce through some trees, squash some skunk cabbage, and then, with the help of my plastic suicide knob with the naked lady on it, I'd manage to get it all back on the track.

At night it was even better because you could see the orange flames shoot out from under the door. Life could have stopped there, but it didn't.

At last I turned 16 and it was time to get my driver's license. I couldn't wait. This meant that I'd be 'street legal' and out on the highways. I'd even be able to drive to Boston if I wanted to. Ryan couldn't wait either because he wasn't 16 yet. I knew I was a good driver and that I'd have no trouble with the road test. So I went up on my birthday, June 5, to take the test, but the one thing that I didn't do was study the driver's manual hard enough. And I failed the written test. I couldn't believe it. I passed the road test with flying colors, but I failed the written test. I was so mortified that when I got home I lied to Ryan. I told him I was caught cheating, because I'd much rather have been thought a cheater than a cretin. The following week, after endless late-night study of the driver's manual, I went back to Providence and passed the test.

Now I was on the road and could really practice in the family car, my father's gray and royal blue two-tone '54 Ford, and that car did not have what I would call a low center of gravity. It was nothing like a Ferrari. But that didn't stop me. I was off. And the first mishap I had was at Barrington Beach. This was what I would have to call an unconscious mistake. It had nothing to do with racing.

One day I was just driving down the hill to the town beach, and instead of turning left to park in the lot with all the other cars, I drove straight out onto the beach and toward the bay. I don't know what got into me that day. Just before reaching the bay, the car sunk down in the sand and stopped, and I just sat there spinning the wheels. As I sat there I could see that the tide was coming in and that the car would soon fill up with water. I jumped out of the car and ran to the pay phone to call a tow truck, and they got it out just as the water reached the front wheels. The brake drums were filled with sand and the car had to go into the shop to have them cleaned. My father didn't seem all that upset. He just couldn't figure out why I would have done a stupid thing like that. And I was no help.

Both my parents dealt with my automotive mishaps very well. They never seemed to get rattled. Once I had to appear in the traffic court in Providence and my mother had to accompany me. It was a snowy day and we were driving down this big hill leading into town when someone put on their brakes way up ahead of us. When I saw his brake lights go on, I hit my brakes and Mom and I just sat there while our car slid out of control and bumped into his. There was no apparent damage, but I'm sure he was crying 'Whiplash.' Mom just said, 'Step it up, Spuddy dear. Do the best you can.' I just pulled out around his car as Mom rolled down her window and called out, 'Sorry, this kind of weather, you know.'

After the Ford got out of the shop, I tried to drive more carefully. I was sure the Marquis de Portago would never get stuck in the sand. My next big mishap took place on Colt's Drive. Colt's Drive had become my favorite practice spot, and Larry Lindberger had become my new copilot. One rainy September day when I was going through my laps, the car slid sideways on some wet leaves just before the stone bridge. Larry was impressed. Back on the road again, I hit another patch of leaves at the corner by the playground and the car went into a full skid and rolled. I don't remember anything after that until I came to. When I did come to, I found that the car was teetering on its side on the small sea wall, just inches away from falling into the bay. And Larry was using my body as a ladder to climb out the passenger door, which he'd pried open above us like a hatch. The radio was playing 'The Girl Can't Help It' full blast, and the first thing I did was to reach over and turn it off. Then, following Larry, I climbed out. We just stood there in the rain, looking at the chassis of the rolled Ford. Larry turned to me and said, 'If my mother knew I was out here in the rain with this sore throat she'd kill me.' And I thought, oh God, Larry's in shock. Then he turned to me and said, 'Shit man, you're a mess. You've got blood pouring down your face.' It was then that I realized that I was also in shock.

We walked together in a daze up Colt's Drive until we reached the National Guard Headquarters and I called Gram Gray to come pick us up while one of the National Guardsmen called the Silver Tow Truck Service.

Mom broke the news to Dad when he got home that night. I was upstairs in bed, depressed, with a bad stiff neck. I couldn't move my head in any direction. After Mom told Dad, he drove down to Bristol to examine the wreck. When he got back, Mom asked him how it looked, and he said, 'Like the two boys inside it should have been killed.' And at first I wasn't sure if he meant that we should be dead because of what we did, or dead from the crash. But I figured he must have meant the crash because the side of the car had been ripped apart by the sea wall and it looked like a can of Dinty Moore someone had opened with a Swiss army knife.

I was depressed for days and didn't want to drive anymore. Once again I couldn't understand why Dad wasn't angry. He just seemed to accept it. I didn't miss any school, and the following day I found out that everyone knew about the accident because a photo of the car had appeared in the *Providence Journal*. There it was, on its side, teetering on the edge of the sea wall. The photo had been taken straight on, so that the license plate was clearly visible. No mistaking whose car it was: G914, the Grays of Barrington, Rhode Island.

The first thing that happened when I got into school the next morning was that Mr Bender, the driver ed teacher, called me into his room for a private chat. I don't think Mr Bender liked me all that much. One of the reasons for this was that I wasn't a good student; the other was that I'd learned how to drive with my grandmother instead of him. Also, by now there were rumors going around school that Larry Lindberger was either dead or in the hospital. It turned out that Larry *did* have a sore throat after all and the day after the accident he came down with the Asian flu. So he was at home in bed.

I think Larry got better in about two weeks. I never saw much of him after that. Between the accident, the way he used to treat his parakeet, and the fact that his father bought him my Gram Gray's '48 Chevy, things were never the same. That was the car I had learned to drive in and I couldn't stand seeing Larry drive it. It wasn't just that he had his own car and I had none. It was the fact that as soon as he got the car, he put Hollywood mufflers on it, lowered the rear, and hung fuzzy dice and a pink chiffon scarf from the rearview mirror. And in the morning he'd just sit there in that transformed car, just sit out there in his driveway, warming it up, revving the engine for the big five-minute drive to school, while I walked.

So Mr Bender just took me in his back office and didn't say a word about the accident. He just sat me down and told me a little story. He said, 'You know, your Grandfather Horton is a fine upstanding man. Once when he was at a basketball game that I was coaching, he left early and accidentally sideswiped my car, which was parked out front. And he left a note on the windshield that read "Elmer S. Horton did this." Then he left his phone number at the bottom of the note. He is a fine upstanding man and you will never turn out like that.' That was all he said.

My Gramp Horton *was* a fine upstanding man and he really knew how to take care of his cars. He would buy a new black Mercury with red upholstery every three years. He knew exactly when to buy and sell so he'd get his money's worth. He'd cover his seats with plastic so they wouldn't get warm. In fact, I used to think his cars were in better shape when he traded them in than when he bought them. Gramp was in advertising and knew all about planned obsolescence. But still, there was something about his immaculate cars that Rocky, Chan, and I just couldn't stand and we'd love it when something went wrong. Like the time Teddy Hike threw up from too many pink Canadian mints in the back seat on the way home from Sunday School. My grandfather seemed more upset about the throwup on the back seat than he did about Teddy being sick. That used to drive me and my brothers wild.

I remember the best joke we played on him. Once when Gram and Gramp Horton came to visit, Rocky and I took one of the fake dog shits that came in a box labeled 'Doggie Done-It'. It was made of rubber and really looked like a big fresh dog shit. The only thing missing was the smell. We took that 'Doggie Done-It' and put it right on my grandfather's front seat, and when he came out of the house and discovered it we thought he was going to have a heart attack. His whole face turned red and the veins popped out from his neck as he cried out to Gram Horton, 'Peg, come quick! The cat's been here. The cat's been in here!' Rocky, Chan, and I laughed and laughed. We laughed until we couldn't stand it anymore. It wasn't so much

Gramp's face we were laughing at as the idea of a cat being able to take a shit that big.

Insurance paid for the '54 Ford to be fixed, and it was back on the road in a matter of weeks. As for myself, I just stayed away from driving for a while. I wasn't so sure about becoming a member of the Ferrari team after all. But then suddenly everything changed. Out of the blue, Dad decided to up and buy an Austin Healey. I couldn't believe it. It was like Walter Mitty had come alive and was working out his major fantasy. I had always known that Dad was interested in Austin Healeys, but I never thought he'd really buy one. Then one Saturday he asked me if I wanted to drive up to Preston Auto, the foreign car place in Seekonk. On the spot, he bought one, this beautiful jet black, secondhand Austin Healey with red bucket seats. He bought it right there and together we drove it home.

When we got home the whole neighborhood came out to see us drive in. It was like a for-real pit stop, right there in Barrington, Rhode Island. Everyone wanted a test ride and Dad began to drive them one at a time, down Chapin Road, along the river and then back. At last I asked if I could take Judy Griggs for a ride and he said, 'Yes, you may.' I was trembling all over. So I drove Judy down along the river and around the back to the waiting crowd at the finish line. As I pulled in, smoke was pouring off the rear tires. I had forgotten to take off the emergency brake and the rear brake drums were almost in flames. Watching the red paint peel off those drums beneath the chrome spokes, I knew my racing career was over.

COLLEGE GIRLS

I was a virgin when I entered college. Freshman year I was at a party, and my friend Stubbs came up to me and said, 'You see that girl? Her name's Sandy, and she goes down. And I'm going to go down with her before the night's over.' I thought I'd try to beat him out. I went up to her and said, 'Hi Sandy, my name's Spud and I hear you go down.' We spent the night together. I began by licking her breasts. She said, 'Who do you think I am, your mother?' Then we had intercourse and I came in about 30 seconds. I ended up lying there for the rest of the night staring up at the ceiling, which wasn't all that bad because it was one of those ceilings in old Boston houses painted with little cherubs flying through the clouds, and it was something to look at. The only bad thing about it was that Zapata, the Latin lover from Cuba, was making love to his girlfriend right on the other side of a partition that didn't go all the way up to the ceiling. They really carried on. I had heard stories about Zapata. I had heard that he had made his girlfriend take a nylon stocking, tie it in little knots, and fold it up and stick it up his ass; then, while she was giving him a blow job, just before he was going to come, she tore it out. I had *that* to contend with.

I hadn't gotten much sleep at all, and in the morning I just wanted to get out of there. I didn't know the right thing to do or the wrong thing, even. Zapata was calling out, over the partition, 'Hey, nothing like starting the morning with a little good loving,' in his Spanish accent. His brother Aroozoo was the same. I was over at his apartment once and Aroozoo had been in bed with his girlfriend for three days and three nights, and they hadn't washed any of the dishes. Zapata started in on them in Spanish about the dishes and Aroozoo got up and said, 'I'll wash the dishes' and took them and threw them out in the hall, smashed every one of them, and said, 'There, they're done.'

So Sandy decided to bring me back to her apartment for breakfast. I didn't want to go, I had no appetite at all. And she served me eggs, baked. I'd never had baked eggs before. She baked them in the oven and after I had the baked eggs, I hightailed it out of there, fast. I went back to my dorm room and rolled around on the floor, praying God to forgive me and swearing I'd never do it again. After that, when I saw Sandy in the halls of Emerson College, I'd run for the men's room, and I never went after another girl my whole freshman year.

My sophomore year, I was allowed to move out of the dorm and get my own place. I rented an apartment like a little house in an alley behind two buildings on Newbury Street. The arrangement was that I would pay only $30 a month for this little alley bunker with window bars, provided I swept the halls and emptied the trash in the two buildings. That wasn't a bad job, except for having to pick up the flaky pieces of shell from the hard-boiled eggs of Mrs Fletcher, the real estate lady. What was worse was that my apartment was in the alley, and those back alleys in Boston were alive with rats. They would squeal and carry on like kittens outside my door at dusk. At night when I'd come home, I would clap my hands to get them out of the way. My friends called the place 'Rat Alley', and girls would rarely visit.

Once a baby rat had crawled into a garbage pail and was stuck in there, just squealing and jumping up on the side. I didn't have the heart to kill or the mind to set it free.

Some girls did stay over, but I don't remember any sexual intercourse. In fact, there was no intercourse at all. One time I lay down on Adele Schreck when we were both naked and I caught crabs. I treated it like a major venereal disease. I went to a private doctor and he prescribed my first A-200 crab lice remover.

Once Monica Moran showed up at the Newbury Street apartment. I knew Monica from Fitchton Academy, where she had chosen me to be her boyfriend during our senior year. I didn't say yes and I didn't say no, until one cold winter night she snuck out of her dorm and came knocking on my fire escape door. I had a single room senior year at Fitchton. It was actually more like a closet than a room, and it had a door that led right out onto the fire escape. I couldn't imagine who'd be out there at that time of night. I opened my door and let

Monica sit on the edge of the bed. She told me she'd come to give her virginity away. I had just been reading Freud for the first time – his essay on narcissism. I said, 'Monica, do you know what a narcissist is?' And she said, 'Of course.' I said, 'Well, I think I am one, that's why I can't respond to you.' We had a good talk anyway.

So here was Monica in Boston. She came to visit me in Rat Alley and she was still a virgin. And I still didn't respond. Then she went off to Cambridge to lose her cherry with some guy and came back to tell me she wasn't a virgin anymore and that she had done it just for me. I tried to go to bed with her this time, with the rats squealing outside. At first I felt nothing, so I decided to get very drunk. Then I felt nothing even more. Finally, I just threw up. So Monica gave up on me as a lover and we became friends.

My junior year I moved up in the world. I got a furnished room on Marlborough Street. It was much more elegant and I felt like I was living in London. I began to read all the existentialists, drink Chivas Regal, and eat sunflower seeds. Some girls came to visit me there, but none that I was really attracted to.

One time Tammy Mahoney, an old girlfriend of Felix Quinn's, looked me up. I had met her once at his place in New York. After she had broken up with Felix she got married and moved to Hadley, Massachusetts. Her husband turned out to be a wife abuser and beat her up. When she got out of the hospital she fled to Boston and sought me out. Tammy was cute and sassy, with small breasts. I had no trouble looking at her nude body; it was like a sweet little nut. But getting close enough to touch her was a whole other thing. It was like a steeplechase.

She began by reading Camus's 'The Myth of Sisyphus', and soon I'd get her down to the buff. She baited me into chasing her as she leapt over the armchair and pranced along the back of the couch. But I never caught up with her. Even if I had, I don't think I'd have known what to do. Then she'd reread 'The Myth of Sisyphus' naked, by candlelight. Or sometimes we'd go to a Bergman movie and come home depressed, drink some scotch and eat some sunflower seeds, and go to sleep in separate beds. After reading 'The Myth of Sisyphus' a few more times, Tammy would go back to Hadley to get beat up.

Then Melanie Truscott came into my life. She was 17, a freshman at Emerson, and a model for *Seventeen* magazine. She was tall, blonde, and thin, with hardly any breasts. Her breasts were so small she wouldn't take off her bra, and I didn't insist. When we made love, she'd always make a lot of noise, and afterward she'd ask me why I was so quiet. She told me her first boyfriend made a lot of noise when he came. I was always under the impression it was a sign of good sex to laugh a lot like Henry VIII – you know, 'Ho ho ho ho ho' and all that, like a sexy Santa Claus, but no laughter was coming, not even an ounce.

But we were laughing a lot outside of bed. I used to play practical jokes on Melanie. I was working as a kitchen boy at the Katie Gibbs Secretarial School in Boston. If you worked at Katie Gibbs you were not allowed to date any of the girls-women, women-girls there at all. That was fine with me; it left me feeling totally free. I felt like a good castrato. I felt more creative because I didn't feel as though I was being led around by my balls. I could make jokes and say whatever came into my mind. Like when I was scraping their plates at the garbage wagon, I'd say, 'What are you throwing your roast beef away for?' (Thursdays we'd have roast beef.) 'Think of all the starving people in the world!' And they'd say, 'We pay for it, we do what we want with it.' So on Thursdays all this roast beef would go into the garbage disposal, which we called 'The Pig', to be ground up and sent out to the Charles River, so the fish were really eating well out there. They were probably hanging around that particular drainage pipe. And on Fridays they'd serve fish, and every Friday their sisters and brothers would come out there ground up. We would have terrific fish on Friday, scrod or cod, well-done. Well-baked. Baked well. Real well. With a little paprika on the top.

And I got on well with the women there, the Irish Catholic women, and all the cooks, until John F. Kennedy was shot and I overreacted a little bit. I came in when they were all weeping in the corner and I went, 'Come on, what's going on? Don't let a little shooting hold up the dinner.' And it took some time to get them back as friends.

The cooks used to give me leftover pea soup, that was my favorite, to take home in a half-gallon milk carton. It'd be cold and gray-looking when you took it out, but when you reheated it, it was fine. One day I was going to heat some up for Melanie and I stuck my arm into the carton, up to the elbow, to scoop out some soup. I looked down and there were globs of cold, gray pea soup hanging off my arm, and I went, 'Ah, ah, ah, ahchew! Oh, Melanie look! I sneezed my brains out all over my—' 'Oh, no!' she screamed, 'not right before dinner.' I didn't know a lot of the time who was fooling whom. For instance, once I went down to the Charles River. I was a sun worshiper, and I wanted to lie in the sun there. When I came back, I opened the refrigerator and peeled the skin off some overcooked chicken that was all black and bubbly. I unbuttoned my shirt and put it on my shoulder. Then I said, 'Oh, Melanie, Melanie, I've got a bad burn. I got too much sun. Give me a little cream rub, please.' And she pulled open my shirt and screamed.

When I was in college, I was always afraid to urinate when girls were around. I was afraid to pee directly into the toilet bowl because I had the feeling that girls judged the size of your cock by the sound of the flow, and I didn't want any kind of judgment going on. So I would always pee on the inside of the bowl and sometimes it would go a little over the edge. But with Melanie, I would take two big empty grapefruit juice bottles, fill them with water and dump them one at a time, very slowly into the toilet bowl. This would go on for five minutes while she was outside, screaming with laughter.

Somewhere along the line, I think Melanie felt I wasn't paying enough attention to her, that I was too self-absorbed. So she staged a fake rape scene in order to get my attention. To this day, I think it was fake. I was studying theater at the time, and I knew bad acting when I saw it. A mutual friend of Melanie's and mine came rushing into my room on Marlborough Street one day and said, 'Oh listen, listen. I'm really sorry. I just got overtaken with lust and accidentally raped Melanie. You've got to forgive me.' I said, 'Oh, that's all right, Danny. I forgive you.' We talked for a while. Shortly after he left, Melanie came running in, and something about her timing made me think she'd been hiding just outside the door all the time. She threw herself on the bed and started screaming. 'Danny raped me!' I said, 'Oh, gee. That's too bad. Is there anything I can do to help?'

Well, we broke up shortly after that. And when we were breaking up told me that she had faked all of her climaxes. Now, I didn't mind that so much as the idea that she might have been faking the laughter over the chicken, the grapefruit jars, and the pea soup.

My senior year I moved into an apartment on Beacon Street. I loved that apartment. It was so simple and empty that it made me feel like a Zen monk. There was a small fireplace, two straight-back chairs, and a single mattress in the corner on the floor. There was a hot plate and a refrigerator, but no kitchen table, so I ate the leftover food I brought home from Katie Gibbs standing up.

Irena Cleveland was one of the first black girls I'd ever known, and it was at this time that I almost got involved with her. She was a virgin and very beautiful. I had never been involved with a black girl before, and I was titillated and confused. On our first date, she came over to my apartment and we got very high on Gallo sherry. Then I got out my new Ouija Board and we began to play. Irena and I were asking the regular questions about when the world was going to end, how many children we would have, and what spirits out there had any important messages for us, when at last the board spelled out I-R-E-N-A. Irena and I asked the board what about Irena, and it spelled out F-U-C-K-H-E-R-A-N-D-F-I-N-D-O-U-T. We both leaned back and laughed. I was sure neither of us were manipulating the board. We were both too innocent and neither would have talked like that. Well, I just turned to Irena and blushed. We got into bed, fully dressed, and I just laid down beside her. Then I put my arm around her and she burst into tears. When I asked her what was wrong, she said that her mother had been encouraging her to lose her virginity, but she didn't know how. Also, she wasn't sure that she really wanted to before she got married.

This was during the Cuban missile crisis, when, after Kennedy's speech, all the Emerson College girls ran out of the dorms, screaming, 'Take me. I don't want to die a virgin! Please, take me!' After that I kept having these obsessive fantasies about how I would go to the girls' dorm all dressed in white lace, with three eunuch slaves carrying bull whips. And I'd just go from room to room deflowering all these flowers.

But Irena Cleveland wasn't one of them. Irena thought she wanted to be a virgin when she got married, so we just spent the night sitting around, drinking sherry, and listening to the last movement of Beethoven's Ninth, over and over again.

Kit Tobin was a student at the University of New Hampshire, and I thought that would be a little safer because she could only hitchhike down to see me on weekends. And since I was involved in a theater production, rehearsing for Molière's *The Misanthrope*, I had a perfect excuse to make her come to me. We had a great relationship, except that she didn't like fish. That was a problem, because every Friday when she arrived from Amherst, I would serve her the leftover fish I brought home from work. I still didn't have any chairs, so we would eat standing up. I was too cheap to take her out. Each Friday she'd come down and I'd serve her a little leftover fish with garlic, a little leftover fish with curry, a little leftover fish with tomato, until one Friday she came down to visit and said, 'Oh, God. Not fish again,' and started throwing up. She threw up all night long.

The next weekend Kit called me from Amherst and said that she wanted to talk, and could she come to my parents' house in Barrington over Christmas vacation. I said yes. When she got down there she said, 'I met someone in Amherst who gives me more.' I didn't know more of *what*. I didn't ask. Then she said, 'I'm going to be seeing him, and I have to tell you something we did together, but I don't want you to tell anyone.' I said, 'I won't.' And she said, 'We went to a barn, a bunch of us, outside Amherst, and we smoked marijuana together.'

So she left. I went indoors, drank about a fifth of vodka and got very drunk. I thought, I've got to go the theater. This is the only recourse, I will go see *The Caretaker* at the Trinity Square Playhouse in Providence. I went to ask my parents for the keys to the car and my mother said, 'What's wrong, dear?' And I burst into tears and said, 'I've lost Kit. I'll *never* find anyone like her again.' And my mother said, 'Well, that's what you said about the last one, dear.' I don't remember ever saying that. They gave me the keys to the car and I drove off to Providence. The road was like a roller coaster, and every five minutes I was opening the door and vomiting my guts out. The next day I had such a hangover I felt like I was going to die. But I loved the play. It was then that I made up my mind. No more booze, no more love, no more girlfriends. I was going to devote my life to the stage.

Now that I wasn't drinking at night, I was much more aware of the Beacon Street noise. I began to close down. It began quite simply with plugging my ears. I did this with wet toilet paper. I would take the toilet paper and run it under warm water. Then I would shape it into two wads, smear a little Jergen's hand cream on each of them, and fit them into my ears.

But the toilet paper wasn't enough. I still felt assaulted by sound. I designed three soundproof shutters for the windows in my apartment. I cut them out of plywood and backed them with fiberglass insulation. Then at night I put the shutters up and plugged my ears with the wet toilet paper.

One morning I just decided to leave them up. The Back Bay

Community Association sent me a letter requesting that I take the shutters down. I didn't. Next they sent a representative who looked like T. S. Eliot knocking at my door. When I asked him what was wrong, he said that from the street, the external insulation on the shutters made my apartment look like a construction site, so would I please take them down. I didn't.

About this time I dreamt I had lost my testicles. Either they had dropped off or someone had cut them off with a scissors, I don't know which. I was searching for them on a football field. I think it was Victory Field in Barrington, Rhode Island. At last I found my balls behind the seats, just hanging there from the bottom of the bleachers.

I went to the student psychiatric clinic to have a little talk with the therapist there. After listening to me for about half an hour he said, 'You are suffering from a drawn-out case of postadolescence.' He talked about how nowadays that sort of thing could go on until you were 40. Thinking I should get a second opinion, I consulted a therapist at Mass. General. After about 20 minutes, he stopped me and said, 'You're just a big existential garbage pail. Go home and relax.'

Then I met Adriana Alexis Glick, the first sensual love of my life. She was brunette and beautiful. She was from the upper West Side of New York City, and she was going to Emerson College. We had a very romantic relationship. I had a fireplace, a working fireplace, but I was too cheap to buy firewood. So after we struck *The Misanthrope* set, I had the crew bring it over and put it in the corner of my apartment. It was piled almost to the ceiling. I burned *The Misanthrope* set while we lay naked on this mattress in front of the fireplace, sipping sparkling rosé out of matching hollow-stemmed champagne glasses and listening to the Fantasia on 'Greensleeves'. The fire would be burning and we'd be sipping and we'd be kissing, having a little sex and a lot of petting. Once she tried to suck my cock. I said, 'What are you doing?' And she said, 'Well, I just wanted to kiss it, you know.' After we made love, I would ask her to go home so that I could be alone and suffer for the same amount of time that I had had pleasure with her. And I would put on some Berlioz and drink another bottle of wine and I would suffer, and I would sleep alone.

Now this was fine. What was so exciting about making love with her was that she would have climaxes just by my cock being in her.

All I had to do was enter her and she would have a climax and faint. Now, all right, maybe she was faking it, but at least it showed that she liked me. The relationship reached its romantic culmination when we ran out of *The Misanthrope* set and I leapt up naked, broke up the only remaining furniture in the room, threw it in the fireplace, and we made love in front of the burning chairs.

On Sundays Adriana would come over to my room to study. I'd get a fire going and she'd stretch out naked to read her botany book. After reading for a while, she'd fall asleep on her belly and I'd just stand there looking down at her exquisite naked ass and back. I could never get enough. This longing to devour her led to atomic bomb fantasies, which most likely grew out of a lot of my reading at the time. I had this fantasy that Adriana and I would commit atomic hari-kari together. I would have an atom bomb under my bed and just as we were about to come together, I would trigger it and the whole city of Boston would come and go with us.

With Adriana I had the sense that I was finally in love because I was jealous, really jealous, for the first time since Julie Brooks exchanged shirts with Billy Patterson. One day an old boyfriend of Adriana's came to Boston from New York and she was going over to pay him a short visit 'just to catch up on old times,' she said. I thought that meant 'good times'. While I was in the bathroom I looked up at the shelf over the toilet and noticed Adriana's diaphragm case, and thought, the sweet little thing, she's true to me. She actually left her diaphragm behind. But I had this little residue of doubt and I opened the case just to check. And the diaphragm was gone.

When Adriana returned that night we had a big fight. I went into a jealous rage. And she said, 'Oh, babe. Don't you trust me? Do you really think I could make love to anyone else but you?' And I said, 'Well, what the hell happened to your diaphragm then? Hey? What happened? You tell me!' She told me that it had sprung a leak, a little hole, and she had taken it into the diaphragm shop for repairs.

Soon after that I graduated from college, and I thought that graduation would mean the end of Adriana. But it didn't work that way, I missed her a lot. I was surprised at how much I missed her and I tracked her down at Block Island. I called her up from the mainland and said I was coming out. And she said, 'Oh, I wouldn't do that.' So I said, 'What do you mean? I'll kill him! Kill him!' I couldn't believe I was talking like that. I was glad I was on the mainland. She said, 'No, I don't think you should come out. I have a bad case of poison ivy.' 'I don't care about poison ivy,' I said, and I went out anyway and she *did* have poison ivy, on her right thigh. We went to bed and made love and then in the morning she got out of bed while I was still asleep. I saw her disappearing through the sand dunes and I knew she was on her way to see him. I couldn't take it. I started crying and wandering up and down the beaches of Block Island, weeping, every so often looking over my shoulder at another woman on the beach.

I decided that this time I was going to become an asexual theater artist, and I went away to the Champlain Shakespeare Festival in Burlington, Vermont, with the anticipation of great roles. I had a roommate there that I didn't like. He was one of those actors who would recite Robert Frost poems by heart – 'Two roads diverged in a yellow wood,' and on and on and on. Both of us had our eyes on the same woman, a long, tall, dark woman who lived above us. But I was sticking to my vows. I was going to take my time even if it took all summer. I'd wait for her to come to me. My roommate didn't waste any time at all. The first night we were there I went off to a rehearsal. When I got back, I heard laughter coming from her second-storey balcony, I heard this Henry VIII laughter, 'Hah, hah hah hah hah.' And I thought, my God, there ought to be a law, you know they just met! I was disgusted. And then I saw a naked leg rise up over the railing of the balcony just as her underwear came floating down and landed on my head. It was like a movie or a play. I took the underwear off my head, went inside and laid it on the guest bed next to mine, and went to sleep. I don't know how I slept.

The next morning when I got up, I took the panties upstairs to return them. I knocked on her door and she didn't answer. But the door was unlocked – it was Burlington, Vermont – and I went in and left them on her bureau with a note. And shortly after that I was drafted.

47 BEDS

I awoke a little anxious to find that I was sleeping on my brother Channing's futon guest bed on his living room floor in Providence, Rhode Island. So, in order to calm myself down, instead of counting sheep, which I thought might put me back to sleep and I didn't want to do that, I started counting beds and realized that I'd slept in about 47 since the first of March. Usually, when I go to visit my brother in Providence, we talk about music, Buddhism, gurus, and the quickest way to enlightenment. We were always practicing the I-am-one-who-is-doing-this method. No matter what you're doing, you say, 'I am one who is picking this up, I am one who is . . .' And eventually, the books say, you get something of a liberating distance, whatever that might be, rather than an aesthetic distance. But we weren't talking about this anymore because my brother had become a land-lord. He had just bought the building he was living in, and he and his wife were upping the rent of the couple above them who had lived there for 15 years. The couple was moving out and no one was speaking to anyone, and my brother and his wife had become more property conscious.

Not that I don't occasionally get drawn in by gurus. When I was in India, I became sexually obsessed. I just couldn't stop thinking about sex. I think it had to do with India. I knew there was a lot going on because there were so many people, but I could never get a sense of how and where it was operative. So I began dwelling on it, a lot. I got interested in the idea of tantric sexuality, where you get locked into a tantric sexual pose and say, 'I am one who is doing this,' and you stay in it, meditating on the cosmic polarity between male and female without discharging the 'precious seed'.

At last I was about to get an introduction to the tantric master,

Gopi Krishna, who was said to be one of the last great tantric gurus in India. But when I got to his ashram in Kashmir, it turned out that he was in the Poconos for the summer. So I shot off to Poona, another town in India, which I thought would be a good place to go because the name sounded so sexy and that old reprobate Bhagwan Shree Rajneesh had an ashram there. Some Indians I met in Bombay had told me that they never even would look inside the ashram gate for fear of the orgies they would see. I thought: That sounds tempting.

Maybe you've heard about Rajneesh. After he left Poona he started Rancho Rajneesh, an ashram about the size of the state of Rhode Island in Oregon, and later fled the US, but at the time I was in India he was residing in Poona and advocating a kind of special sexual liberation practice for Westerners. His theory was that Westerners are all hung up on sex and that we really have to just do it a lot and get it out of our systems so that we can get on to something bigger and better. I was wondering what that bigger and better thing was.

So he was running workshops in which he'd say, 'Now we're going to turn out the lights and you just go to town.' You know, do things, freaky things, things you never dreamed of doing before.

Now I could understand the theory of indulgence of desire as a cure – you know, fighting fire with fire. I had a heavy relationship with champagne in 1955 in Barrington, Rhode Island. I thought it had a grip on me and that I was not in control of it, and in order to cure myself of its power over me, I drank two bottles of it on a hot summer afternoon. That took care of champagne for the rest of my life. But it was very difficult to do that with sex in Barrington, Rhode Island, in 1955. So here I was coming full circle.

Friends in New York who had gone to see Rajneesh had told me, 'Look, he's gonna want you to wear orange. That's his trip. Just go along with it. Treat it as a piece of theater.' I thought I knew what theater was – because I'd been involved with it for 20 years – until I got to Poona and couldn't put on the orange. In fact, it made me sick, and I only got as far as putting on beige pajamas. I was wearing beige and teetering. I was the only one in the ashram in beige.

If you were dressed in orange and were not wearing the *malla* – which consisted of wooden beads with a glossy black-and-white photo of Bhagwan hanging from the bottom – that meant you were about to bow down to him to receive it.

After a few days I decided to request an audience with him. His secretary warned me not to wear any scented soaps, perfumes, shaving lotions, or to carry any cut flowers, because the smell might overwhelm Bhagwan and cause him to leave his body. He had been slipping in and out of it accidentally, off and on, and his followers wanted to make sure that he'd return. Otherwise they'd just be stuck with this shell of a guru. So we were to wash carefully and go to the back gate to wait. And to make sure that we weren't exuding any of the forbidden smells, they had these guys stationed at the gate I can only call sniffers. They looked like those little woodpeckers people used to put on the edge of a glass that bob down toward the water. There were two sniffers at the gate who would just gracefully bend and sniff behind your ears as you passed through.

When we got through the gate, we all sat on the ground just outside his back porch, quietly waiting for him to appear. The group was made up of a combination of resident disciples, called *sinasis*, who had already taken the *malla* and had been living at the ashram for some time; several wide-eyed initiates dressed in orange who had not yet received the *malla*; and me, dressed in my beige pajamas. We were told that when we had our audience with Bhagwan we were not to get too close because that might also cause him to leave his body. Finally, he came out, immaculately dressed, a really beautiful looking guru with a full beard and a clean white robe with gold guru cuff links. Then his Shakti, his female tantric counterpart, entered and sat cross-legged at his feet. She was from New Jersey, I think, and looked about 23 years old. Meanwhile, all of Bhagwan's sniffers, who were looking more like henchmen, were standing around photographing and tape-recording the event so that the following day you could buy tapes and photos as mementos.

The first person to come and kneel down at his feet was this pretty young female *sannyasin*. Bhagwan just sat there with his eyes glowing and his hands folded in front of him as she knelt and spoke. 'I've come to you because I've fallen in love with Paul Krishnon, and I'm in pain because he's married to Mary Jo Ellen Annanda and refuses to leave her and I don't know what I should do.' As I was sitting there I realized that I had seen this woman before – one day out in front of the ashram she had tried to convince me to give up all my worldly possessions and come live there. She told me that Bhagwan was like this wonderful father. I told her that I was in conflict, torn between staying on at the ashram to take one of the encounter workshops and going on further north to see some of India. I asked her if she had seen any places in India that she could recommend to me. She told me that she didn't like Indian people much: they were kind of sneaky and nodded their heads no when they meant yes. The furthest she'd traveled into India was her two trips to downtown Poona to buy handpacked ice cream. So I remembered her. After she finished speaking to Bhagwan, he pulled back and, gracefully moving his hands into his lap and adjusting them into a tantric *mudra*, said, 'Don't get involved with Krishnon. He's married and can only cause you pain. Don't seek pain. You deserve so much more. You deserve great pleasure. And if, in two weeks time, you don't find a man, please return and tell me. I will find you one because I have lists.' Then he gestured to her to go back and rejoin our group.

Next a very impressive French hippie with long dreadlocks came to Bhagwan's feet and knelt. I realized that I'd seen *him* before as well, swimming in a pool at the hotel where I was staying in Bombay. I had taken notice of his orange bathing suit and spectacular head of hair. And now here he was coming to kneel down in front of Bhagwan and telling him in this heavy French accent that he felt so much energy in the base of his spine that he could no longer sleep. Whereupon Bhagwan asked him to manifest this energy for all of us to see. The guy began trembling all over, like he had an incredible killer fever. It looked like an earthquake had suddenly struck the little patch of ground he was kneeling on. Bhagwan quickly pulled back his chair, as though he thought he might catch something from him, and all the time the Frenchman is vibrating on his knees like an old GI Joe windup toy, vibrating closer and closer to Bhagwan. Suddenly, Bhagwan rallied his forces, and in a firm, commanding voice called forth the woman who was in search of a boyfriend and asked her to place her hand on the head of the French hippie and draw all his turbulent energy through the crown of his head. She did as she was commanded. She stood over the Frenchman and placed her right hand on his head and within seconds he fell into repose. Bhagwan folded his hands again and smiled, and then said to the woman, 'You see how good you are. You're such a fine-tuned receiver. You will indeed find the right man.' Then, like some high priest who had just performed a marriage ceremony, he gestured to the couple to return together to the group.

After that, it was time for the new initiates to come and kneel down to receive their holy names. Bhagwan would shine a little penlight into the initiate's eye and then, quite simply, give him a new name.

For instance, he'd say, 'You will be called Krishnababaddas, which means "always walking the razor's edge". Does that make sense to you?' The initiate would always enthusiastically nod yes, no one ever nodded no.

At last it was my turn to come and kneel down in front of him. I really wanted to ask him, 'Where are the orgies?' but I was too intimidated by the place. It probably would have been more honest to fly directly back to New York and go to Plato's Retreat. Finding God there would've been a surprise for sure. So I kneeled down and he said, 'What can I do for you?' And I said, 'I'm an actor from New York City and I don't know what to do here. What workshops should I take?' And he said, 'We have many actors here from New York City.' Well, that was the old dime-a-dozen theory, which I expect to hear around New York. But in India. . . He said, 'Take some of the encounter groups, the deprivation therapy or Primal Scream, then come back to me in two weeks' time and we'll talk again.' Now I knew that Primal Scream was going on because I had heard it. Also, people were wearing buttons saying: 'Don't speak to me, I'm in preparation for Primal Scream.' All of this seemed like it could be better done in California. The following day I decided to give up on liberation for a while and see India instead.

Back in the States, still longing for liberation, I ended up in a Zendo in the Catskills. I happened to fall into one of those intensive *sesshins* that go on for seven days, where you're not allowed to speak at all. Well, that was a new experience for me, and it caused great disruption. Luckily it was a beautiful environment, because when you can't talk, reality comes rushing in on you very strongly. The sunset was beautiful, but you weren't allowed to talk about it to the person next to you. It was just there, rushing in. At meals you'd just sit there, looking out the window, chewing your food and not having to discuss it with anyone. And the food was wonderful. It was cooked with love.

I can remember about the third day I began to notice a little wooden tray being passed down the table with what looked like dessert on it, macaroons or something. I always took it off with my chopsticks and thought: strange dessert. It tasted like the rest of the food. One day I looked up and saw that people were *putting* little clumps of food onto this tray with their chopsticks, and then I realized that all this time I'd been eating the offerings to Buddha. When I realized this I had two strong reactions. One was very familiar: guilt. The other was that I might be enlightened before anyone else as a result of my eating. It gave me great courage to go and meditate, which was done by sitting on a cushion, staring at a white wall, counting your breath from 1 to 10.

Often when I travel, I bring one book with me that I wouldn't read in any other circumstances. This time I had brought along the *I Ching*. Every day at lunch I'd throw the coins, and about the fourth day into this I threw the hexagram, The Well. I went back to meditate. Up until then there had been perfect conditions for meditation, very quiet, but all of a sudden this unbelievable pile-driver sound began. It was like putting up a building in New York City, and the Japanese Roshi (the high priest of Zendo) got up and said, 'I must apologize. The people have come from Pennsylvania to dig the new well. I told them not to come until next week, but what do they know of *sesshin*?' I thought, I'm on to something; and this really intensified my meditation. Before that all I had been seeing were hallucinations of black-and-white pornographic films on the wall. Sucking and fucking to beat the band. I realized this was probably how the monks create their *mandalas*. It's all a psychic projection from sitting so long in a cave: they finally project their psychic pattern on the wall and they just color it in like paint-by-number pictures. They probably start with pornographic movies and throw that away like lower *chakra* footage left on the cutting room floor.

About the fifth day there, something happened that I'd only either read of or experienced on LSD. I was sitting there meditating, and everything all of a sudden just emptied out. I was only an outline. Just an outline, like a Matisse drawing. There was no me, which was a treat, a real treat, like a little vacation, and it wasn't scary because I was with all these other people doing, or trying to do, the same thing. I was just this breathing outline with the room floating through me. And I wanted to understand it, make it go on forever, so I leapt on it like a tiger, ate it right up, and it was gone. I spent the rest of the time there trying to figure it out. Thinking about the past, the future, watching pornographic films on the wall, trying to figure out how to get back to that outline.

The first bed that I slept in was in Amsterdam. I was performing my monologues and staying at the Terminus Hotel. It wasn't a cozy Dutch hotel. It was a Greek revival. I had stayed there once before and wanted to go back. They had given me a room with two beds, a place to cook, and a big bathtub with hot running water (unheard of in Amsterdam). It was perfect. So I asked for it again, and this time I got a closet. I mean, I assume it was a closet because there was no closet in it. There was just a bed and a little window looking straight out at a wall about 6 inches away. I had to put my suitcase under the bed. There was no room even to do my yoga, and the only book I had brought to read was *Ulysses*. And it was raining all the time.

I thought, I have to do something to spice up these performances. I can't do these old monologues anymore. I must try a new tactic. So I decided to interview the Dutch audiences. At the performance, I asked the audience members to write their names on little cards, and then I'd call them up and ask them what happened to them on the way to the theater. And we'd go from there. Either it would take off or it wouldn't. Everyone said to me, 'Listen, this is not gonna work.' The Dutch said it. The Americans said it. They said, 'The Dutch do not like to talk about themselves.' Now they're *always* talking. I'd seen them at café tables, rolling Drum cigarettes and talking in Dutch. I didn't understand what they were saying. Maybe they were talking about American cruise missile bases in Holland or talking about how the Dutch don't like to talk about themselves. The same had been true in Belgium. I was performing my monologue called 'Sex and Death to the Age 14' there, and I went to a bar. In Belgium they have beer bars, with six hundred different kinds of beer. It's the greatest beer country in the world, and they have different glasses for each kind. This woman there said, 'Hey boy. Over here. I recognize that you're an American. I've lived in Los Angeles, come over here, I'll buy you a beer.' I came over and she said, 'What are you doing in our country?' I said, 'Well, I'm doing this monologue called "Sex and Death to the Age 14",' and she said, 'Oh, you've got it. You know all about our country.' I said, 'What do you mean?' and she said, 'Oh, I thought you said *deaf*, because we have a saying over here that whoever has too much sex before they're fourteen will go deaf. What are you anyway?' I said, 'Well, I'm just doing these monologues,' and she said, 'Oh. So you're a preacher!'

The two people that I remember interviewing in Amsterdam were the man who talked the most and the woman who talked the least. The man was a Dutchman who said he'd gone to Hollywood to start a magazine for the people: a blank magazine for which the readers were to send in stuff to fill it up. The first item they received was a picture of a guy in a bathtub up to his neck in his own shit that he'd been collecting for months, and it read: 'Help, help, is anyone else into this?' They got enough pictures in response to publish a whole magazine of photos of other people bathing in their own shit! He said that the Manson gang had such a strong reaction to this that they threatened to kill him, and he left Hollywood and fled to Jamestown, Rhode Island, of all places, to try to set the magazine up there. But they got busted and there was a big trial. It was like the plight of the religiously persecuted in reverse. He had started out in Hollywood and was working his way back to Amsterdam.

After his trial in Providence, he returned to Amsterdam to work for ART Radio, where he said he broadcast 'happenings' all over Belgium and Holland. For instance, he would tell his listeners to get out their flash cameras, get in their cars, and drive out across the countryside. At midnight he would count to three and say, 'Push the button,' and the entire Dutch landscape would light up blue. That's what he was into.

The woman who spoke the least was a very beautiful, traditional Dutch woman with gray hair who looked like she'd stepped right out of a Rembrandt. She was with her sister, who had come with Dutch Radio to tape-record certain sections of the show. When I called the woman up to be interviewed, her sister said, 'It's too late in the evening for an old woman to go up there.' But this Rembrandt-like woman said, 'I would like to!' So I said, 'Oh, please, just for five minutes?' She came up and she said, 'You know, the first thing I want to tell everyone is that all my life, my sister has told me what to do.' That was her opener. Then she went on to talk about how she really liked to talk about herself but never had the chance, and would've been interested in going into psychoanalysis but didn't because the Dutch don't talk about themselves. After we had talked for a few minutes I said, 'Do you have any last words?' And she turned directly to the audience and said, 'Yes, to the women out there: Don't feel responsible. Most women think it's their fault when it rains at a picnic.' And then she returned to her seat.

Next I went to Paris where I stayed in a houseboat on the Seine. Paris is a beautiful city, at least that's what I'd been told; the only problem, as I hear it, is that everyone speaks French. I really have problems with the French language because in boarding school my French teacher's mother died and he went into a terrific slough of despond. He would send in all these different substitute teachers. He came in for the final exam and never looked up for two hours. He just put his head down on the desk, and everyone just passed the vocabulary words up and down the aisle.

So I didn't get off my houseboat. I was so intimidated by everyone speaking French in the city that I stayed on my houseboat and read the only piece of literature that was close to the bed, the May 1981 issue of *Playboy* magazine. It had a incredible interview with Elisabeth Kübler-Ross, who'd been working for years with the dead and dying, and now she was seeing spirit manifestations down in Escondido, California. She insisted that she was a sane Swiss scientist and was going to follow this through. She had thought she would retire and go hiking, take up pottery and weaving. But the spirit guides came to her and said something like, 'Honey, it's just begun!' And it had. Her husband of 20 years left her, $30,000 worth of her workshops were canceled, and her entire life changed. What she was saying in the interview was that we all have spirit guides who are born with us, right next to us, like guardian angels. We each have three or four. We're not in touch with them because we're moving around so much, we're so agitated, but the guides are working overtime to produce positive energy because we're on the brink of nuclear disaster.

She also said that after we die, before we go to the Godhead, we pass through a nonphysical state called the ethereal body. After we leave the ethereal body, it's determined whether or not we have completed our destinies. If we haven't, and in most cases we haven't, there's a reincarnation process in which we, as the ethereal spirit, have the choice to come back. That was the exciting part, to me, because I'd never been aware of choice in my life, and I thought, well at least I'll have the chance to come back and work out my destiny in the best of all possible conditions, in the right family. Of course, the interviewer asked her, 'What about Hitler?' You know, Hitler always comes up. Hitler and Jesus. 'What about Hitler?' And Kübler-Ross told how Hitler entered the realm of spiritual energy and had no feelings of guilt at all, was able to say 'I am one who is doing this, I am one who is doing this, I am one who is doing this . . .' And he's able to look back and see the whole Holocaust without guilt. He's able to float around out there until at last he finds the most tender, nurturing, loving family through which to enter back into the world. This may take three to five thousand years to happen, but when he finds it there are no questions asked. Zoop! He's in and he becomes the greatest leader the world has ever had.

The first spirit guide that appeared to Kübler-Ross was named Anka. He was a Bedouin, 7 foot 10, dressed in a burnoose, and he advised her that her *personal* spirit guide was about to appear, and his name was Salem. When Salem appeared in front of her she thought: If this thing touches me I will die. And it vanished. But it came back again and began to bathe her in incredible love, touching her hair, touching her body, touching her in a tender, loving way as she'd never been touched before, and she completely gave herself over to this. After she was touched by Salem, another spirit guide, an American folk singer named Willy, appeared and began singing songs. She got very nostalgic and started thinking about her deceased father's favorite song, 'I'll Be Loving You Always', and just then Willy began to sing it.

At Christmas time the spirit of Santa Claus appeared to her and she actually pulled on his beard, so she was convinced more than ever that the spirits really existed. And down in Georgia a spirit guide named Mario appeared from the waist up and gave her an incredible 15-minute massage. She so doubted this that when Mario came to her weeks later she tested him by asking, 'Mario, what happened in Georgia?' And he said in a gruff, sensual voice, 'Don't you remember that incredible 15-minute massage?' Then the interviewer asked her, 'Don't you think this is a psychic reaction to having worked with the dead and dying for so long?' 'Not at all,' she answered, 'I've never been afraid to die.' Which was an amazing thing for me to read, particularly coming from a Westerner who is chain-smoking cigarettes, and the interviewer asked, 'Aren't you afraid of getting lung cancer from smoking so much?' And she said, 'No, you only get cancer from fear of it, fear's the thing. I enjoy my cigarettes, I'm not afraid of them.' Which reminded me of my mother.

My mother was a Christian Scientist, and she was big on that fear thing. In fact, she used to think that when the winter wind off Narragansett Bay froze the pipes in our bathroom, it had been stirred up by the disturbed thoughts of the Red Chinese. And she once told me that Mary Baker Eddy had said that there had been a guy on the operating table who was so afraid that he started to sweat and thought the sweat was blood and died of fear. So we were always afraid of being afraid.

Well, I was about to be 40 years old, and I was really in need of a spirit guide because I wanted to take a vacation. I'd never taken a real vacation before. I'd always admired those 40-year-old men who just say, 'Hey, babe. Pack it up and we'll go down to Haiti for a long weekend. We'll just put it on the plastic and turn on the answering machine. Whaddya mean you're sleepy? We'll sleep on the plane!' I'd seen pictures of them flying on Philippine Air. There's an entire bed in the place and they're in their pajamas. Who the fuck is that?

I was about to be 40 and I needed a spirit guide. I needed someone to tell me where to go for a vacation, just a good spirit guide-travel agent would've done. So I'm reading through this *Playboy* and I realize how schizophrenic these magazines are, because I'm right into the print, I'm not looking at the pictures. Then my eye wanders, and the first thing I see is a Camel ad. The guy's 40 or older and he's alone. Maybe he's on vacation. He's got a jeep. I turn the page and there's another Camel ad, and this time there's a windjammer with all these men at the stern. I turn the page and there's yet another Camel ad, and I'm wondering if they're trying to tie this into Elisabeth Kübler-Ross smoking Camels. Also I realize that all these men are able to just be out there, alone – 'Where a man belongs!' But then I realize they're not alone, of course, someone's there with a camera, and that makes me feel a little better. At least they're not completely alone. Meanwhile I'm thinking, I've got to take a vacation, and I'm hearing voices, not spirit guides. More like Furies.

All these people were advising me. Leonard Pitt was in Paris, and he said, 'You've got to go to Greece!' You've never been to Greece? Oh, you only live once, go.' He shows me books on the Greek myths, books on the Greek ruins. I'd never read them, and I didn't feel I had the time. It felt like homework and made me feel nervous. Aggie said, 'Look, go. Oh, Greece! Beautiful! You walk on the beach and make love under the stars.' Stewart Sherman said they had to tie someone to a ship's mast in Greece because he was hearing Sirens. Scott said he knew a guy that got laid in Greece with a different woman every night. Dale said she would only go with a lover. To go alone would be torture because it would be such a sensual experience you'd go mad. Alice said, 'What are you gonna do, go down and dance on the rocks like Isadora?'

At last I got myself together and charged out of the houseboat onto the Paris streets, determined to make a decision about where to go on my vacation. As soon as I got on the sidewalk, I realized I had reverse seasickness. I had been on the houseboat so long that I had adjusted to its motion, and now the entire city of Paris was rocking up and down as I stumbled like a drunk through the Place de la Concorde, dodging cars. Starting up the Place de l'Opéra I was bombarded by travel posters and Greece lost my attention. I saw Swiss travel posters and thought: Switzerland! Oh, Switzerland! Oh, the Alps! I've always wanted to go there, and I could take a train because I'm afraid to fly. I could take a train there! I'd be a good boy! I'd be a good boy! I'd walk, walk, walk in Switzerland. I'd climb, climb, climb the mountains there. I'd drink only two beers a day, get into bed early, and spend time with my Thomas Mann reader. I'd be a good boy! Under an eiderdown. I'd be a good boy. A good boy. But everyone said, 'Don't go to Switzerland, they're all Fascists.' And I said, 'That's not so bad – two weeks with Fascists can be very relaxing as long as you know you are going to be getting out.' Then I thought it might be too cold there that time of year, and Italy came to mind – flashes of Tadzio in the Lido – and I thought it would be warmer there, and I could take a train.

I went to the Italian travel agency, but it was three o'clock and they were still on their lunch hour. So I went over to the Air France and said, 'Have you still got that ticket to Athens, you know, the special two-week ticket?' This was an all-day project. Each time, the travel agent punched it up on the computer and said, 'Yes, we have it Mr Gray. Do you want it?' And I'd say, 'No, I'll be right back.' Then I went back to the Italians and there were 50 people waiting outside the door. When they opened after lunch hour, everyone rushed in and started grabbing at all this travel literature and reading it, and I thought: If this is indicative of Italy, I'll go to Greece. So I went to Air France and I put down the $285, and the ticket woman said, 'Mr Gray, for three hundred sixty dollars you can have an open ticket, be a free man, come back when you want.' (Moment of temptation). Then I said, 'No, no, no, I need my frames. I need my frames.'

After I bought the ticket, I decided the best thing to do would be to buy hiking boots, because if worse came to worst and I wasn't having a good time, the only therapeutic thing to do would be to walk. I would walk, walk, walk. I'd walk over the water, walk over the islands; walk, walk, walk until I was just a skeleton – with a tan. Just pure bone, pure flexible tan bone. So I rushed off to a French mountain climbing shop, a real fancy one on Saint-Germain, and no one there spoke any American. I was so afraid of flying that I'd lost touch with my body and couldn't feel whether my toe was touching the end of the boot. And this French shoe salesman was saying, 'Ooh, ah, ohh-la-la, c'est parfait.' I just couldn't believe him, let alone understand him. I needed a good American authority shoe figure with a confident voice to say, 'Yes, right. This is the shoe for you. The toe is right there.' And I was so sure that the plane would crash anyway, as punishment for taking a vacation, that I thought, how silly it would be to go down wearing a $90 pair of boots. So I walked out in my old Puma joggers.

I woke up early the next morning and went out to the airport to get the Air France charter flight. The takeoff was smooth. I held my breath and promised to be good until we were well into the clouds. Then, slowly, I began to relax and feel almost like a normal person on vacation. Three quarters of the way to Athens, I realized that the plane was most likely not going to crash, so I started to worry about Athens. I remembered someone saying, 'Whatever you do, avoid Athens at all costs. Do not go to Athens.' And I wondered: How do you do that? How do you avoid Athens if the plane going to Greece lands there? That's going to be a hard one. So I got real nervous and began talking to this American expatriate. His name was Robert. He was living in Paris and had a friend in Greece, so I asked him about Athens. 'Look, no problem. I know the city well, I've traveled there a lot. You take a hotel room next to mine, we'll go out, we'll have dinner, you can see the ruins, and I'll show you where to get the bus in the morning so you can go down to the docks and choose an island.' Great. I took a room next to his and went up to see the Acropolis in the late afternoon. Same problem as the Grand Canyon: too many postcards too early in life. I couldn't take it in. It looked like a collapsed wedding cake. I met Robert in the Plaka for drinks. I was beginning to sense that he was gay, because he was telling me about going to see his lover on a Greek island. He was also saying, 'It's much better to be gay if you're gonna do a lot of traveling. You meet more people and sex is more available.'

So we just sat there drinking, watching the cruising going on and then we went to have dinner. After dinner we returned to the Plaka for more drinks and more watching. Robert said that Athens was a homosexual city and that every so often the bars got busted, but all they did was interrogate people about whether they were passive or active in sexual relationships. It didn't seem that different from Christopher Street, except it had quite a history behind it.

After some walking around we decided to retire early. We went back to the hotel together and I said goodnight to him and goodbye, because I never expected to see him again. Robert went into his room and I went into mine, and as I started to get undressed I got that weird springtime feeling all of a sudden. A little itch in the base of my spine. Then I got down to my underwear. I usually sleep in my underwear: I don't like to get aroused by the cotton sheets. But it felt like spring, and I thought, oh well, what the heck, I'm almost 40, why not . . . celebrate? I stripped all the way down and just stood there naked. Then I caught a glimpse of myself in the mirror and thought, wait a minute, not bad, I'm not all that bad. Maybe a little belly fat from all that Dutch beer, but still. And then I thought: I wonder why he didn't try to seduce me? What's wrong with me? What's wrong with him? Maybe I ought to go ask him. So I got dressed and went to Robert's door and knocked. 'Who is it?' he said. 'It's me.' 'Come in, what's up?' I kind of edged in along the wall and said, 'Um, we've got to do something. We've got to try something. I can't sleep.' And Robert said, 'Go take a shower and relax.'

I came out of his shower all dripping and naked and just stood there. I figured he was clean, he was nice, I might as well get initiated since I was going to be traveling a lot in Greece. Also I thought something like this would be safer in a private room, better than one of those steamy New York City gay baths. And who would ever know? Well, Robert turned to me and said, 'What do you like to do?' And I said, 'Huh, I don't know, what do *you* like to do?' he said, 'Well, I like to get my cock sucked,' and I said, 'Oh, I would never do a thing like that!' The next thing I knew I was in bed with him and so surprised because he was warm, his skin was soft like a woman's, his body had contours. He was warm and alive and it felt good to be with someone after traveling alone so much. At first I put my arms around him, but I couldn't deal with that at all and I just went right down on him. I kept thinking over and over: I *am* a homosexual, I *am* a homosexual, I *am* a homosexual . . . Then this mad raving passion burst like a bubble, and I found that I was choking on what felt like a disconnected piece of rubber hose. Some of you may know what I'm talking about. He could feel that I wasn't into it, and he called out, 'Spalding, Spalding, come on up. You don't have to do anything you don't want to do, you know. Take it easy.' He was real nice, real understanding. He said, 'Go to bed, relax, and uh, whatever you do, don't go to Mykonos. You just won't have a good time there. Why punish yourself?'

I went back to my room, got in bed and thought: Good God, what have I done. All of these faces came at me, like on a Rolodex: Ernest Hemingway, what would Ernest think? Henry Miller, what would Henry think? Sam Shephard. Lou Reed. Sartre. What would my father think? What would the *Village Voice* say? And then I thought of a joke that was going around Paris. You'll have to imagine it in a French accent. 'So! I sail six sloops across the Atlantic Ocean, do they call me Pierre the sailor? No. I help build the Eiffel Tower, do they call me Pierre the architect? No. I cook a French meal for five hundred people, do they call me Pierre the chef? No. But suck one cock . . .'

So I got out my Mykonos guidebook and read myself to sleep: 'In the evening Mykonos offers either relaxation and quiet or uninhibited enjoyment. At the restaurants people dance, eat and drink, debate, sing, talk, fall in love, just as they do anywhere else in the world.' I got out my pencil and underlined 'debate' just to be safe. I thought: This is something I could do in a pinch.

When I got on the boat in the morning, I was determined not to get involved with any tourists. I was looking for an authentic Greek experience. I went right for this guy who was dressed in black because he looked like a real Greek. I stayed away from the people in white. He was a 26-year-old Kashmiri. He was wearing a black T-shirt with 'Chinese Rocks' written on it. His name was Arjuna Aziz. He had grown up in Kashmir and had been educated in Dublin. He said he had gone to Athens to teach English. But the job had fallen through, so he was going to Mykonos instead. He'd been there before, and he said, 'Spalding, it's fantastic, it's the queen of the islands.' He was right. We got there and it was beautiful, except it was overrun with tourists. People had Super-8 cameras with little microphone booms and were posing their wives with donkeys, the natives acting as extras, and Zorba-the-Greek music playing from all the shops provided the sound track. But it seemed like a good place to stay for a while before going on to some of the more authentic islands. And it was beautiful.

Arjuna said, 'Let's take a hotel room together,' but I said, 'Oh, no, no, no, I'm going to take my own room and we'll explore the island together.' I thought if he'd been there before he could give me a tour. But it turned out that he wouldn't go out in the sun until he found some Oil of Olay, and there was none to be had on the island. He said that every other lotion made you fry like a pig. He had to send to

London for the Olay and said he was staying in his room until it came. I figured I would have to explore the island myself. So in order to keep my sanity, I set up a seven-part ritual. Number one, I'd wake up in the morning, completely anxious and rigid, thinking about what other islands I should have gone to instead of Mykonos. Tinos, the religious island, with more churches than any other island. I pictured myself climbing up a hill in the hot sun with a heavy cross on my back. Naxos, a working island, beautiful olive trees, an authentic experience. Siros, also a working island, but boring. Ios, ah, that was the one. Arjuna said there were honey-dipped thighed hippies dancing in discos everywhere in Ios. He said the Greeks wouldn't even come out of their homes because of the noise. But I'm not a hippie, I thought. Santorini, volcanic rock. I could walk over the volcanic rock, I could walk, walk, walk. Crete. I could learn to be alone like a real man and like it.

Next I would get out of bed and pack up my sleeping bag. I was traveling light. My head was completely full, but my arms were empty. I'd leave my hotel and go down to the harbor and see where the boats were going that day. I'd ask the tourists which islands they were going to and why. But I would never be able to make up my mind what boat to get on so I would wave goodbye to everyone and feel this incredible sense of loss.

Then I'd wander out to the hills to do a little Primal Scream activity. It would always start with some little involuntary moans and groans until it grew into a full scream, and I'd just stand there screaming at the tourists who were so mellow that by the time they turned around to see who was screaming I was back to normal. One day I discovered this slaughterhouse. I didn't know it was a slaughterhouse at first. It was just this junky little house that wasn't white like the others. It was brown. Then one day I saw this guy pulling a cow toward that house and I noticed that the cow did not want to go. It was dragging its hind legs like it had a good idea of what was going on. I watched the whole thing. He pulled it through the doorway and didn't even bop it over the head. He just took a huge knife and *whink*! Slit the poor cow's throat, left a gaping hole. The cow just kept breathing through the slash in its neck as it went down on its knees, and in no time it was skinned and hanging up. He did this to cow after cow while I was standing in the doorway, ashamed, but he didn't mind. Then I had this fantasy that he was doing it that particular day, but I realized he must have been doing it for 50 or 60 years. The blood would flow out the back of the house onto the beach until there was this great puddle of blood that would dry and feather like red seaweed.

Number four, I'd go into town and have my Greek yogurt with fresh strawberries and then head out for Paradise or Super Paradise Beach. Actually I never made it beyond Paradise. It was a peaceful hour and a half walking. I didn't take the boat or the bus. But when I got to the beach, the pressure began again, because Paradise was a nude beach. Nudity was forbidden on the Greek Islands, but the Archbishop of Greece, for tourist reasons, gave a special dispensation for Mykonos. And as much as I love to think that I like to go to nude beaches, I can never really relax. I think I really wanted just to sit down in peace and read Thomas Mann. But I felt compelled to interview every pretty woman from one end of the beach to the other, probably in some shady hope that somehow romantic love would take flame. But romantic love was getting more and more difficult to find. On a nude beach everyone's just roasting out there in that bright light.

So I'd start at one end of the beach, talking to every lone woman I came upon. At first I didn't know what to talk about. I thought the best thing, because everyone was island hopping, would be to start by asking, 'What islands have you been hopping to?' The first woman said, 'I come from Copenhagen.' I was so nervous that I didn't understand her, so I said, 'Oh, really? What island is that?' That was the end of that conversation. You can tell when those things are over by the way they go back to their books. The next woman I chose was a nurse from Vancouver who worked with blood and urine samples and rode one of those indoor stationary bicycles in front of the TV to lose weight. She was very talkative, but I wasn't into that topic. The next woman I came to looked like a hippie, and I thought: 'Hey, maybe *I'm* a hippie. Also it's very difficult to tell when someone is naked whether they're a hippie or not. I said, 'What islands have you been hopping to?' and she mumbled, 'Ios.' 'Oh,' I said. 'Really? I was about to go there, what's it like?' She said, 'It's different.'

Then I walked back into town. I was getting like a skeleton, losing weight, and I was feeling good about that. I would go wake up Arjuna and we'd go for our cocktail hour, which was number six on the list: Wake Arjuna up. His room would be completely shuttered, dark. He'd have been lying there all day. 'Spalding, Spalding,' he'd say, 'What time is it?' I'd say, 'It's six o'clock, Arjuna.' And he'd say, 'Am I peeling? Am I flaking, am I getting any darker? Listen. Tell me the truth, am I any darker?' He had a real problem with his color since he was a Kashmiri who grew up in England. And he said, 'Am I any darker? Now tell me the truth.' I was beginning to realize that one of the reasons I was hanging around with him was that he was, in fact, a living Greek myth. He was a real live walking Narcissus who only came alive when he was seen by other people.

After he finished preparing himself, we'd go to this gay bar called the Castro Bar and watch the sun go down. As soon as we walked in all eyes went to us. Are they gay or not? We'd come in, sit down, and have ouzo and 7-Up as the sun set and classical music played. Soon we began to collect a little group of odd people who would drink with us every cocktail hour. Brigitte, who was a 22-year-old German, very beautiful, could have been on the cover of *Stern* magazine. Her boyfriend Volker was one of the most beautiful men I'd ever met – people said he looked like James Hunt, the English racecar driver. He was like Billy Budd. He was from Germany and had been a cowboy in Wyoming. Then there was Elford Elliot from England, who had something to do with producing garden gnomes. He was tripping on acid all the time and going out to Delos, this little island off Mykonos, chipping little pieces off the ancient ruins, which he then brought back in the pocket of his jumpsuit. Then there was Bryan, an IBM operator from Australia, who fancied himself as a kind of Oscar Wilde figure. I don't know why. The only story of his I remember was about some Australians who stole a garden gnome from the front lawn of a very elegant mansion and took it for a trip around the world. They would send postcards back to the owner saying things like, 'Having a lovely time in the Fiji Islands' and sign it, 'The Garden Gnome.' After six weeks, they brought the garden gnome back and left it on the lawn with little suitcases full of tiny clothing they'd knitted for it.

I also remember a story Brigitte told me while Mahler's Fifth Symphony played in the background: 'May I speak with you?' she whispered in my ear. 'I cannot give my heart to one man. Volker loves me and has given me his entire self. He lives for me. Last night I rejected him and he broke down and cried. He said he was going to kill himself. I like falling in love. I like the feeling of passion. I like lying on my bed at night and not being able to sleep because I am thinking all the time of my new lover. I am thinking of his eyes. May I tell you briefly of my father? He is a judge and works very hard. When he was thirty-nine years old he had his first heart attack, and now he expects another one any day and this one will be fatal. I am his only daughter and he adores me. People say his whole being lights up whenever he sees me. He will do anything for me. He is sure that the USSR will invade Germany soon. The German economy is in a state of collapse and the chancellor is about to resign because of this. My father desperately wants me to leave Germany, but I can't. I am a German. My father gets very depressed about this and pleads with me. He was going to help with the building of a collective bomb shelter, like the ones the Swiss have, but when he found out that it was forbidden to bring dogs into these shelters he said, "What's the use?" '

Everyone told me that I was not fitting into the island well because I was not wearing the traditional garb. I was wearing dungarees and a tee-shirt. So the last night I was there they said, 'You've got to go out and buy the white pants, the Hawaiian shirt, and the hat. A panama hat.' They got me a little drunk on ouzo, and we went out and bought the pants, shirt, and hat, and I put them on. I walked around the island and felt in total control, like I had arrived. That night I went to bed early.

The following morning I woke up in total panic. I was so afraid I was going to miss my boat that I found I was holding the alarm clock with both hands on my chest. I thought: Hoo, I am in desperate shape. When I got down to the dock I saw that Arjuna had come to say goodbye. He said, 'Spalding, you look great. You look like Bob Dylan in that hat. You could go to Ios and pick up any honey-dipped thighed hippie you wanted.' I said, 'No, Arjuna. I gotta get back. I'm a busy man. Besides, my ticket is up.' He said, 'Wait just a minute. I'm going over to the post office to see if my Oil of Olay has arrived.' It had arrived, but the top was broken.

I said goodbye to Arjuna. I thought I'd never see him again. Goodbye to Mykonos. And as the boat pulled out I saw that it was, indeed, a beautiful island. I began to feel this terrific sense of loss, but I didn't know what it was about. I couldn't figure out what it was I'd lost. At first I was afraid I'd lost my sense of humor. Then I realized it wasn't that. I'd lost the experience of Mykonos. I hadn't had one. I began to moan and groan. I was pacing up and down on the boat, dressed only in my ocean briefs, letting out little groans as the boat docked and left each of the islands on the way back to Athens. I could feel what might be an involuntary Primal coming on, but I thought that the deck of the boat might be the wrong place for one. Then I realized that none of the tourists would hear me because they were all wearing stereo headphones. But just before I let out a scream, one of those tourists, who was American, took off his headphones, came over to me and said, 'Aren't you Spalding Gray?' And my ego all at once came together like a diamond in the center of my forehead and I said, 'Yes. Why do you ask?' He said, 'Oh, I've seen all your work, I like you very much. In fact, I'm writing film scripts now and I'd be glad to try to get you a role in a movie.' I said, 'Do it! I'm ready.'

He was traveling with some archeologists, and they were staying at the poet James Merrill's house in Athens. They invited me to come stay with them. I thought: Oh, boy, an authentic experience at last. Suddenly a red light lit up on the map of Athens. Instead of returning to a hotel, I was going to stay at the poet James Merrill's house.

When we got there, I was given the royal tour. They took me to the archeological digs the next day, and all the Seven Sisters were there in their madras Bermuda shorts, sifting and sifting for little pieces of ancient ruins. The archeologists took me into a vaulted room where all the artifacts were filed in drawers. They got out a two-thousand-year-old skull and put it in my hands. I held it and thought: This is a two-thousand-year-old skull, this is a two-thousand-year-old skull, this is a two-thousand-year-old skull. . . I put it back in its box and took a cab to the plane. I was so excited to have had an authentic experience that I thought: Oh God, now the plane's going to crash! So I started making up little prayers – not exactly prayers, more like conditions, little promises. I was thinking: All right, all right, all right . . . if this plane doesn't crash, I promise, I promise, I promise I will make Art out of this experience. No entertainment. No more entertainment! I didn't know who I was making conditions *to*, maybe the *Village Voice*, maybe the *New York Times*, maybe God. When the plane landed in Paris it was raining and I found that I was locked out of the houseboat, so I took the train to Amsterdam to catch my KLM flight back to New York City.

In Amsterdam, I went to stay with friends. When I got to their apartment they were very excited because they'd heard a rumor that the chancellor of Germany had just been shot. And I said, 'The chancellor of Germany? You're kidding! I just heard he was resigning because there's no more money in Germany.' And they turned on the TV and we found out that it was *Ronald Reagan* who had been shot, and everyone started laughing. I was a little depressed. I thought: It's one thing for *me* to laugh, but when the Dutch start laughing . . . I went up to bed early and slept in this 11-year-old boy's room. On the bureau there was a large model of a KLM Royal Dutch airplane in takeoff position, and all night I kept sitting up in bed thinking it was my plane taking off without me.

The real plane landed safely, as always, and I found myself in Hell City. I understand why people travel all the time – you know, teach a little English in Bombay, a little in Athens, a little in Iran. It's possible just to keep hopping around the world and not ever have to touch down. Because it's hard to come back to the hot New York City summer and find that the rents have tripled and the streets are still filthy. So off I went to my father's home in Rhode Island.

My father and stepmother were living in their retirement dream home. It's like a very fancy motel. You drive into the asphalt driveway and on the right is a tennis court. You push a button, one of the three doors in the three-car garage goes up, and there are three cars in the garage. You go around to the front door, press the doorbell, and it plays 1 of 20 different tunes (my father changes it every day). This day it happened to be 'The World is Waiting for the Sunrise' with a polka beat. Another day it might be Bach's B Minor Mass or the *William Tell* Overture. At Christmas it was always 'Jingle Bell Rock'. The whole house is wired with a burglar alarm system that my father says can be heard in New Jersey when it goes off. As you walk into the house, the first thing you see is an entire weather station on the wall, with instruments showing the barometric pressure, wind velocity, and temperature. There's wall-to-wall carpeting and Muzak in every room. You go into the bedroom and in between the twin beds is a sound box that makes the sound of wind or water or just white noise. My father can't get to sleep without it. Down in the basement there are two freezers filled to the top with meat. The attic is like a liquor store, with rows and rows of bourbon, vodka, and wine as well as tonic, soda, and Mr T. Bloody Mary Mix. In the garage is a gasoline generator which automatically goes on if the electric power goes off. There's an automatic ice machine, a trash compactor, an electric bread box, a cordless telephone . . . Cocktail hour begins in front of the TV at five o'clock. We start with 'Zoom', then the 'Six O'clock News', the 'Seven O'clock News', and somewhere around 'The Odd Couple' we're eating dinner and I don't know whether I'm talking to my father, the TV, or to Tony Randall and Jack Klugman. It all gets blended together.

But this particular day we are eating outside because it is summer. The only problem is FLIES. 'Flies!' my father cries out. 'Look out, don't leave the door open, the flies are getting in.' He gets out the Fogger, a big poison fog bomb that he sets off right next to the picnic table. Meanwhile my stepmother, who collects antiques, rushes into the house to get her antique fly gun – a little metal contraption shaped like a gun, with a swatter you pull back and hitch to the top of the trigger. If you aim it right, it will mash a fly. Everything else is going fine, except that my father's flagpole has been stolen twice, both times with the flag on it. He had to cement the third one in. Everything is going fine, except the gypsy moths are chomping at the leaves. And everything is going fine, except there are cracks in the swimming pool and it's beginning to leak and the Astroturf is shrinking. And everything is going fine and everything is going fine, except the neighbor, Rocky, has pigs, and even though he lives a good ways away, when the wind is blowing wrong and you're in the swimming pool, you smell garbage. They're trying to get this to be the perfect home, so they've got to get rid of this guy, it's a problem. Not only is he a pig farmer, but his name is Rocky and that's my father's name also. So they figured out this plan: they bought, at a great cost, the property between theirs and Rocky's. And then they took him to court and said, 'You can't have pigs next to our property.' He said, 'But you don't own that property.' And my father said, 'We bought it this morning, my friend.' And everything is going fine, except people are dying. My father and stepmother read the obituaries every morning. It's the first thing they read. They talk about cancer like it was the common cold: 'Well, Tony and Lucy Gardner were over the other day and they *both* have cancer. Lucy's doing fine. She's got a wig, she's holding up well, but . . .' Then: 'Well, Tony's gone, but Lucy's going back down to Florida without him, she's such a good sport.' My father heard through the grapevine that one of his neighbors had cancer, and he wanted to ask him about it. So he called him up and said, 'Hi, uh, Ted. I hear you're a little under the weather, not feeling up to snuff.' My father told me that a friend of his came over for lunch one day and died of a heart attack that afternoon. He said, 'But these people are seventy-four, and I'm just seventy.' I thought: Gee, what must it be like to know that you may only have four years left? And then I realized that a big part of living is conformity. For years my father conformed to the styles and rhythms of his friends and colleagues, and now that they were all beginning to die, he was wondering if maybe he was supposed to go along with them.

After I left Rhode Island I wasn't ready to go back to New York so I decided to go to Dover, Delaware, to visit my friend Ryan Ryder, who had just become a 39-year-old grandfather. I hadn't seen him in 15 years and he sent me a card announcing that he had just become a grandfather. I thought I should go see him because I had been with him when he lost his cherry to Bonnie, now his wife. She was 20 and he was 17. He went wild for her – she was one of those lusty singers. She'd go to all the fraternity parties. Well Ryan fucked her for the first time in the rec room of my parents' basement when they were away and Pete, Webb Webster, and I watched it through the louvered door from the other room. We saw this primal scene. People can now go see it on Eighth Avenue for $1.98, big deal. But then, in Rhode Island, this was unheard of, and on top of that it was my *best friend* and I was seeing it for the first time. There was a party, and we were all drunk. 'Them Dirty Blues' by Julian 'Cannonball' Adderley was on the hi-fi full blast. The record was stuck, which was adding to the atmosphere, and Webb, Pete, and I started creeping in to get a closer look. There they were, doing it, right in front of us, and Webb freaked out . . . He was very conservative, a cautious type. He was a weightlifter and the first in the neighborhood to discover health food. And he yelled out, 'Stop them, stop them, the police are gonna come, the police are gonna come!' like he thought the police could pick up all the fucking on radar. Pete just got right in there with both hands and started mixing and shuffling like a sex mechanic, feeling the different body parts. Bonnie was yelling, 'Do it right, goddam it! Do it right, Ryan, do it right!' And I didn't know what 'do it right' meant. I wondered what Ryan was doing wrong. From where I stood it looked right to me. I was making a study because I wanted to know how to do it right. Maybe Bonnie felt that something was wrong because she was feeling four hands instead of two. Then somewhere in the middle of it all I realized that my parents might come home at any minute, and I told Ryan and Bonnie, 'You gotta get out of here, my parents are coming back. You can use my motorcycle.' So they got dressed, rode the motorcycle to the Rhode Island Country Club and went down near the ninth hole, in the back of the nunnery off Barrington Beach. They started rolling drunk and naked in the poison ivy and fucking up a storm. Well, they both got poison ivy, Bonnie got pregnant with Zachary, Ryan dropped out of high school, and they got married. Ryan got a job on the assembly line packaging cough drops at a factory in Dover.

I hadn't seen Ryan since then. Over the years he and Bonnie had four kids, and they were crazy about them. Bonnie wanted to have more, but Ryan said no. Instead they started taking in foster children – they took in 18 in two years – and, of course, they fell in love with them, too, and couldn't help adopting two of them. So they had four kids of their own, two adopted ones, and a whole lot of little suckers passing through all the time in this tiny suburban home.

When I arrived, Ryan wasn't there. He was out somewhere in town at the local bar. I just walked into the kitchen and there was Bonnie, sitting on a stool like a big earth mother, drinking a can of Pabst Blue Ribbon. She didn't even seem surprised to see me. She treated me as though I'd just come in from around the corner. She was wearing this big muumuu that went down to the floor and I had this vision of her perpetually giving birth, the children flying out like little bats from under her dress. She was real happy to see me. She said, 'Ryan's just gone out to the bar, he'll be back, take it easy, walk around, do what you want.' As I'm sitting there this little girl is running in and out. She's this little towhead, about 5 years old, with frizzy hair. She looks cute from the top, until I get down to her level when she comes running in again. I think, oh my God, this girl looks like the 90-year-old 6-year-old in the *Enquirer*. You know, '*6-Year-Old Girl Ages 90 Years?*' There in front of me is the incredible little face with the skin hanging down like an old woman's. And there are these little bright eyes shining through. I said to Bonnie, 'What's that? What was that?' And Bonnie told me the story of Jennie. Jennie had been recently diagnosed as having multiple sclerosis and they had to take her in for an operation in which the doctor took a piece of bone from her thigh and transplanted it into her ankle. While she was in the hospital, they gave her too much of the right medicine or too much of the wrong, they didn't know which. And this had caused Jennie to lose all the elasticity in her skin, her face, her knees, her ass, and her elbows. To correct the condition the doctors were now using plastic surgery.

The first thing Ryan did when he got home, after he greeted me, was to go into what he called his 'power corner' in the kitchen. He began drinking Pabst Blue Ribbons, just one after another, and rapping with the whole family. It's a tight little family unit and they rarely go out of the house. Bonnie doesn't even have a driver's license. When I asked her why she said, 'I knew if I got one I'd have to go to the supermarket all the time.' She stays in and takes care of the babies and Ryan goes to the supermarket once in a while. So we're rapping, and I said, 'Ryan, Bonnie, come on, how did you make it through all these years, you know, all the changes? What kept you together?' And Ryan said, 'What changes? I worked on the night shift at the cough drop factory, I came home, I slept, and the kids just grew up like little plants.' 'Didn't you have *any* problems?' I asked. And he said, 'Yeah, one problem. Zachary came home once with a bunch of kids and they were going down to the basement to smoke hash and listen to Pink Floyd. I thought I was going to tear my fuckin' hair out!' I said, 'What'd you do?' He said, 'I went down and got stoned with 'em and Zachary and I have been best smokin' buddies ever since, right Zach? Hey – let's get out the water pipe!' He got out the water pipe and started passing it around. While we were smoking, he told me they had only taken one vacation in 20 years. 'My God,' I said, 'only one vacation in twenty years? What did you do?' He told me that they all went to L. L. Bean's in Freeport, Maine. They stayed in a Holiday Inn, run by Chinese. They had Chinese food every morning for breakfast. And they loved it.

After a while, Ryan got a little competitive and belligerent. He saw that I was drinking Jack Daniel's straight from the bottle and said, 'Gray, how can you do that, how can you drink that shit straight?' I reminded him he was a thimble-belly and should stick to beer. He got pissed and said, 'What do you mean, a thimble-belly?' And I said, 'Come on, don't you remember? Barrington, Rhode Island? Mr Boston Vodka? Walking down Chapin Road? Falling down suburban lawns? Getting arrested when you told that cop, "Drunk? What do you mean, drunk? You can't smell vodka!" ' Ryan remembered and we both laughed.

By now it was getting really late. It was about eleven o'clock and we hadn't eaten yet and I felt an attack of hypoglycemia coming on. I started looking to see if Bonnie had set the dining room table yet, and I noticed there wasn't even a dining room. I *had* noticed a turkey in the oven earlier, so I said, 'Bonnie, do you think I could take a little turkey?' 'Oh, go ahead,' she said. 'We never sit down to eat in this house, we just pick. We just run through and pick. I'll set you a place.' She put out a plate for me and a plate for Ryan at this little breakfast table. Then Ryan left his 'power corner' to come eat with me, which may have been a mistake. He lurched across the room and hit the table, knocking over the bottle of red wine I had brought for dinner. Then he put his face down in the middle of his turkey dinner, ate a few bites, sat back up and said, 'I'm going to bed. Put a blanket on the floor for Spud.' And I said, 'Bonnie, what happened? Is he pissed at me?' She said, 'Look, I don't think it's you, it's Jennie. You know, Ryan cried when he found out about Jennie. I'd never seen Ryan cry before. And also, why would you want to come see a friend after twenty years? . . . Well, anyway, let's sit down and talk. I could talk all night. I haven't talked with another *adult* in twenty years. What's happening?' I said, 'Oh, you know, everything and nothing. I started therapy.' 'You're kidding,' she said, 'I didn't know you had an unhappy childhood.' 'No, I don't think I did,' I said, 'I just, well, lots of people in New York go to therapists.' She said, 'You're kidding.' I said, 'No, they do, they call it "doing therapy".' And she said, 'Well, what is it that you do?' I said, 'Well, at the end of the week you get a chance to reflect and go over everything that happened in front of a witness, try to put the puzzle together, you know?' And she said, 'Reflect? Reflect? I haven't had time to do that in twenty years and everything's going fine down here! I don't know why you don't get hypnotized and find out about your past incarnations. Bypass your parents. Go right back to the source.' I said, 'Look, everyone I know who's been hypnotized to find out about their reincarnations finds out that they were one of the slaves who carried the rocks up the pyramids. And who wants to know about that, anyway? Furthermore, if there's a nuclear holocaust, how the fuck are you gonna have an earth to reincarnate on?' She said, 'Well, you have a point there, but you know, if I had one wish, I'd just wish for the genie in the bottle to come and make Jennie the way she was again.' She got out an old picture and showed it to me, and there she was, this cute little kid.

'You know, it's really upsetting,' she went on. 'When Jennie was in the hospital, doctors came from all over to observe her because her condition was so unusual. One day three hundred doctors came to examine her. At last she got so fed up with it that she pulled the sheets up over her head and only stuck her foot out – the skin on her foot is normal. And she said, "That's all you're seeing of me today!" ' I said, 'When did she find out that she looked like this?' Bonnie said, 'Well, it was a while after she got out of the hospital, because she was too short to look in any mirrors. And one day Ryan was down on the floor with a hand mirror fixing the water heater and Jennie came over, saw her reflection and said, "Hey – wait a minute. I look like that king." And Ryan says, "What king?" And Jennie says, "You know, that king that got shot? King Reagan. I look like a lizard." And that was the end of it, that's all she said.' It was late and I was tired. I said, 'I think I'm gonna hit the floor, Bon.' I went into the living room, where there was one blanket and a pillow on the floor. She said, 'You go on to sleep. Don't mind me, I'm just going to turn on the dishwasher.'

The dishwasher went off around 3.30. Shortly after that, the children were awake, all those little suckers, and they were all out in the kitchen. I began to understand how Ryan made it through all those years. He was a great father. He does a routine with them: OK, kids, line up. Who's gonna have the sugar this morning, the Sugar Pops? Who's gonna have white sugar and not tell their mother they had it? Then he sings this little song to them: Mr Toothpaste and Mr Toothbrush have very often said, 'Please use me in the morning and before you go to bed.'

I came into the kitchen and said, 'Ryan, my God, man, don't you have a hangover?' And he said, 'A hangover? Who has time for it?' And then I realized – all these hangovers I have, and this problem with my right knee, and the little twitch in the base of my spine – it's because I have so much time! I've got to start having children, quickly, lots of them.

After breakfast, I wanted to see where Ryan worked. So we went to the cough drop plant together and Ryan gave me a tour. They turn out thirty thousand cases a day with only five men, all automated, and Ryan counts the cases. I said, 'Where's it all going?' He said, 'Most of it's going to the American armed forces in Germany because they're too paranoid to use the cough drops over there. They think that's where the first espionage is going to start, with the KGB putting nerve gas in the cough drops.' After the tour I asked him to walk me to my car and as we were walking I said, 'Ryan, how *have* you made it through all these years?' and he said, 'I don't think about it. And, I astral project.' I said, '*Now* you tell me! What do you mean, you astral project?' He said, 'Each night before I fall asleep, I find that I'm flying five-hundred-miles-an-hour over the telephone wires, headed for downtown Dover.' I said, 'You're kidding, how do you know it's not a dream?' He said, 'Because I feel the wind on my face. I actually feel the cold wind on my face. It really happens, and I've learned how to will it. I can do it myself, anytime I want.' 'Oh, wow,' I said. 'Really? You must do it all the time, then.' He said, 'No, I've kind of given it up.' I said, 'How come?' He said, 'Well, you know, we got this stereo, I don't use that anymore. I got this gold Cross pen and I don't use that anymore, either. It's the same with astral projection.'

When I got back to New York I was trying to put these stories together, and one day the phone rang. It was Arjuna Aziz calling from London. 'Spalding? Spalding. This is Arjuna. Do you know how much this phone call is costing me? I'm coming to see you.' He called from Kennedy airport. 'Can you pick me up?' I said, 'No, no. I'm a busy man, I'm a busy man. You'll have to take a cab.'

So Arjuna arrived in a cab and he's wearing this smartly cut English tweed overcoat, he's had his hair cut, he's looking real dapper, and he's got a bottle of champagne. He said, 'Have I got the look? Have I got it? Am I peeling, am I flaking? Tell me the truth, Spalding, am I getting any older, any darker?' I said, 'Come on in, Arjuna. You can stay at my place for a few days, about five days, but then you'll have to find another place or a hotel or something.'

I went and stayed overnight with Renée. The next day I came back to my loft and found Arjuna all stirred up. He wanted to call a skin specialist. He told me he wanted to call Dr Norman Orentriech. Whenever Arjuna checks into a new city, he calls the best skin specialist to find out if he's peeling or flaking too much. Then I saw that my desk drawers were all open. He was trying to use my desk as a bureau. My razor was missing, and I asked him about it. He said, 'Did I use your razor? Oh my God, man. Once I used my father's razor and I got this incredible rash. I've got to call Dr Norman Orentriech.'

Arjuna came to opening night of this monologue and sat way up in the dark. At the end of it, I asked the audience if they had any questions, and a woman raised her hand. 'Yes, I'd like to know, are these people that you talk about real? Or are you making them up?' I said, 'As a matter of fact, we're lucky enough tonight to have one of them here and his name is—' I got nervous and called him Arguna. He was a little upset about that, but he came down out of the audience and I offered him my chair. He told how he perceived me in Greece and I sat next to him. The audience thought that he was a plant.

After the show was over, Arjuna went around the corner to La Gamelle for a drink. I was hoping he would be discovered, and he was. Some of the audience who were drinking there came up to him and said, 'You looked great under those lights!' He's one of those narcissists who thinks he has to respond to everyone who comes up to him. He doesn't know that he can just walk into a room and let it roll off like water off a duck's back. He met a blonde he called 'The Vacuous Blonde'. The next day he called me up at Renée's and said, 'Spalding, you won't believe it! The Vacuous Blonde called me and she wants a date. She wants to go to a bowling alley!' By now I was getting into it. 'A bowling alley! In New York City, a bowling alley? Go!'

Well, I came back the following morning hoping to find my bed empty, but he was in it, alone. I said, 'What happened?' And Arjuna said, 'Oh, she was weird! God, she had her hair dyed pink and green, and she was talking weird to her friend.' 'Weird, like how?' I inquired. 'A guy came walking down the street and she said to her friend, "Broom Alert! Broom Alert!" ' I said, 'What did she mean by that?' 'It means the guy is "sweeping her off her feet". If he's rich, she goes: "Rich Broom Alert, Rich Broom Alert!" If he's poor it's "Poor Broom Alert, Poor Broom Alert." And then she wanted to know if I was "draped".' I said, 'Draped? What do you mean, draped?' He said, 'Whether I was circumcised or not.' I said, 'Look Arjuna, it's time to go, the five days are up.' He didn't seem to believe me. He went into a panic. 'Am I peeling, am I flaking? Wait – am I growing older?' I said, 'Arjuna – we're all peeling, we're all flaking.' For the first time, I heard this adult voice coming out of me and I realized that at last I had gotten the narcissistic child outside myself. I had that child right there in front of me in the form of Arjuna. I said, 'You've got to find a hotel now. Calm down.' I checked him into the Pickwick Arms up on 51st and Lexington.

Later that day he called me up. 'I left my glue at your place. I'm coming down to get it.' I said, 'No! Buy some glue up there. What do you need glue for anyway?' He said, 'I have to glue certain things together, you know.'

The next day I thought I would confront him because I was just too busy to do this anymore. He called and asked if we could have lunch together. I told him to meet me at Eva's on 8th Street. After we settled down to lunch, I said, 'Arjuna, listen, what is it that you're looking for? What do you want from me?' He said, 'Actually, now that you ask, I'm looking for an epiphany.' I said, 'What do you mean, an epiphany?' He said, 'You know, like in the Catholic Church, when your whole life suddenly comes together and everything is meaningful, and it's in order, and it makes sense.' I said, 'Well, listen, don't have one of those here at Eva's because I'm not gonna be the one to take you to Bellevue. The Catholic Church exists for a reason: so you can have epiphanies in a safe, supportive way. Also, I think you're going to the wrong kind of doctor. You need something other than a skin specialist.' He said, 'Listen, Spalding. Being up in front of those lights was better than sex! I think we should do a duet.' After I didn't respond to this, he said, 'Spalding, something did happen, didn't it?' I said, 'Yeah it did.' At this point I thought I should just hug him and say goodbye because it seemed like he was ready to go back to London, and I felt I needed to finalize it. At last we parted in a vague, undecided way. When I got home I took the phone off the hook so that I wouldn't be interrupted. I put it back on around six o'clock and got this call from Arjuna. He said, 'Oop! Spalding! I'm out here, I'm out at the airport and there's this beautiful blonde looking at me. She's from Ireland and she's gonna be on my flight. I'll be back soon.'

Now I get a call from him about once a week. He claims the transatlantic cable is his umbilical cord to me. He'll call me just to say, 'It's snowing here.' The next week he'll call me and say, 'Oscar Wilde said that you can have epiphanies when you travel, and I'm going down to Venice to try for one there.' The next time he calls and says, 'I've been out to Elford Elliot's vicarage and he has garden gnomes that walk and talk.' The next time he says, 'I've found the perfect skin cream! Cedar Macragola, with cebum.' Then he called me and said, 'Spalding? I've gone into a heavy narcissistic period. I haven't been able to go out in three weeks! I had a charter flight to Venice and I didn't even bother to pick up the ticket.' I was kind of worried about him until the next time he called. He was in Venice. 'Spalding, I'm in this fantastic hotel with three different kinds of toilet paper in it. I'm watching *Dallas*, with subtitles, on TV. But you know, when we left Mykonos, the soul went out of that island.' I hung up the phone and thought: I wonder if I'll ever get in touch with any normal people?

NOBODY WANTED
TO SIT BEHIND
A DESK

The summer was completely planned. All I had to do was get safely from Amsterdam to New York, where Renée was to meet me with a car. Then we had three solid weeks to drive to San Francisco, where I was to perform.

I had had trouble getting out of Amsterdam before. It was not so much the city itself, but the airport, the Schiphol airport, where I had a tendency to get bogged down. In 1976, when I was returning from India with an open ticket on KLM, I decided that I wanted to avoid the bicentennial and spend the summer in Amsterdam instead. Just as I was about to board, I told the stewardess at the gate, 'Take the luggage off the plane. I'll stay here.' She said, 'I'm sorry, Mr Gray. I'm afraid it's too late for that.' Then I said, 'Very well, send the luggage on to New York. I'll stay on without it.' She said, 'We can't do that, Mr Gray. It's a rule, you have to accompany your luggage on the flight.' So I flew all the way back to New York to accompany my luggage.

This time I was determined to get out to the airport early, maybe 6 hours early. I was buying traveler's checks at American Express when I ran into a friend from New York City. It turned out that he was also flying back to New York that day, on Swissair. I said, 'Why don't we share a cab out? Although I'm going quite early.' He said, 'That's all right. I'm taking an earlier flight. All I have to do is pick up my bags first.' I said, 'I'll go help you with your bags. Where are they?' He said, 'They're at the Hotel Terminus.' On the way over we fell to talking, and everything was going fine. The bags were in the foyer and I picked them up, and we took a cab to the airport. When we got to Schiphol he said, 'I'm going to check in at Swissair.' I said, 'Don't you want to take your bags with you?' He said, 'What bags?

Those aren't my bags!' 'Not your bags? Well, whose bags have I been carrying all this time?' I looked at the label. It read 'Quintero', or some Spanish name.

I rushed to a row of public telephones to call the Hotel Terminus. There were five phones in a row, and the first phone didn't work, which was a surprise to me, because everything works in Amsterdam. You can stand in the train station and watch the clock, and the train comes in just as the second hand hits 12. So I tried the next telephone booth, and it didn't work either. Five booths, and none of them worked. I went up to the guy with the mop and said, 'These phones don't work.' 'Impossible,' he said. He went and checked each of the five booths with a coin. He said, 'I think they're all dead.' I said, 'Don't use that word around me.'

I took the bags and went to Information. I said, 'Look, call the Hotel Terminus.' They did. It turned out that this guy, this Spanish man, was going to Madrid, and he spoke no Dutch and no English. So they couldn't tell him his bags were at Schiphol airport. Besides, he was taking the train.

The plane was packed, but I wanted to be able to see the tip of Greenland when we passed over, so I was trying to get a seat near a window, but not near a door. Sometimes I think it's a good idea to sit next to the emergency door, sometimes I don't. That particular day I was thinking about James Dickey's poem about the stewardess who gets sucked out the door. It's one of his best, and it's a lengthy one because it takes so long for her to hit the ground. But my brother had told me that he'd recently heard of someone being sucked out the window. So, door, window, it didn't matter.

I ended up next to a window, just one seat back from the emergency door. An Indian man sat down next to me. He was very nervous because he wasn't sitting with his wife, who was sitting by the emergency door. He said he would buy me a drink if I switched with her and sat by the door. I'd do anything for a free drink, so I agreed that after takeoff I would switch. I moved, and to my left, standing in the service alcove, was a huge man from Salt Lake City in a T-shirt, with a big pot belly. He wasn't watching the movie, which happened to be 'The Seduction of Joe Tynan'. A little kid who looked like Swee' Pea was crawling around at his feet. The guy was in with the stewardesses, chugalugging those little bottles of Bordeaux. After a few of those, he slid down and sat with his back against the wall at the stewardesses' feet, stroking their ankles and saying, 'Nice Fräulein' as they passed.

We got over Newfoundland and up went the shades because the movie was over, and the whole plane was filled with light. By that time the man was very drunk. He leapt up and started for the window of the emergency door. He was going for it like a moth to a flame, crying, 'Light, light!' He collapsed against the big plastic bubble that says 'Do Not Sit'. He spent the rest of the trip sitting on it with the little kid on his lap, who was playing with the handle that opens and closes the door. I kept saying (trying not to sound like a fool), 'Looks like your little boy wants to get out of the plane early.' 'No, he doesn't,' he said.

Miracle of miracles, we landed safely, and Renée met me at the airport. I had left her $1000 to buy a car, anything she could find. She got one of those Volkswagen squarebacks. Both of us were aware that to re-enter New York City was to risk being caught up in the vortex again, and not being able to escape for the whole summer. It happened to me after India. It could happen again. I'd told her, 'Have the car warmed up at the airport, we'll just leave.' But she said, 'Look, I've got some bad news for you. After I bought the car, the transmission went, so I got a rebuilt one. Then all the fuel injectors went. So I put five hundred into that.' I said, 'All right, we'll work it out later. Let's just get out of here.'

But back at Renée's apartment, trying to pack up, we decided to take the car uptown to see *The Shining*. On the way we heard the sound of ripping metal – the flywheel, it turned out. In repairing the fuel injectors, the Volkswagen repair place up on 125th Street had put the flywheel on crooked. We took the car back and said, 'Fix it.' It was Fourth of July weekend, and it felt like it was taking forever. After it was fixed, we took it for a test drive and it broke down in Harlem. We had it towed back and they said, 'It's probably your computer box.' That was the first I'd heard of a computer in a Volkswagen. 'Must be your fuel injector computer box. It's broken, and you can't get it fixed over Fourth of July weekend.' We just left the car there, and I insisted that Renée and I walk most of the way back to her place. All the way back, people were throwing firecrackers at us out of their windows. It felt like a war zone.

After about two weeks we were able to get out of the city. We had decided to try to avoid the heat by taking the northern route. Neither of us had driven cross-country before, so we just took a map and decided to make up our route as we went. It was good to get out of New York and out on the open road. Driving through the rolling Pennsylvania hills we got hungry and stopped at a supermarket for cheese and cold cuts, which we ate while we drove. After lunch we both got horny at the same time. Renée went down on me, but it was hard to concentrate with the semitrailers looming up behind. The drivers had a perfect bird's-eye view down on us. At last I swerved off onto a dirt road and we both charged into the woods. There we did it, all sweaty in the sun, on a big rotten fallen tree, with flies buzzing all around.

The first stop was Saltsburg, Pennsylvania, a little redneck town about an hour and a half outside Pittsburgh, where my brother Rocky had just landed a job teaching at a boys' school. Rocky is a specialist in the history of thought, so he'd had trouble finding work in the United States. He ended up teaching English at this school. There was the town of three thousand rednecks, a faculty of 27, and all those boys, so he was feeling a little claustrophobic. He was teaching his favorite book, *Walden*, and most of his students, who had strong business careers in mind, couldn't understand how any guy could waste so much time just hanging out in the woods.

The headmaster had built the place up from an old resort and now he rode around in a leftover golf cart, cheering on the students. 'Hey boys! That's the way we do it. Kick that goal. Pass that ball. Swim that lap!' He ran the whole place from that motorized cart. He spotted us arriving, drove right up to the door of my brother's house, came in, had a couple of beers and said, 'We got it all worked out here. It's a beautiful place. Now all we gotta figure out is how to get rid of the boys.'

We drove across Ohio and on into Michigan. We couldn't find any place to stay near Ann Arbor because the Republican Convention had overflowed out of Detroit. Renée was in a bad mood because her period was coming on and we couldn't find a place to eat. At last we found a Ponderosa Steak House where we fought over the fact that I had smuggled in cans of beer under my armpits to save money. Then, right in the middle of the medium-rare Manhandler's steak special, Renée's period came on full blast and she started to leak through onto her chair. She didn't have any Tampax, so she had to take some Ponderosa napkins and go into the ladies' room to build a makeshift stopper. After dinner, cranky, Renée drove while we looked for a motel. About an hour later we found one with a single room left for $25. I bitched and moaned about that being too much, so we went on until we were both exhausted, and we pulled over at a rest stop somewhere south of Saginaw, where we slept in the car.

The sun woke us early. I felt triumphant that we had been able to save money by sleeping in the car. Renée felt cranky and dirty and wanted to wash up. We went into our respective restrooms at the rest station. The men's room was without toilet paper and Renée said the ladies' room was filled with pizza puke. The only place we could find for breakfast was a horrid doughnut shop with coffee that looked like weak tea. You could see straight down to the bottom of the Styrofoam cup.

We decided to try to get cleaned up in Lake Michigan. Everyone had said, 'Oh, you can go swimming anywhere along Lake Michigan.' But we couldn't get down to it. The shoreline was all private property covered with 'No Trespassing' signs. Renée said, 'This looks like Gerald Ford country.' So we finally trespassed through a narrow empty lot and got down to the lake, where we found a band of what looked like human shit just floating there a few feet out. You could get out past the line if you wanted. People were swimming. It would just leave a little brown crust around your ankles. Renée didn't go in. I did. I was hot.

We stopped in Escanaba on the Upper Peninsula to spend the night with friends, and they said, 'Let's walk down to the lake.' We got out to the lake and there were clumps of dead fish in the water, feathering like flowers. Out in the parking lot, four-wheel-drive vehicles were circling endlessly, their radios blaring 'Funky town. Funky town'.

We finally made it to Fairmont, Minnesota, by about 8:30 one night, where we checked into a cheap motel at $16 a night. The town was flat and hot and the whole place smelled of bad industrial pollution. After a greasy fried chicken dinner, the evening's floor show came on, Danny and Claudette. Claudette did all the singing ('Killing Me Softly') while Danny played a muted steak house organ in the background. We were the only ones on the dance floor. We went back to our motel early to watch the Republican Convention on TV. I drank can after can of 3.2 beer while wild-eyed reporters hyped the whole thing up like cheap theater. 'Bush is going to do it! Look out for Bush!' Bush this, Bush that, until completely bushed, we fell asleep.

The following day was an exciting one for us. In Mitchell, South Dakota, we got to see the world's only Corn Palace. It looked like a big Russian Orthodox church, made entirely of dried corn. We had BLTs for lunch and headed for Murdo. In Murdo we found the Sioux Motel, one of the best so far. Our place mat at dinner read: 'Sioux Motel, Murdo, SD, AAA, on US 16 & 23, Phones, Color TV, In-room coffee. Relax to stereo music in your room. Your hosts Tom & Helen Wheeler. See one of the largest collections of ballpoint pens in the area'.

The next morning we pushed on into the Black Hills of South Dakota. My dentist in New York City, Sheldon Stutzke, had suggested that I stop there. Sheldon is a swinging dentist. He wears his shirt open, with a medallion, and he has graffiti up on the wall that say things like 'Gas Is Better Than Grass'. He was the one who gave me gas for the first time and in the middle of it all left to take a phone call. He said, 'I'm just going to leave this gas on low. You relax and go with it.' I did, and after he was through filling and drilling I rushed to the nurse to ask for a pencil. (I felt a great American epic poem coming on.) When I got the pencil I felt that the dentist's waiting room was not the right place to write, so I raced over to Central Park and collapsed under a cherry tree. Just as I sat down, the gas wore off, leaving me sitting there stupefied, holding the paper and pencil.

Sheldon had told me, 'You've got to go see this guy, Jim McBride. He lives in the Black Hills. I met him at a toastmasters' convention when I was in the Air Force out there. He's a great guy.' I didn't know what toastmasters were at the time. I found out later they're people who get together and talk about anything. They just talk.

Just the other side of the spectacular Badlands, we started seeing sign after sign for Wall Drug, the biggest drugstore in the world. We couldn't wait. When we got there it turned out to be like Rexall, only twenty times bigger. Renée bought some toothpaste and I bought one of those little plastic bottles of Listerine. Then I called Jim McBride to see if we could stay with him and got Jim, Jr., who said, 'C'mon up.'

Jim McBride was the son of an Irish immigrant and he had married an American Indian. They had raised six children together in a log cabin. She had just died, and he seemed to be coping with the loss by working overtime as a railroad engineer. He was doing a 14-hour shift. He came home, found us in the yard, sat down and started talking. His father had been an Irish immigrant, came out to the Black Hills on a train, and was so hungry that he was tempted to steal a chicken and eat it. At the last minute a voice said in his ear, 'You haven't stolen anything yet,' and he put the chicken back and went to bed hungry.

After Jim told us this story, he went to bed. He said, 'You can have the teepee out back.' I said, 'Wait a minute, wait a minute. I'm petrified of rattlesnakes, and I hear you got a lot here.' He said, 'Oh, that's nothing. Take some rope, run it under your armpits, get your body smell all over it, then put it around your body. A snake won't go over anything with a human smell on it.' (Later I found out this was a joke.) When Renée and I got up to the teepee, I saw that it was so open that anything and everything could crawl right in. We didn't have any rope, so I rubbed rocks under my arms and put them around the base of the teepee. Then I made a magic protective circle of rocks around the bed.

We got through the night all right. Over a breakfast of steak and eggs I asked one of Jim's daughters, Jana, 'What about that house down there below, the funky little one in the shade? Who lives there?' She said, 'Would you believe it? One day a woman came up to our house completely fried, and fell down dead when we opened the door. She had burned. They found no evidence of fire in her house. The only report we heard was that there was this terrific *flash*. Her toaster melted, her TV melted, even her stereo melted, but nothing else was singed.' It sounded like real flying-saucer activity to me.

And there was more. She told us about this other guy living in the Black Hills. He was a new age doctor and he lived just up the hill. He was using every kind of perverse method to reduce women's weight. One of them was to administer the larvae of tapeworms to his patients. He'd disguise them by cutting them up, mixing with baking soda, and putting the mixture in gelatine capsules. When the women would quit because they thought his practice was outrageously un-ethical, he would drive by them on the street, give them the finger, and cry out, 'Hey, fatso!' Jim's daughter said the women told her this. Then a big flood came and lots of people had to leave their homes. They didn't want to move back because this doctor was such a pig that they felt it wasn't worth it to return and fix up their houses. So now he was buying them all out in order to turn the whole area into one big health spa.

At this point I was beginning to wonder where we could find some normal people in the area. Jim, Jr., said we had a few choices. We could go to 'The Gathering' to protest local uranium mining or go up to Hill City for the sportsmen's open competition. If we didn't want to do either of those things, we could drive up and watch the four-hundred-acre forest fire that Jana's boyfriend Billy Longfox was fighting. We opted for Hill City.

Hill City was a true Western town that looked like a set for 'Gunsmoke'. All the townspeople were having some sort of celebration on the outskirts of town. Loggers were carrying on with chain saws to see who could cut through a giant tree fastest. After that they rolled logs in a giant trough and had a contest to see how many whacks it took to split a log with an ax. Then there were payloaders pulling thousand-pound cement blocks through the mud. We watched all that for a while and then went back into town to see the 'Shootout'. When we were having lunch we'd seen signs for a real shootout that was to take place at four o'clock. The sign read: SHOOTOUT TRIAL AND REAL HANGING. We waited around, but nothing happened. Finally, this guy swaggered down the main street wearing holsters that looked like they had real guns in them. He tore down all the posters and spat on the sidewalk.

We weren't sure whether we'd be in the teepee or have to sleep in the car that night. Jim had forewarned us that Jana and Billy Longfox might need the teepee. It turned out Billy had to work all night fighting the forest fire. After a bean and frank supper and a lot of beer we went right to sleep. But I woke up in the middle of the night with a new fear: people. I was sure I heard human footsteps in the bushes outside. I woke Renée and whispered, 'Shhh, listen, listen! Someone's walking around out there. C'mon, just take the flashlight and go to the doorway and look out.' She said, 'Give me a break,' and rolled over to try to get back to sleep. But I shook her again and said, 'Just take the flashlight and go look out!' She said, 'No.' I said, 'Yes.' She said, 'What's in it for me? What are you going to do for me?' I said, 'All right, all right, I'll let you drive all day tomorrow.'

In the morning we said goodbye to the McBrides and headed out toward Sheridan. Renée got to drive for the whole day, all across Wyoming. For three hundred miles we saw nothing but landscape. I lay in the back sulking, daydreaming of Greece. Just before the cocktail hour we reached the Bighorn Mountains and they woke us up. Surprise, surprise! Cattle grazing at fourteen thousand feet. How did they ever get up there?

We slept in the car at a campsite near the road. We didn't even have time to make a fire. Just before bed we walked over to a nearby campsite and visited a family man standing by his campfire. He was surprised and intrigued to find a New York actor straying so far. I got a little panicked and began to wonder what I was missing back there.

We drove straight for Yellowstone the next day. I had been excited about Yellowstone ever since Ralston Russell and I had read *Mickey Mouse Sees the USA* when we were 8. We'd planned to take a trailer across America as soon as we could drive. We wanted to give special attention to Yellowstone because Mickey'd had so much fun there. I was also excited about Yellowstone because I'd always wanted to see those wild bears up close. I had a real fear of bears and wanted to get over it. I used to have recurrent dreams where bears would chase me up trees, I figured maybe if I could see one up close it wouldn't be so bad.

We stopped for a pancake breakfast at the Old Faithful Motel, where the place mat advertised 21 deluxe units as well as an adjacent 'shopping maul'. Something about the misspelling made me queasy.

Renée and I drove through Yellowstone and didn't see any bears. We saw some trout. We made it to Old Faithful and stood around this steamy, bubbly hole in the ground with bunches of other people until it gushed. Before the last of the spray hit the ground, everyone ran for their cars like the LeMans start. Not wanting to get caught in it, we ran too. We got out of the park through a back road as fast as we could. It was nothing like *Mickey Mouse Sees the USA*.

In Bozeman, Montana, we stopped for a lube job and I called Randy Boulton in Missoula to find out if we could stay there. No problem. So we headed off for Missoula and stopped in Butte for lunch. Butte is an old copper-mining town that has something to do with Dashiell Hammett. At lunch – smoked clams and bean dip, which we ate in the car – Renée told me a story about Lillian Hellman and Dashiell Hammett. It seems Lillian called him in LA from New York and a strange woman answered. When Lillian asked Dashiell who it was, he said his secretary. But after she hung up she figured that given the three-hours time difference, he was certainly in bed with whoever answered. In a jealous rage she flew out to LA, and when she found Dash wasn't at home, she blew away his prized antique soda-fountain bar with one blast of his twelve-gauge shotgun. Then she got on the first plane back to New York. After Renée told me this story, I wondered what she would do to me if ever I crossed her. Also, I couldn't believe the story, because what man would ever allow a woman he was sleeping with to pick up a ringing phone?

After lunch we drove in silence to Missoula. When we got there we sought out Randy Boulton at the University, where he taught theater and was rehearsing a summer production of *The Amorous Flea*. After rehearsal he took us back to his little house, which was kind of stuffy. It had been shut up in order to be fumigated for fleas. I wondered if it had anything to do with the play he was directing. Randy was one of those exuberant, positive types who love Missoula because it's so close to the wilds. There was a small mountain in back of his house. After his first child was born he climbed up the mountain, where he chanted a good luck benediction to her and created his own little birth dance under the great Montana sky.

Randy fed us venison stew for dinner. Then some local friends of his who worked at Anaconda came over for beers. They told stories about how they'd get real drunk in the winter and go for moonlight hikes in Yellowstone. Listening to them talk I thought these men could be my native gurus. I dreamed of the day I'd have the time to return to Yellowstone some winter to hike with them.

God was it hot the next day. It must have been over a hundred degrees, but Renée wanted to shop for cowboy boots. Missoula was filled with hot, flat streets, and at last we headed for an air-conditioned magazine store. I skimmed through a detective magazine (why would someone stab an 11-year-old boy 69 times?) while Renée bought a copy of *Red Harvest*.

Renée couldn't find any cowboy boots she liked, so we went for lunch at Alice's Restaurant. Then to escape the heat we went to an adult bookstore and both got so turned on by the books that we raced back to Randy's for hot pornographic sex. It was great because his bedroom was like an anonymous motel room in a cheap porn film.

To try to stay cool we spent the day lying in the shade down by Rattlesnake River. Randy came home from rehearsal all upset because he'd just heard that Mt. St. Helens had erupted again. Determined to get his mind off the volcano, he decided to cook a wild Canadian goose a friend had shot the past fall.

By now it was Wednesday, July 23, and Randy got us up early for a big buckwheat breakfast. We were off by 8:30. Renée went into a big funk and launched into a long diatribe about how I'm a control freak and how it's *my* trip. She said she felt like she was just driving me to work, only my work was three thousand miles away in San Francisco and she wasn't even doing any of the driving. She was enraged and couldn't take it anymore and she missed her support system in New York City. She said we weren't cut out for each other and that I traveled too much. She wanted to go home and demanded that I drive her to the nearest airport.

All this time we were driving beside a rushing clear river that runs right through the heart of Idaho. At last, when I couldn't stand it anymore, I stopped the car, tore off all my clothes and dove in. It was ice cold and Renée was standing by the car in her black overalls yelling, 'I hope you drown! I hope you fuckin' well drown!'

After I got out of the water, I drove Renée to a pay phone and she called the nearest airport in Portland for flight information. But the fare back to New York was $300, too much for her. We drove on in silence for some time and then she apologized. I refused to talk about it. I told her I didn't care if she *did* go. I'd gladly make the rest of the trip without her. I said I was fed up, but the combination of my naked swim and the assertion of my power began to make us both incredibly horny, and we started reaching over to touch each other (depending on how close the semitrucks were.) At last the windows were steaming up and we couldn't stand it anymore, so we pulled right into this dry, hot field, tore off all our clothes, and went at it in the back of the car. We both felt much better and headed out across the rolling wheat fields of southeast Washington, while Renée read out loud from *Red Harvest*. I got high just from the view.

Renée drove, and we reached Oregon during cocktail hour. As we passed over the border into Oregon I was suddenly happy. I felt like we were in the right spot at the right time.

In Oregon I wanted to find the perfect lake, one where we could stand on the edge of a dock and look all the way down to the stones shimmering on the bottom, a lake you could dive into with your mouth open and just let it fill up with pure water.

We saw signs for Shuttle Lake and thought we'd give it a try. On the way we bought chuck steaks to cook out, but the supermarket didn't sell beer. At the lake we found a beer store and camped right across from it. We charged down for a swim. The water was full of some kind of algae that had turned the lake brown. The dock was filled with all kinds of kids yelling at their fathers, who were driving speedboats with huge outboards, and pulling their wives or girlfriends all over the lake on water skis.

At night the campground was filled with the sounds of chain saws, babies crying, and four-wheeled vehicles driving in and out. After that died down one lone dog would not stop barking. At last Renée got up and threw our leftover steak bones at him and we slept.

The next day I was in despair over not being able to find the perfect lake. Walking through the campground, I stopped in front of a trailer to ask a man about clear lakes. He knew where one was. It was called Scout Lake, and it was just up the road. Before letting me go he insisted that he give me a Cook's tour of his trailer, during which he told me briefly of his recent history. He had been a lumberjack until a rotten treetop fell on him from two hundred feet up. It took 20 minutes for his friends to dig him out. He ended up with six broken ribs and most of his spinal discs destroyed. The doctor fused his spine and the company wanted to make him a foreman, but he said he'd rather not work than watch others work. Now he lives on a small pension and does wood carvings, which he gives away to friends. He and 'the little woman' were on the road most of the time, he said, because they belong to a group called the 'Good Sams', which is short for Good Samaritans. They drove all over the United States in long caravans like covered wagons. They liked their life and had no complaints.

Scout Lake was indeed clear. It was a small man-made lake, so small that you could swim to the other side with no problem. Renée said it was too cold for her, so she sat on the edge while I swam out to the middle. When I got back on shore I was so turned on by all the swimming and cold water that I dragged Renée up into the pine forest and proceeded to ravage her. She wasn't really into it, but she put up with it to please me, even with pine needles jabbing into her back. After I had my way with her I apologized and made up for it by buying her a can of the 100 percent pure Blue Bird orange juice that she loved to drink through a straw.

We drank the OJ and I put the pedal to the metal. We headed as fast as we could to the coast. One hundred fifty miles later, we popped out in Newport, Oregon, and drove right up to land's end. And there it was, under a racing fog, the vast silver Pacific. We had made it to the other side. We both got out of the car and stood there looking. Then Renée turned to me, extended her hand and asked, 'Still friends?' And we shook.

We wound our way south along Highway 1 toward San Francisco. After two days of wretched wet camping along the Oregon coast, we arrived in Bodega Bay. I was excited to discover that it was a real live fishing village. At last, I thought, no more landlocked junk food for me. I pictured a steamy hot bowl of homemade clam chowder instead.

We went into a restaurant and I asked, 'Are the clams in that chowder fresh?' They said, 'No, lucky for you, they're not. A guy just died eating clams out of Bodega Bay.' So I had a frozen fish sandwich. We decided to skip San Francisco and go straight to Santa Cruz to unwind. Santa Cruz was thought to be the spiritual center of the universe by its residents. Baba Ram Dass lived there before he moved to Santa Fe. His original guide, the surfer from southern California who had led Ram Dass to a guru in India, had just returned to Santa Cruz and set up a Chevy franchise. So he's there. And a famous Tibetan *rinpoche* had just passed through, taking his whole band of monks for a screaming ride on the Santa Cruz rollercoaster. And there was a real Indian guru who hadn't spoken in seven years, who gave answers to his disciples on a chalkboard every Sunday at an empty Catholic school. So the place was *buzzing*.

We stayed at my friend Jim Bierman's house, the perfect solar house, which he'd built right into the side of the Santa Cruz Mountains, on a hundred acres overlooking the Pacific Ocean. His only problem was that he had covered his roof with sod so that it looked like an extension of the hill, and the ground hogs and prairie dogs were digging their holes right through into the electrical wiring and shorting out all the lights. One of them made it all the way through to the kitchen and dropped out of the ceiling onto the floor like some kind of China Syndrome.

Jim rented out his land to farmers to graze their beef cattle on, but ate only vegetables from his own garden. He was involved in shooting a film about the Moonies – a real exposé. All of the film crew were staying there at the house, and I was very nervous. One night we were talking and I told them how I had been fantasizing about giving up theater and becoming a fisherman in Gloucester. Jim said, 'Don't do it. The Moonies have taken over the entire Gloucester fishing fleet.'

Because Santa Cruz was the murder capital of the United States, per capita, and Renée and I were sleeping out on the deck, I started sleeping with a knife by my bed, a big carving knife, and I stopped plugging my ears with toilet paper. I had plugged my ears with wet toilet paper ever since I was 16, and I finally broke the habit in Santa Cruz.

While in Santa Cruz Renée wanted to have a real California experience. So we picked up a copy of *Good Times*, the alternative newspaper. We read:

> For many Santa Cruz spiritualists it's suddenly hip to travel to Mount Shasta, a looming snowcapped dormant volcano fifty miles north of Reading. Says Barry Tellman, 'Yes, there are beings. These beings are masters, and, whatever they are, met me.' He said, 'I believe deeply in God, and whatever is going on spiritually. But there's a part of me that's skeptical, and I went out to see for myself. I was backpacking up a trail when this guy came the other way, looked at me, and said, 'You're supposed to go to Panther Meadow.' I was so startled that, by the time I thought to ask him some more, he was gone. I hiked into the valley in the evening, and I suddenly saw that the entire place was filled with incredible, luminous light. Then I felt these beings, that didn't actually have bodies, but I could feel their presence. Their touch was very loving, sort of enfolding me. I got the impression they were about twelve feet high. What they share is, everything is perfect, it's all right. These beings are very much like us, and they care about us. They showed me that all that happens is part of God's plan. Then he says, 'Ascending masters, or whatever they are, will be welcoming visitors to Shasta through September.' Tellman says, 'After that, who knows?'
>
> Tellman, incidentally, will recount some of his experiences at a series of workshops he's holding in Marin and elsewhere, called 'Manifesting'. It's a pot-luck supper, so bring drink and dessert. For further information phone 429-9166.

Then Renée went on to read out some of the other choices of community activites – homemade isolation tank, a lecture on UFOs, *est* meeting, things like that. She wanted to try the isolation tank. She called the first ad she saw in *Good Times*, and it turned out to be in a downtown condo, which seemed perfect to me. We arrived and the guy, who was a psych major at the University of Santa Cruz, had on an open shirt and a gold medallion. He said, 'Come right in, I'm just fixing dinner.' The TV was blaring, 'Kung Fu' was on. In the living room, under a picture window covered with black drapes, there was a huge homemade deprivation tank, or isolation tank, or tranquility tank, depending on your point of view, covered with sleeping bags. From where I was standing it looked like a giant coffin filled with water. He said the sleeping bags were for light leaks, because the tank was a homemade thing.

Renée wanted to get right in. She wanted to go first because I had gotten to do almost all the cross-country driving. She had to take a shower and pass naked in front of the tank owner before she got in. I watched 'Kung Fu' with him. I said, 'Look doesn't this "Kung Fu" bother her? I mean, doesn't she hear the sound in there?' He said, 'No, your ears are below the water. These tanks are filled with water and eight hundred pounds of dissolved salt.' After only five minutes, there was a knock on the tank, and the guy went to open it up. Renée said, 'I want to get out.' He said, 'You've only been in there five minutes.' She said, 'I know. You know how you get in some places and you just *know* you don't want to be there?' So she got out, and I rushed up, took my shower and got in. I thought: This is my cup of tea. I could stay in here for a couple of hours. Maybe all day even. Maybe the rest of my life.

Now it wasn't deprivation of smell. I could smell the sleeping bags. Very musty, like a gym or a coffin, like I was buried alive under the damp earth. It took me a long time to get used to floating with my neck bent back, too, suspended on top of the water. And 'Kung Fu' was bothering me a little. I *could* hear it, way in the distance. But it was comforting. I was glad I wasn't totally deprived. After about an hour I thought: This is really good. I could go on in this thing for two hours. I began to sink into it, my body and the water became one, like I was cast in a solid block, waiting to be carved out.

Suddenly there was a scream. I jumped. I thought at first it was an auditory hallucination. Then I realized he was piping in the sound of dolphins through speakers mounted under the tank. After that came Paul Horn playing the flute at the Taj Mahal, like the Muzak they turn on in a plane. I figured I was due to come in for a landing. Renée was screaming at him outside, 'He's been in there an hour! Don't play those dolphins like that, it sounds like a baby crying!' So I got out. Then he wanted to sell me some magic mushrooms, but I didn't buy any. I got out of there for just $6. I left my shampoo upstairs, which was $2, so it all came to $8, and we set out for a UFO meeting.

We got to the UFO meeting and found it was canceled. The speaker didn't show up. So we wandered around and ended up at an *est* meeting, but we were two hours late. We said, 'Could we please get in?' They sent out this guy who had a wonderful smile. Smiling all the time, he kept saying, 'You really want to get in, don't you?' We said, 'Yeah.' They kept sending notes backstage, and more people would come out and kind of interview us. We gave up and left before they gave us permission. Then Renée talked me into getting on a rollercoaster for the first time in my life, which was sort of hideous.

The last California experience we had together was watching the cheerleaders at UC Santa Cruz. This was a real phenomenon. All the cheerleaders in California come together for a week-long cheer-leaders' convention. They all learn the same basic cheers. It's *Big Red*, or *Big Blue* – or whatever the school color is – *you can do it!* The energy those girls put off, you could run the World Trade Center off it, easily.

I stayed for about as long as Renée could take it. All the cheer-leaders wore T-shirts with USA printed on them, which stood for 'United Spirit Association'. They've got it, they've got the spirit. After breakfast, they cheer all the way down from their dormitories to the field to begin practice. They cheer about everything. A drink of water – 'C'mon Big Red, Hey Big Red. Let's hear it for the water!' 'Let's hear it for the day!' 'Let's hear it for the sunshine!' 'Let's hear it for the football field!' They pass the cheer back and forth, call and response. After cheering for the sun and everything under the sun, they make up this game to cheer for. They call it a 'pork-out'. I didn't know what a pork-out was. They'd have two cheerleading teams, A and B, and they'd have two pork-out groups, the Red and the Blue. Their task was to devour big bags of junk food, baby food, M&Ms, and Snickers as fast as possible. They'd stand in a row, fill their mouths as fast as they could, pass the bags back over their shoulders to the next person. All the time the cheerleaders are going, 'Bite it! Chew it! You know how to do it!! Bite it! Chew it! You know how to do it! . . . ' After they ate it they'd have to come and open their mouths wide to show that they had swallowed all that shit.

After that, Renée flew back to New York and I went up to San Francisco, which is a beautiful city without my glasses. Very impres-sionistic. My first fear there, as soon as I arrived, was earthquakes. I never know what I'm going to be afraid of until I get to a place, but then it's amazing how quickly it manifests itself. I said to friends there, 'How can you live in this city?' It reminded me of Thomas Mann, the West Coast version. Death and Beauty united. They answered, 'Oh, what a beautiful way to go.' The earthquake was overdue, it's *factually* overdue, and everyone was having a good time. It's the city of encounter groups, the city of therapy, still.

The newest one is Lomi Therapy, which is a combination of all the new therapies, updated. Another therapy that interested me was called the Gideons. The Gideons are millionaires who feel guilty for having so much money. They invite all their poor friends to big dinners and after all their friends eat, the millionaires get up and talk about how they don't feel guilty for their millions. They tell their poor friends this. It's a kind of testimonial dinner. And the new money-saving idea in cryogenics is if you can't afford to freeze your body, you can just freeze your head.

I got very earthquake-obsessed. I was staying out on Bernal Hill, and the people I was staying with, Jim and Muniera, said it was safe because they'd just bolted the house onto the foundation – and Bernal Hill is granite. So instead of taking my walks through the city, I'd walk around Bernal Hill and look down, thinking what a great view I'd have when the earthquake came. My only fear about Bernal Hill was the telephone microwave transmission station on the top. I was told that I might go sterile if I spent too much time near it. I wasn't so worried about that – sterility might be a blessing in this day and age. I was more worried about my mind. I was told they use the telephone microwaves to reprogram people's minds, because the human mind, they say, is something like a transistor radio. If you zap it with the right waves, you can get people to move like robots. In San Francisco they told me that was how they emptied the Fillmore area of blacks – they used the big telephone tower they call Godzilla. They were zapping down the message 'Move to Oakland' so they could gentrify the area.

When I went for a walk in the city I'd always think: What would be a good place to be if the earthquake came? In Washington Square, at the base of Nob Hill, it'd be way over on the far side, so if that giant church fell, it would only reach three-fourths of the way across the square. When I'd get into that square I'd be able to breathe. It was about the only place I can remember where I was able to just relax and take it all in.

When I had the courage, I'd drive around the city, listening to my radio. There's good music in San Francisco and good talk shows, too. My favorite talk program was Organic John's 'Beside the Garden Wall'. He would have guests on who would talk about things like aseatropic raw glandulars and wheat-grass juice therapy. Every day there was a new kind of therapy that could cure you of anything. Wheat-grass juice could cure you of cancer. John would remind you not to drink too much milk because, after all, it's designed for a two-thousand-pound animal. One woman lectured on enriched bread. 'Look at it this way. Say a hold-up man came up to you and said, "All right, take off all your clothes." And you did. You were standing there naked. And then he said, "Okay, now put on one sock." and you did. "All right, now put on one shoe. All right, now put on your undershirt. Put on your glasses." And there you have enriched bread.'

While I was in San Francisco I began to get reacquainted with Sam Shepard. The playwright, not the murderer. He asked me out to see Lou Reed. I was real nervous, kind of like on a first date. I had been involved for two years in his *The Tooth of Crime*, which is about a styles match between Hoss and Crow – two styles meeting and having a stand-off, a word battle, a styles match. Suddenly, it was like the play had come to real life, which was much more exciting for me than the play itself, because here was Sam Shepard himself, who had a very different style from mine. He was very West Coast. Most of the time I was in San Francisco I couldn't figure out how to get shoes to make me feel more like a man. I'd been feeling more and more light, light, light on my feet – too light for my age. I'm always winding up with Puma joggers, and the ones I was wearing at the time had air soles, which gave me a really bouncy step. The point was that I was feeling very light that particular night and Sam was very heavy, in his cowboy boots, and we were going to see Lou Reed.

Sam picked me up in his Ford Bronco, which smelled of wild horses. In fact, he had his saddle in the back seat. He was smoking Old Golds and going through the gears, saying to me, 'You guys in the East are too pessimistic. You should see what it takes to get a *horse* down.'

Before the concert started we went into the dressing room to visit with Lou. Sam introduced me as Spalding, and Lou Reed said, 'Oh, Spalding balls.' I came in and sat down. They had a pinball machine and a pool table and whiskey and beer and fruit and rare roast beef. They even had deviled eggs with paprika on top. And all the men in

Lou Reed's band had the right shoes – I think maybe Capezio black dance shoes, jazz shoes. The drummer was standing at the pinball machine, tight-assed, with his knees locked, ringing up those points. I was feeling assless and out of it. I couldn't get the right posture. I was standing kind of like an amoeba, soft and overflowing at the edges.

Sam was very considerate of me. He could see that I was a little uncomfortable. He came over and said, 'You know, if you want to go, we can, it's cool.' I said, 'Oh, that's all right. I'm having a good time just watching.' I felt like I was melting in my chair, getting softer and softer. He said, 'Anyone wanna play a game of pool?' The drummer jumped right in, and Sam beat him quick. It looked like they were going to play another game, and I thought: This is the time. I've got to do it. I've got to force myself. I've got to challenge him to a game of pool. It's the working out of *The Tooth of Crime*, finally. It's in the stars. I don't play pool, but I figured I could give it a try. So I said, 'I'll, hmm, uh, try.' I took the pool cue and did a pretty good break. Then it was his shot, but nothing went in. Then I made this total freak shot. I hit one ball, it jumped over another ball, and hit *another* ball, which went in. Sam took a long pause, looked down at it and said, 'That must be what you call a New England shot.' Then he put every ball in, *bing, bing, bing. Bing. Bing.* All the balls. That was the end of the game. Then we went in to see the Lou Reed concert, which I liked very much. I'd always wanted to see Lou, and he was very good. For someone his age, I thought he was very talented.

A couple of days later I was lucky enough to land a house-sitting situation in Berkeley. Berkeley is a wonderful city. It's the only place I've been where you can see 'Kitty Found' signs hung up around the neighborhoods. All I had to do was baby-sit a dog named Stanley, a cat named Colleen, and a bird, a catatonic bird in a cage. I don't remember the bird's name. It was sad, all the time. It looked stuffed. There was an animal virus going around Berkeley. If a dog smelled shit, it would die immediately. Before the owners left, they warned me to be careful. 'All you have to do is keep Stanley away from sniffing shit.' I didn't know anything about dogs. That's all they do when they go for a walk.

In Berkeley I felt like a good guy, a nice guy, because people looked like me. I was feeling good. No more knife, no more ear-plugs. Everyone was happy, everyone was white, everyone was

looking something like me. I would go out on the streets and say
'Hi.' I was feeling good.

One day I was out for a walk and I saw this checkbook lying on the
sidewalk. I thought: *Ah!* . . . No, I'm a busy man, I'm a busy man.
Don't get involved. I'll let some Berkeley person pick it up. No, no, I
should do something good. But every time I try to do something
good, it makes me feel panicked inside. Then I thought: Wait. I'll
take it back. The checkbook had the guy's name and address right on
it and I figured: I'll take it over to him. It's close by. He'll know I'm
good. I was so over-anxious to do the right thing that when I parked
the car I forgot to turn the car wheels into the curb and put on the
emergency brake. You're supposed to do that there. As I looked back
across the street, I saw that the car was rolling down toward the
intersection. I dropped the checkbook, ran back, reparked the car,
and ran back to the house. He wasn't home. I stuck the checkbook
through the mail slot and figured: He'll probably just think he left it
there in the morning or dropped it in the hall on the way out. I'll
never get any credit for my good deed after all. So I went back to my
house. And everything was going fine until Stanley the dog set the
bathroom on fire by accidentally switching on the bathroom wall
heater. I smelled smoke and ran in and the towel was in *flames* and it
was nine o'clock in the morning. I had to beat them out in the sink.

You never know. You never know where it's going to happen.

Before returning to Santa Cruz I was scheduled to do a week of
performances in San Francisco. As part of the performance program,
I decided to tell this story – the story of 'The Great Crossing', about
what happened to Renée and me on our way cross-country. Also,
because I had no time to drive our car back to New York, I decided to
announce after each performance that it was for sale, as of now. I sold
the car after the first performance. Someone couldn't wait to get his
hands on all that history. I sold it to him with the stipulation that he
drive me back down to Jim Bierman's in Santa Cruz. And he did. We
drove down that spectacular coastal road on a lovely Sunday.

When we got there I found Jim standing in his kitchen, distraught
and wide-eyed, just standing there with a garden hoe in his hand. I'd
never seen Jim like that. For me he'd always been a classic Type-B
person, but now he was looking like a raving A.

'What happened?' I asked. He just pointed to a snake head in the
corner of the kitchen, then he told me to go out on the deck. There

was the headless body of the largest rattlesnake I'd ever seen. It just lay there, headless, coiling and coiling around on itself. Jim said it had slithered across his kitchen floor while he was wokking the vegetables. He had rushed to get the garden hoe and just cut the head off. I wanted to roast it over an open fire and have it with beer, but Jim was a vegetarian.

In Santa Cruz there was one person from my past I was trying to avoid, but somehow he had a telepathic approach to me. His name was Evan. He was teaching at UC Santa Cruz, but I had first met him when I was artist-in-residence at Bennington, two summers before. He was doing research at the college library and staying at his parents' home, and he was shopping for a new wife. He had married a very pretty woman in Santa Cruz. They'd had three children, but she decided she didn't want to be a mother anymore and fled to South America to seek her fortune. So he was left with these three beautiful children, and he was looking for a wife. He found out I was an actor and thought he could play the seducer if he learned the techniques of acting. So he would follow me around, taking notes. We were both particularly interested in a girl-woman named Nora, and we wanted to see who could get her first.

Because of Evan's childlike openness, I had begun to grow fond of him back East, but now I felt that the whole male competitive sparring trip we had been into there had run its course. At first I thought I'd want to see him in Santa Cruz, but after I got there I had second thoughts. Now that I was in California, I wanted to practice being a good American Buddhist and give up on telling tales out of school. So I was trying to avoid Evan because I didn't want to gossip about Nora and I didn't want to compare male chauvinist notes anymore with him.

Since I was without a car, Jim Bierman was kind enough to loan me his Chevy pickup to take to the beach. I decided to be a good guy and put some gas in. It was a big tank. I thought: I'll really splurge, I'll fill it up. I was filling up the tank when the thing broke open. Gasoline poured out of the bottom of the truck. It was like a Molotov cocktail down there. The guys at the gas station were really mellow. They just closed off that whole section of the station and helped me push the truck off to the side. They sprayed down the area with soap and water and covered it over with sawdust. I said, 'What am I going to do?' This guy comes up to me and said, 'I'll go to an auto store and get epoxy for you.' Out of the clear blue, he's just doing me a favor. I

said fine. I'd never fixed anything in my life. I'd never made a cake.
I'd never made a model airplane. I hate directions. But I was reading
Zen and the Art of Motorcycle Maintenance, and I had the idea: Hey,
maybe I can do it. Maybe I can get in touch with my machine.

He came back with the epoxy. I felt good vibes. I tried to stick the
epoxy on the hole and it fell right off, leaving this big, gaping, rust
hole in the gas tank. I thought I'd better read the instructions. It read:
'Ball up the epoxy until it's all one color of green.' I thought, this is
something to do. This is a real Zen exercise. It's simple. I will also
stand in the sun and get a suntan while I'm doing it. So I balled it up,
and at last it fit! It fit! It stuck perfectly. And while I was still under
the truck, I looked up, and there was Evan. He was standing over me,
smirking, like he'd been sent. Like it was a plot. Like shit to flies. Or
flies to shit, I don't know which. He was standing over me and he was
saying, 'You wanna come for lunch?' What could I say? I had to wait
two hours for the epoxy to dry.

I did go with him and at lunch he told me a long and complicated
dream he'd had about his father. It was difficult to follow, but it had
something to do with Evan being in the car with his three kids trying
to get over a big toll bridge, like the Golden Gate. And it turned out
that the man in the toll booth was his father. But Evan couldn't come
up with the right change. Then he told me about the four different
women in Santa Cruz with whom he was having relationships. He
wanted to show them off to me, he wanted me to meet them. None of
them was home. At the second house he said, 'Let me at least show
you her bedroom.' He took me around to the back where we peeked
through the bedroom window, and he said, 'This is where I have
fucked her hundreds of times.' I said, 'Hundreds, Evan?' He said,
'Yes, if you count the strokes.' We went on to the next place and the
cleaning woman was there. Evan started coming on to her. All the
cleaning women in Santa Cruz are very young. He said, 'You go in
there and see the bedroom. I was there last night.' I said, 'No, no,
that's all right. We'll let that go.'

I thought a good way to get out of there would be to turn on some
of my acting technique. At last I would be an actor for him. I barked,
'*Look*, Evan, take me back to my truck. It's the first time I've ever
used epoxy, and I want to see if it's sealed. You understand? Don't
give me any more of your shit. I don't want to see any more of your
women, now take me back to my truck.' He took me back to the
truck. When I got there I found that it had dried and made a firm seal.

It had worked! I drove back to Jim's and said, 'Look. Look what I've done! I broke your tank! And I fixed it.' And he said, 'That tank? That's an old tank. Ripped a hole in that one a year ago. We got another one on the other side.' So now they had two gas tanks, and he was going to make a gas line between them because he had about $20 worth of gas in that one. Maybe a little more.

I hopscotched my way back across the country, flying as little as possible, taking the train most of the way. At last, I was rolling home on an Amtrak out of Buffalo. It turned out to be Columbus Day, and at Rochester a whole bunch of kids got on with amplified guitars. They had their own portable amplifiers. The train started filling up. I wasn't getting any of that much-needed quiet autumnal meditation before re-entering New York. I had expected to be so high by the time I came back to New York City, but everything began to break down early. It's not supposed to break down until at least Grand Central.

So the train was totally packed, and I was in a line two cars long trying to get food. When I got there, they were out of sandwiches, so I had to get four beers and a scotch. To go. I sat down and started drinking them. There was a woman across the aisle from me, and a little boy, a beautiful little boy. He opened a 7-Up, and it sprayed all over the place. She whapped him in the mouth and he started going, 'Ah, oh, ugh, ah.' He was convulsing. And I thought: What am I going to do? I've got to say something. He was convulsing and going, 'I want, I want, I want . . . ' He finally got it out, 'I want my mommy.' I thought: Holy shit, this woman isn't his mother. And she's hitting him in the face. I was sitting across from them watching this. The boy was convulsing. She looked around for the best authority figure in the car – not looking at me at all – and she turned to an older man and said, 'Look, what am I gonna do? I got my own problems. I got a vegetable stand in Brooklyn, and lettuce is a dollar a head.' She just went on like that. By then I was quite drunk, and we arrived in Grand Central Station. I tried to put the blinders on and get down to Renée's loft as fast as I could without seeing too much.

I took the Lexington Avenue subway, and walking across town on my way down to Renée's, I saw a guy I used to pass on my way to Unemployment. He used to write messages in chalk on the sidewalk below Canal Street, on the corner of Chambers and Broadway. Rather articulate Marxist messages. I'd always pictured him living in a lean-to in the Catskills, taking a Trailways down to New York City to do this. Now he'd moved uptown, he had a knapsack and a dog with him. And his message had evolved. This one read: 'The Devil's nun is a topless waitress who works in the Devil's church. The top looks good but the bottom smells like the Devil.' This was written in chalk. I was trying to imagine what the devil smelled like, and the best I could come up with is the orangutan at the Central Park Zoo.

By now I needed a sanctuary. I was so happy to reach Renée's loft and be in her arms again. She said, 'Hi, hon! How you doin'?' And her whole body welcomed me like a big flesh couch, but the hallways were dirty and the loft was dark and her neighbors were playing 'We Are Family'. I wanted out. I had to get out and get some light. I told Renée, 'I gotta get out. I gotta get out and get some of that stuff they loosely call air!' No green trees in downtown New York, and she was living in the Cancer Belt.

So I walked up to Washington Square to sit on a park bench in the October sun. I was just sitting there trying to relax, and there was a guy next to me, a young man with a beard, dressed in a business suit. But as I sat there I began to notice out of the corner of my eye that he had no socks on and that the entire suit was coming apart at the seams. And he was deep into the process of delousing himself. In fact, when he lifted his arm I saw a whole nest of them seething there in his armpit. I was thinking: Why, why am I seeing all this madness? I turned to my right and a woman started in on me. She said, 'The safest place, the only place I can go to now – I can't go any further – is Washington Square, because I'm afraid they're gonna lock me up for being crazy. I had a friend who came up from Virginia and she disappeared into a mental institution. So Washington Square, that's about as far as I can walk.' She had wanted to become a good secretary. That had been her ambition. She'd been married twice – both of them had been one-night stands. The second time she was married, she had a real big wedding, and they got divorced the next day. She kept saying, 'And it was a big wedding. A big wedding.' Now she was married again. She said that she was crazy, and I asked her how she got that way, and she said a friend of hers talked too much. It drove her nuts.

Then I saw the flag man. He was wearing a construction helmet with American flag decals all over it and had a rolled-up flag between his thighs. He had no teeth, and every so often, he'd pull the flag out from his crotch, unfurl it, wrap himself in it and sing 'I Love America'. Beautiful. I went over to talk to him and he said that he had gone crazy when he smoked his first marijuana cigarette and realized that the system was corrupt. Now he was getting paid for being crazy. He was on welfare. He was a virgin, and he slept with the American flag. I said, 'Don't you realize the American flag is just a symbol?' He said, 'Not for me. I sleep with it. And one of these days I'm going to get such an erection here in this park, that I'm going to be able to hang the flag on it.' He also had love letters to President Carter stuffed in his crotch. Love letters proclaiming his love for America.

I walked over to the Dance Theatre Workshop on West 19th to look over the space. I talked to Bob Applegarth about my upcoming performances, and left. I started down the steps and saw a woman collapsed at the bottom of the stairs. It looked like she had fallen. She had one hand in her pocket and with her other hand she was twisting her hair. Her eyes were rolling, looking up at me. Totally mad. I could smell her two flights up. I stopped. I thought she had a gun in her pocket. Then I thought, no, no, no, it's too small. It's too small a pocket. But she had a kind of intensity, a silence. Her eyes were young, and they were still soft, and they were rolling like an animal's. I was scared. I thought she'd scream and leap on me. So I came down the stairs, and I knelt beside her, and just as I did she blurted out, 'Ya gotta cigarette? Ya got some reefer?' I said I didn't have either of those things. She said that she used to be a dancer in Florida and that she was 26 years old. I said, 'Do you realize that you're in the hallway of the Dance Theatre Workshop?' She said, 'No, no.' I thought she was an ex-DTW dancer. But she slept in different doorways. She said, 'Look, all I need is a million dollars. Then I can get an apartment.' I thought: She's not crazy. I said, 'Where are you from?' She said, 'Las Vegas. I love it there. I've got to get back.' I said, 'Why do you like it in Las Vegas?' She said, 'Because there are no hoodlums.' I said, 'Why not?' She said, 'They lock them up.' I said, 'I know, I've been locked up for six days there myself.'

I thought of taking her home, to wash her, to clean her up. And then I thought . . . No.

After this long tour I went to visit my father in Rhode Island. I was curious how he felt about the fact that none of his sons had chosen to go into business like he had. So I asked him. He thought for a while and then he said it wasn't a major issue. For a long time he had wondered when I was going to give up what I was doing and go to work. But then, as time went by, he began to see that it wasn't going to happen. And he said, 'At first I was a little confused. But then I thought, well, if you're happy in your work, that's fine. And besides, I figured nobody wanted to sit behind a desk.'

TRAVELS THROUGH NEW ENGLAND

Why do people often feel bad in good environments and good in bad environments?

Why do people often feel so bad in good environments that they prefer bad environments?

Why is that a man riding a good commuter train from Larchmont to New York, whose needs and drives are satisfied, who has a good home, loving wife and family, good job, who enjoys unprecedented 'cultural and recreational facilities', often feels bad without knowing why.

Why is it that if such a man suffers a heart attack and, taken off the train in New Rochelle, regains consciousness and finds himself in a strange place, he then comes to himself for the first time in years, perhaps in his life, and begins to gaze at his own hand with a sense of wonder and delight.

What is the difference between such a man, a commuter who feels bad without knowing why, and another commuter who feels bad without knowing why but who begins to read a book about a man who feels bad without knowing why?

Why is it that Jean Paul Sartre, sitting in a French café and writing *Nausea*, which is about the absurdity of human existence and the nausea of life in the Twentieth Century, why was he the happiest man in France at the time?

Why do more people commit suicide in San Francisco, the most beautiful city in America, than any other city?

– Walker Percy, *The Message in the Bottle*
© 1954, Farrar, Straus & Giroux

All happy families resemble one another, but each unhappy family is unhappy in its own way.

– Leo Tolstoy, *Anna Karenina*

Just before I went on my two-month tour of New England, interviewing the audience in non-performance spaces, including golden age drop-in centers, paper mills, clothing mills, historical societies, and Grange halls, I went to see *Death of a Salesman*. At first I saw it as a good omen for the tour because Willy Loman was talking about the New England route. He's just gotten in and he's talking to Linda. 'Oh, New England is a *wonder* in the spring! I opened the windshield, let the wind blow over me and went to Hartford and it's a lovely city and on to Providence and I met the mayor and I said, "Hi, Mr Mayor. You've got a lovely city here!" We had lunch together. Then on to Boston, the cradle of the Revolution. Then up to Portland, Maine, and straight on home to you, Linda.' So I was feeling real good about the tour – until the intermission. And this scriptwriter friend of mine comes up to me and says, 'Hi, Spalding. I'm working on a new film about a sociopath. It's modeled on a photographer who poses as Richard Avedon to get women to strip and pose for him and then he rapes them. I'm thinking you're perfect for the role. What are you up to now?' I say, 'Oh, Dawson, I'll tell you. Dawson, listen it's great: I'm about to do a tour of New England. Grange halls, paper mills . . . ' 'Oh, really? Very well, Spalding, it's your choice. If that's what you want to do with your career.'

The rest of the play was kind of down for me. I kept seeing Willy as this outsider trying to get in, all the time wandering around the neighborhood going, 'What's the answer? What's the answer, Bernard? What is the *answer*?'

The first stop was Hartford, Connecticut: home of insurance and

inspiration. Inspiration because my favorite American Poet Wallace
Stevens had lived there. The first thing I wanted to do was to touch
down and see where he lived. But no one seemed to know where his
house was. Everyone knew where the Mark Twain house was, but no
one knew about the Wallace Stevens house. Someone suggested that I
go to the local bookstore. I went in and cornered three of the
salesmen. The first one I asked about the Wallace Stevens house had
never heard of him. The second had heard of him but didn't know
that he had lived in Hartford. And the third one had heard of him *and*
knew where the house was *and* drew me a little map. I took the bus to
the outskirts of town and wandered into this semisuburban community, very upper middle class, with block-patrol signs up all over.
The streets were empty, except for one guy walking a German
shepherd on a leash who ran me off the sidewalk. This all made me
feel like I didn't belong there, like I was a weird kind of killer, like Joe
Kallinger.

I don't know if you remember Joe Kallinger, but he was a very
insane visionary shoemaker out of Philadelphia, back in the seventies. Went quite mad. He had visions. His daughter was born with
these blue sores all over her body, and he had a dream about how he
could cure those sores. In the vision he saw himself walking down
this golden highway. Little shoes, golden shoes, were dancing all
around the highway, singing. A shower of golden shoelaces came out
of the sky and hit him. Butterflies were bouncing off the walls and
angels were flying up through the clouds above snowcapped mountains singing, 'Joe Kallinger, master shoemaker and God of the
Universe. O Healer and Destroyer, we sing your praises. Halle-
lujah!' Then the head of Christ appeared to him, impaled on a
butcher knife, and it talked, but no words came out of its mouth. He
looked over and saw a woman's black pubic delta and it turned into
the face of the devil. The delta began to speak to him in a gruff,
sensual voice: 'Take my fluid, mix it with your semen and with
perfume. Put the liquid on Bonnie's sores.' So Joe Kallinger went out
to suburban neighborhoods, in a grand frantic search for delta fluid.

I kind of felt like Joe Kallinger because of the way people were
responding to me in this neighborhood as I wandered past these
$400,000 homes in search of the Stevens house. At last, quite lost, I
decided to go up to one of the least imposing houses to ask directions.
I rang the bell and a little girl came to the door. Something about the
way her mother swooped down, pulled her away, and latched the

screen door made me feel like I *should* be a murderer or a rapist. 'Can I help you?' the mother asked. I said, 'Oh, yes, uh, the Stevens house, I'm looking for the Wallace Stevens house.' This seemed to put her at ease. 'Oh, the Stevens house? It's just about three or four houses up the way. You'll recognize it by the big holly tree in the front yard.' And I thought: Of course, a holly tree. Wasn't Holly his daughter's name? That makes sense.

I walked three houses up and there it was, this two-story white and slightly peeling clapboard house with a giant holly tree in the front yard. The tree was as high as the house. I'd never seen a holly tree that big before. Instead of going straight up to the door, the front walk curved around it. The house was obviously lived in. It was far from a museum. There was no special plaque or landmark on it. I went up and knocked on the door and all these dogs began snorting and barking like they were going to suck me in under the door. I pulled back and went to the front window to try to get a look at the inside of the house, and all the dogs ran to it and began gnashing their teeth against the glass. I left.

The interviews went well in Hartford. I asked some members of the audience to come up, one at a time, to be interviewed. I asked them simple questions about their personal lives, why they chose to live where they did, and what they did for fun and work. Occasionally I threw in a few questions like, 'Do you believe in God? Have you ever taken LSD? How do you get on with your neighbors?' Everyone told me that things were going fine. No one seemed to worry about the bomb. They'd given up thinking about it. At the end of the interviews, when I asked if there were any questions, there was no response. But after it was all over, some people grabbed me in the corners and in the halls. A young man said, 'I think about the bomb all the time. I'm terrified.' And a young woman said, 'How could you have mentioned the fact that your mother committed suicide? How could you have said such a thing in public? Is nothing sacred?'

On to Providence, Rhode Island. The Shortline bus wove through the lovely backyards of farms, where streams flowed out of the melting spring snow. Now Providence I thought I knew because I grew up outside of it. I used to think of it as a slum because I grew up in Barrington, Rhode Island, and Providence was just another big dirty city. Spike Claxton and I used to bunk high school and go into

Providence to see World War II movies. We'd just walk out of school
at 10 in the morning and start hitchhiking in. After a while, if no one
stopped, Spike would start yelling at the cars, 'Hey Bob! Hey Bob!'
and it wouldn't take long before someone stopped. We'd get in, and
after a short silence the driver would say, 'Hey, how'd you know me,
anyway?' And we'd say, 'We go to school with your son.' He'd say,
'I don't have a son.' By the time we got that settled, we'd be in
Providence. We'd have a vanilla Coke and a piece of lemon meringue
pie, then go off to see some movie like *Heaven Knows, Mr Allison*. If
we didn't like the film, we'd throw water balloons at the screen from
the balcony. If we had any left over we'd go up to the top of the
Outlet Building and hurl them down at the people below.

One day we were watching *Cheaper by the Dozen*. The film opens
with a pan of a train pulling into Providence. You see the Christian
Science Church up on Benefit Street. And I thought: Whoa! Providence is really a beautiful city, now that I've seen it on film.

In Providence I was doing interviews at the Rhode Island School of
Design, and all I remember vividly was one of the graffiti I saw in the
men's room just before I went on. It read: When the world runs out
of money and we start using shit instead, the poor will be born
without assholes.

On to Boston, cradle of the Revolution, where I was supposed to
pick up my rental car. It was a beautiful gray Plymouth Reliant that
smelled all new inside. Searching on the radio for the appropriate
music by which to exit Boston, I headed for the mighty Cape,
extending like an arm out into the Atlantic, with clenched fist and
flexed bicep. Along the way I got hungry. I saw a Bickfords and
thought: When in Rome . . . why not eat the native food? The
special for the day was a hot openfaced turkey sandwich, so I ordered
it. It was fantastic – slices of hot turkey with gravy on Wonder Bread
and even a little cranberry sauce in one of those cardboard cups on the
side. I thought: This is great. I'm eating the food of the pilgrims here
at Bickfords. And as I ate the food of the pilgrims, I began to muse on
Plymouth Rock. I remembered that my friend Steven Snow was
working at the 1627 Colony there, which is a complete recreation of
the original colony. They have a stockade that surrounds a group of
houses with thatched roofs. Anthropologists, sociologists, and
actors and actresses work there and each makes a study of a particular
historical family. Then they re-enact members of those families,

taking on their names and habits and speaking in Early American. They live right in the stockade.

It was one of those cold, early spring New England days, one of those days that makes you want to take a shot of scotch at nine in the morning. There were no tourists because of the weather. The woman at the ticket booth told me I could find Steven at the Warren House. I thought: That's strange, why isn't Steven playing a Snow? The Snows came over on the *Mayflower*, too. So I walked down to the far end of the stockade where the Warren house was, went in, and there was this woman dressed in a pilgrim outfit working over the sink. I said, 'Hi. I'm looking for Steven Snow.' She turned to me and said in this Early American accent, 'Methinks you've come to see my husband, then?' I said, 'Yes, is he here?' She said, 'No, he's down by the strand, tending to the chillun' and the pigs.' I knew she meant down by the water, and I tried to put that together, whether she meant that Steven Snow was having a day off or that he actually was down by the water, which was a whole other reality because the beach, or the strand as she called it, wasn't even inside the stockade. I was debating whether to stay or not. I said, 'Well, maybe I'll write him a note.' 'Well you could do that, then, but none of us reads here. Only Pastor Bradford reads.' I said, 'Well, I'll write Pastor Bradford a note, you take it to him and have him read it to Steven – I mean, to your husband.'

While we were talking, in came this barrel maker. And every time I'd refer to a contemporary issue, they'd both look at me with these beautiful wide eyes and say, 'Oh, no, we know not of what you speak. Curious, but we know not of what you speak.' Then they asked, 'Where is it, then, that you're headed?' I said, 'Well, Provincetown, actually, where you people originally landed, supposedly. There's a tower down there commemorating the landing.' So they said, 'Oh, no. We know of no such Provincetown. We hear there's no fit drinking water down there. We know of the Cape of the Cod, but we know of no Provincetown. And how is it, then, that you're traveling? By foot?' And I said, 'No, as a matter of fact, I'm driving a Plymouth Reliant, which is named after your colony.' 'Oh, no. We know of no such thing.' I said, 'I'll be there in an hour.' 'No. We know of no such thing.' So I said, 'Well, you take the note to Pastor Bradford, I'm getting out of here.'

I walked out of the little house, and all sorts of things were going on in and around the main street – a funeral, musket practice, people working in their gardens. Still there were no tourists. And I was drifting deeper and deeper into this pilgrim Twilight Zone. At the top of the road, I decided to go into one more house. There was a dirt floor and a real cute pilgrim woman was kneeling down in front of the fireplace, basting a real duck. I realized that I was attracted to her. I mean, I was starting to feel like a horny pilgrim. I started asking her questions about her sexual practices. 'Good morning, ma'am. Could you tell me, please? Do you bed with any other than your husband, then?' She turned from the duck in surprise and said, 'Oh, no. Never. Only when he commands. And then often.'

I was getting more and more attracted to her until I heard the sound of a motorcycle in the distance, and tourist voices woke me, and I drowned.

Back on the road in my Plymouth Reliant, I headed for Province-town, Land's End, place of desire. It's where all the tourists end up after driving up the Cape, and when they get there, there's nothing to do but circle around and around out there and eat and circle and eat again and circle and eat a little more and circle. If you get too full, you can go in and drown yourself. Or go in for a swim. In the summer the tourists are like ants crawling around the head of a popsicle.

I've been there a number of times. Three times as a matter of fact. The first time was in 1965. I'd just graduated from Emerson College and was reading Alan Watts's *Psychotherapy East and West*. It was my Bible. I had read it through a few times, underlining certain passages in red and inserting asterisks with little comments like 'Oh wow! Right on! Too much!!' At the time I was torn between taking LSD and dropping out to become a hippie or going to New York to pursue my acting career. I was staying with Gideon, a friend who was the night manager at the Breakers Motel. Since he didn't use his bed at night, he let me sleep there. Occasionally he'd bring a woman home with him that he'd picked up at the Breakers Motel and ask for his bed back so he could make love to her. I'd get out and go to the other side of the attic to sleep on his roommate's pallet on the floor. His roommate's name was Sesquash-Yeti.

Sesquash was living in a teepee in Maine at the time. He was a total pacifist. He was so against killing that he wouldn't even cut the hair on his body, lest he kill the cells. He had ass-length hair. I don't know what his nose hairs were like, but basically this guy was a walking jungle. And not only that – he refused to kill any of the crab lice on his body, of which there were a number at this point. So his whole bed was hopping with them. I think that's part of what made me decide *not* to take LSD and to go directly to New York City and become an actor.

The second time I visited Provincetown was in 1976, the bicentennial. I had just returned from traveling in India for six months, and I was suffering from a bad case of reverse culture shock. Everyone in America seemed wealthy, gross, and overfed. The vegetables in the supermarket looked like they'd been inflated with a bicycle pump. The cauliflower looked like it was about to explode and the artichokes seemed to be breathing. I was overwhelmed. But I couldn't stop moving because I had been traveling for so long. So, of course, I ended up at Provincetown, Land's End, circling and circling and going kind of mad. I thought I'd become some kind of wandering mendicant. I didn't want to work anymore, I wanted to beg, like the Indians did. I had some beautiful Tibetan finger cymbals that I'd bought in Ladakh. And I thought that a good way to stop all the motion would be to sit down in front of the Town Hall with my legs crossed and just begin begging and chanting. Every so often someone would put a dollar into my hat. The dollars were adding up. And I was very proud – until the police came and told me to get out of there. I took the money I had made from begging and went down to the foot-long hotdog stand to buy one of those long dogs. I'd lost a lot of weight in India, and I was so thin that my shirt kept coming untucked. So I got into the habit of opening up my pants to tuck it back in. I did this while waiting for my hotdog, whereupon the woman at the counter called the police and accused me of exposing myself to her. I swore to them I'd done nothing wrong. I thought she'd been working around those foot-long hotdogs too long. They took me down to the police station and said they were going to book me if I didn't leave town. So I left.

The third time I was in Provincetown was when I was artist-inresidence at Bennington College in 1979. I met a beautiful dancer there named Nora to whom I was very attracted. I just assumed that we would eventually sleep together, but I didn't want to rush it. So I waited for the second date. When I suggested it she said, 'No, I can't.' I said, 'Why?' She said, 'I'm shy.' I said, 'Well, I'm shy, too. We can work it out.' She said, 'Maybe someday.'

Because of this I got more and more obsessed with her over the summer. I just couldn't take my eyes off her. And at the end of the summer session, afraid it would end, I said, 'Listen, what are the chances of us traveling together? Can I come home with you? (She lived in Newton.) I have time, you have time. You have your car.' She said, 'All right. I'm open to it – on one conditon: that you in no way try to seduce me.' I said 'All right. Agreed.'

I knew that was going to be difficult because Nora was smoking a lot of marijuana then, to get in touch with her spine. After she smoked, she would lie on this huge yellow beach ball to stretch out her spine, just lie there in her leotards. Now when I smoked, it would unlock my *kundalini* in the worst way. I would get this terrific sexual energy coiled in the base of my spine, which was kind of masochistic because she wasn't feeling it. She was polymorphously perverse – she was able to spread it out over her entire body.

When we got to Newton, I found out that Nora's mother and father had broken up. After the divorce her mother suffered from extreme agoraphobia and didn't go out of the house for a year. At last she cured herself by putting this house key in her shoe so she could focus on the pain whenever she went out. This slow cure led to a torrid affair with the local sexton, which brought her back to her wits. Now she was taking a course in writing and watching a lot of television in order to develop her style and structure.

Her favorite show featured actual doctors. Each week it would follow a different doctor through his daily rounds at the hospital. They showed actual operations, in which the blood flew up and hit the camera. If the patient died, they'd interview the nearest relative; if the patient lived, they'd interview him, right there. At the end of the program they'd show the doctor relaxing on the porch of his vacation home. If he was from the seacoast, he'd be contemplating the seagulls and sipping scotch; if he was from the Southwest, he'd be roping heifers on his ranch, talking about the stubbornness of life. That was Nora's mother's favorite show.

I was torn between Nora, who by now was out in the kitchen practicing modern dance, dressed only in her leotards, and her mother, who was trying to lure me back into the TV room by crying out, 'Oh look! The blood! The blood!' And I'd run in to see what was going on. After the program was over, while Nora was still doing dance steps in the kitchen, using the counter as a barre, her mother told me about Nora's anorexia. Nora had also told me on the way up that she had been anorexic and that she never felt better than when she was starving to death. It was like levitation. She was so light she felt she was floating, and she couldn't understand why her parents were so concerned. At last they had to hospitalize her, and the doctor told her mother, 'You've got to put your daughter in a room with other anorexics. She'll die if she stays in this private room.' They did. A friend of Nora's who stayed in a private room died shortly after.

At last we took off traveling in Nora's Plymouth. We went to Salem, where we visited Laurie Cabot, the last witch, but she was booked up until September, so we couldn't get a consultation. We went to Concord, Lexington, Walden Pond. We finally ended up in Provincetown, Land's End, place of desire, where I watched Nora eat steamed clams in slow motion, dressed in her three-quarter-length English black leather coat. We were taken in by an abstract expressionist and his wife, who let us stay in the guest apartment at the back of their house. By now Nora and I were sleeping naked in the same bed, without touching each other. It was some kind of strange New England tantric exercise, I'm convinced, looking back on it. At last I couldn't stand it anymore and I left.

My fourth visit to Provincetown was to interview the audience at the Provincetown Art Center. It was off season and a wonderful time to be there, but, my God, it was melancholy. Instead of the tourists, there were other kinds of nuts. The first thing I saw pulling into the driveway of the house I was to stay at was a huge station wagon completely covered with sand – I mean, the sand had been glued to it. Inside the station wagon was an entire family of mannequins that looked like the perfect American family, with coolers, portable radios, beach balls, and blankets. They, too, were completely covered with sand. The owner, Jay Critchley, told me it was a work of art. He was a sculptor. Every summer he would take this car down and park it on the dock and every summer the police would try to tow it away. Finally, Jay went to court to prove that it was an official work of art. So every summer it was there.

The first thing I saw when I got into his house was a console TV entirely covered with popcorn. Above it, suspended from the ceiling, was a popcorn bra and a popcorn football. What he was into now, besides organizing a whale watch, was taking soil from Truro and sending it to Russia. Children were digging up soil from the town of Truro and writing little notes with it and sending it off to a town in

Russia. And hopefully, the Russian children were going to dig up some soil in their town and send it back to Truro. We had a lovely visit.

The interviews went fine, except some of the people were a little testy and confrontational. One woman arrived on a bicycle completely covered with plastic flowers. She happened to be one of the most outspoken town characters. She started in on me about my tie and jacket. 'You should loosen up. Take off your tie and jacket. The only person who wears a jacket and tie in Provincetown is the local liquor salesman. So, loosen up your tie and go out on the dunes – then you'll be able to talk to us. You're acting like some sort of therapist.' I said, 'I know what the dunes are like. I wandered in them today. I'm wearing a tie and jacket as a costume.'

They couldn't understand this concept. The point was that I was trying to dress as *though* I had grown up in New England and had stayed and not gone to New York City. So I had on a Harris tweed jacket, a white shirt, and a tie.

From Provincetown, I went on to the real cradle of the Revolution – Acton, Massachusetts. Acton was where the first Revolutionary soldier was killed by 'the shot heard round the world'. He was Isaac Davis, a gunsmith.

The place where I stayed in Acton was a former dairy farm. It had been in the same family for a long time but had recently been gentrified by my host, a retired insurance man. He and his wife came to the door to give me a warm greeting and apologized for being a little hung over from overindulgence at a Hearing Ear Dog benefit they had attended the night before. They wanted to give me an entire tour of the house, right away. They were so proud of it. They told me it was a 'raffle house'. A Harvard student in the 1800s won $10,000 in a raffle and built three houses – this was one of them, built on three hundred acres of fields where the cows had grazed. Now it was just an immaculate museum of the home it had been.

I went inside and they gave me the Cook's tour of the West room, the East room, the music room, the parlor with its straight-backed horsehair chairs, the dining room, and a huge kitchen that looked out onto those three hundred acres of rolling fields. Then we went down into the basement, or the cellar as it was called. The ceilings must have been 10-feet high and there was a wall of solid New England stone.

Driscoll, my host, turned to me and said, 'Look, now, here's a jar of preserves from 1942.' He blew the dust off. 'We don't want to eat it, do we? It's too old. And we don't need to throw it out. We've got plenty of room in which to keep it.' And he gingerly put it back on the shelf. Then we went up into the parlor, which was so filled with historic geegaws that I got dizzy. It was like trying to locate a can of Campbell's tomato soup in the supermarket. I was looking everywhere and my eye stopped on a real rhino's foot sitting on the desk. Driscoll noticed my interest. 'Open it and see what's inside.' I opened it. Inside was a note that told the date the rhino was shot, how many men shot it, how many bullets it took to knock it down, how long it ran before it fell, what the weather was like that day, and how many men it took to pick the damn thing up and carry it away.

It was almost dinner time. Some guests had arrived and we sat around drinking a little sherry. I was talking to a mathematician who had recently moved to the area from Groningen, Holland. He said, 'I am *so fed up* with the fact that everyone will only talk about 1776 around here. Is that the only idea they have of history? We just bought a nice house that we heard was built on the site of an old turkey farm. There used to be a turkey farm there back in the 1800s, and darn it all, we would love to *know* about that turkey farm, but no one can tell us about it because everyone's talking about 1776!' Then it was time for dinner. We prayed: 'Bless this food to our use and us to Thy service.' And we had a lovely big roast beef, real rare, and asparagus and ice water.

The interviews went fine at the Acton Public Library – nothing very eventful, but sweet and interesting. The following day, Sunday, Driscoll asked if I'd like to stay over another day because it was Patriot's Day and they thought I might be interested in seeing some of the celebration, like the re-enactment of 'the shot heard round the world' and a shoot-out at Lexington Green. All of that was going to start at six o'clock in the morning. I decided to stay.

When I woke at five a.m., it was pouring rain. Driscoll cried up from the bottom of the stairs, 'What's your pleasure?' (which at five o'clock in the morning I assumed meant a Virgin Mary). All bright and cheery, he said, 'You know, when the sun shines we call it a blessing. When it rains, we dress to match.' He brought out all this foul weather gear and yellow slickers. And he didn't come with me.

I went on the Isaac Davis Camparee. The Boy Scouts, three thousand of them, had gotten up at four o'clock in the morning to begin marching in the rain along the actual trail that Isaac Davis took, all the way down to the Concord Bridge. I fell in with them. It wasn't exactly a march, it was more of a shuffle. Everyone seemed kind of depressed. They had only eaten a granola bar at four o'clock for breakfast, and it seemed the only thing they wanted was to get out of the rain and get some bacon and eggs.

Down by the bridge was a museum, and everyone went into it to get out of the rain. We all stood around looking for history, gawking at the maps, muskets, and soldiers' hats. And I wondered why I didn't feel anything. We were all looking at the maps and looking at the pictures and I wondered why I couldn't feel anything. We were looking at the Minuteman statue and taking photographs of the Minuteman statue and I wondered why I couldn't get in touch with history. We were looking at the 'raffle house' and looking at the rhino's foot . . .

Since it was raining and I didn't want to hang out with the Boy Scouts looking at the Minuteman statue anymore, I decided to go to Walden Pond to try for communion with the spirit of Thoreau. I drove down and parked in the empty lot across from the park. It was exquisite, and I walked down through the sound of rain on rotten leaves. As I saw the pond in the distance through the bare spring trees, I thought of that other time, with Nora.

It was one of those clear, dry August days, with high fluffy clouds, and Nora and I went down to the far end of Walden Pond, away from the public beach. We lay down, and she lit up a marijuana cigarette, toked it and passed it to me. Then she started writing a letter to an 80-year-old naturalist in Minnesota. I turned to her and said, 'Nora, I'm starting to feel all that sexual energy again in my spine, what should we do?' She said, 'Why don't you lie down and I'll give you "Touch for Health".' I took off everything but my jockey shorts and lay face down and she put one finger right at the base of my spine, and another right at the base of my skull, lightly. She said, 'Now I'm going to draw all that awful old sexual energy right out of you.'

And, by God, she did. I could see the flames. It looked like a blowtorch, shooting out of my coccyx, going up her fingers. Her fingers were red hot. The flames went up through her and I could see that her arm was hollow inside. I could see all of this with my eyes closed. Her forearm was like cool, hollow alabaster. Sure enough, the flames had closed out by the time they reached her elbows. She was draining that energy out of me. I had visions of witchcraft because we were so close to Salem and also of Samson and Delilah. When she finished with me, I was like this big, cool, sexless blue blob, like a beached whale, lying there by Walden Pond.

But it came back, as it always does. 'Nora, look out!' I said. I got up and I was bucking like a satyr. I put my shoes on and started galloping back through the woods, briars, leaves, sticks ripping at my flesh. All of a sudden I came upon the chains that mark off Thoreau's cabin. Inside, at the hearth, was a little plaque that read: 'Go, Thou my incense up to Thee'. Bucking and snorting, I ran up on a knoll in a grove of trees in back of the cabin, and standing on that knoll I looked out over the cabin, through the branches where the wind was flashing like a green fire, and out onto the pond beyond. I went down on my knees, I tore down my shorts, and I felt that dappled light bursting through the trees and running across my chest . . . and I masturbated. Just as I was about to come, I positioned myself on a big pile of soft moss and stuck my cock deep in and shot into the earth. I lay there, exhausted, completely fulfilled, thinking: What a fantastic union with Mother Earth. Then I thought: I wonder how many times Thoreau did this? Maybe in this very spot even.

But soon the mosquitoes and the itchy bugs and the brambles and everything else that was sticking to me began to get to me. I needed to cleanse myself, purify myself, and I thought of the Pond. I galloped down again, pulled my boots off, threw my shorts on a bush, and dove into that quicksilver water. It buoyed me up. It was like magic. For the first time in my life, I had no fear of sharks, no fear of drowning. The setting sun cast a line of shadow that cut across the Pond. I could hear the whistle of the Budliner as it made its way toward Conway. And I could see the head of a man swimming out of the shadow toward me and I could see that he was *angry*. He swam right up to me and he was *angry*, and he dived down two feet from my body. I felt his eyes examining my body under water. He surfaced and he was *angry*. He swam to shore. He stood there with his wife, his arms folded, waiting.

I waited and waited and waited, but the sun wouldn't go down fast enough. Finally, I had to charge, bent and naked, out of the water, covering myself as much as possible with my hands, making a run for my shorts in the bushes. He started yelling, 'You've ruined it for us all. I'm calling the police! Don't you ever do this again! If I ever catch you like this in front of my wife again, I'll kill you!' I said, 'I'm sorry, I'm sorry. I'm from California. We all swim naked out there!' I really wanted to say, 'Listen, Jack, you're part of the reason I left Rhode Island in the first place.'

On to Groton, Massachusetts. I was supposed to do interviews at the Shirley Golden Age Drop-in Center. I went to stay in nearby Groton, with one of the most perfect American families I'd ever met – totally devoted mother, two children, and a devoted father who ran a little factory that made vacuum furnaces. He was good friends with all the people who worked for him. She was a great cook and a great mother. When I asked her why she moved to such a small community, she told me, 'In small towns, the community takes care of their old, and I have full intentions of gracefully growing old in Groton.'

The next day I went over to the Shirley Golden Age Drop-in Center. Now, I thought I knew what it was like to work with old people: I had two grandmothers who lived to be 94. I had this image of myself helping these shaky old women up on stage, sitting them down, and asking them a few simple questions about what it's like to grow old. But when I arrived at the Shirley Golden Age Drop-in Center, it was *popping*. These weren't old people, they were senior citizens. They were carrying on like it was a big party, and the chairperson was trying to gavel them to order. At last they calmed down and the chairman said, 'Now, I'm going to read the minutes. Last week we voted *not* to have the world-renowned talk-show host, Mr Spalding Gray, come to interview us because it would cost too much. Then the New England Foundation said that they would subsidize it up to fifty dollars. Then it was voted that that was still too much. So then they said they'd cover the whole fee. So we have him here today.' Some mildly enthusiastic murmurs. He went on. 'As you know, we're about to have our next club luncheon in Boston and it's going to cost one hundred sixty dollars per person, including round trip on the bus and all food. Now, I'd like to take a vote on what people want. How many want ham? Turkey? How many for roast beef? May I please see hands? How many hams? All right. Please, please, I don't want to have to be a policeman. How many turkeys? Wait a minute, can we have that again? Gloria, did you raise two hands for turkey?'

This went on for 20 minutes. There was great debate over whether the combination of ham and roast beef would be digestible. Finally, they settled on ham and turkey. Then there was the saluting of the flag, a little American flag, tacked to the wall, that looked like it was wrapped in Saran Wrap. Then there was the prayer. Then the meeting was gaveled to order yet again, and the chairman said, 'Since Mr Spalding Gray is here and waiting patiently in the corner, I think we should interrupt the meeting for today's entertainment.'

By now I realized that I was a kind of filler, a court jester, the obligatory entertainment for the day. So I tried to draw on some of the 'principles of expression' I got from my Emerson College toast-master education: Try to employ material that has been mentioned, and so on. So I said, 'Well, it's nice to be here today. It's the first time I've ever been in competition with a bus to Boston and lost.' No response.

In the course of the interviews it came out that I hadn't saluted the flag since the seventh grade, that I'd never voted in my life, and that the last time I prayed was in Acton. When asked where I came from, I said jokingly, 'An island off the coast of America,' referring to Manhattan, but by then I think they thought I meant Cuba. Speaking of my interest in Buddhism, I referred to it as a philosophy without a deity, and that did it. No longer able to contain himself, a man jumped up and said, 'Mr Spalding, you talked about questions. I have some questions. Now you say you don't salute the flag, you don't pray, and you don't vote. Well, would you mind telling us all here what exactly it is that you do do?' And all I could hear in my head, over and over, was: *do do, do do, do do, do do* . . .

Then I pulled out of it and said, 'Wait a minute. It takes only about two minutes to salute the flag, a little bit longer to pray, and I don't know how long it takes to vote because I haven't done it, but that leaves a lot of time left over for other things.' And he said, 'Well, we don't want to hear about them. We don't talk about religion and politics in public here.' Then a woman piped up, cutting him off. 'What religion are you, anyway?' I began, 'Well, I grew up as a Christian Scientist,' and she started shaking her head and clucking. I said, 'What's wrong with that?' She said, 'Well, that explains it. That explains a lot.'

By now the whole place was in an uproar. I was trying to shout over them like some sort of college radical, crying, 'Now wait. Please, please. Listen, listen. I'm not a foreigner, really, I'm not all that unlike you. I grew up in Rhode Island, was born in Providence.

In fact, listen, listen! My Gram Gray was born in *Cambridge*. She was born in Cambridge, Massachusetts!' And one woman yelled, 'Cambridge! My good Lord, down there they'd even *make* you salute the flag if you didn't want to. They're a bunch of Communists! Get him out of—'

I might as well have said Hanoi.

I headed for the door as fast as I could, with the taste of chemicals in my mouth. In the foyer a woman called out, 'Mr Gray, Mr Gray, could I speak with you a minute, please? I have a nephew who lives in Hawaii with a Hawaiian gal. They're not married. I went to visit them and they have a Buddha Bible right by the bed. Every time my nephew has an overwhelming problem, he runs out, opens his arms wide to the heavens and says, "Father, Father, Thy will be done." So I think there is a God. I think there is a Buddha God, don't you?' I said, 'I dunno. Tell me this: You went all the way to Hawaii and you're still wondering about this? Did you ask him?' And she said, 'Oh, no. I would *never* do a thing like that.'

The following day I was nervous because I was scheduled to do more interviews at the Golden Age Drop-in Center in Pepperell. I was surprised and happy to find the senior citizens there much more open. I talked with a woman named Harriet who told me that she had worked with cows all her life and wanted to retire and mix with people. So she went to Canada for a vacation, where she found out that cows weren't so bad after all. And she came back to the cows. I asked if she had any last questions, and she said, 'Yes. When are you going to get a hairpiece?' I was thrown by that one. 'What? Do you really think I need one?' She said, 'Well, you're a world-renowned talk-show host. I don't know how you can do talk shows with that bald spot.'

On to Lawrence, Massachusetts: immigrant city. I arrived when Lawrence was having a particularly bad day. They had just been voted the worst city to live in in America, besides Fresno, California. So they were feeling a little on edge and I don't think they wanted any investigatory reporters coming around. Also, the people who had arranged my accommodation weren't very politic about it. Instead of putting me up with the workers in Lawrence, they put me up with a couple in Andover, where the mill bosses had traditionally lived.

After I got settled, I was driven over to Polo Mills to meet the boss's PR agent. Polo Mills was a very beautiful old factory that had been refurbished very skillfully to keep its original look. The workers seemed to have a real sense of loyalty to it. They proudly told me about making the suit in which Robert Redford received his Oscar. They took me on a tour and treated me like a visiting dignitary, but all the same I felt a little under the gun. I would have preferred to wander around, talking to the workers at random about any topic that came up. But the PR director insisted that I be escorted.

I accepted the boss's dinner invitation for that night. Then I felt like I needed some air, like I had to get out and wander the streets, so I went over to Lowell in search of Jack Kerouac's grave. I wanted to check in on him and pay my respects. The Town Hall actually had a map showing how to get there. I've never seen so many graveyards in my life. There were three huge graveyards right in a row, and Jack's grave was in the third, in the family plot. I was surprised to find there was no headstone, only a little plaque flat in the sand that read: Ti-Jean, John L. Kerouac, Mar. 12, 1922-Oct. 21, 1969. On top of the plaque people had left wine corks, beer bottle caps, joss sticks, a little prayer wheel, and other weird things. I hadn't brought any offerings. I felt awful. The only thing I had in my pocket was a Marriott matchbox that read: 'We did it right'. I tore that off and stuck it against the plaque.

Back in Andover, I was picked up for dinner by the mill owner and his PR agent in a black four-door Cadillac with chrome-spoked wheels. We drove over to Lawrence to a popular Lebanese restaurant. Dinner conversation was awkward. I didn't know what to talk about besides business, until at last the PR agent asked, 'Is this the first mill you've done?' I said, 'Yes, it is. I'm interested in doing interviews in mills and other places where I'm not on top of the situation. Where I'm dealing with people who are different from any I've known before – like prisons, for instance. I would very much like to do prisons.' She said, 'Prisons? What would you talk about in prisons? What do you know about them?' I said, 'Actually, I was in a Las Vegas jail for refusing to give an officer my name, so I had a good taste of it. I was in with 30 guys for seven days.' She said, 'They put you in *jail* in Las Vegas? How could they arrest a famous person like you?' I said, 'Real easy. They knocked me down on my knees, put my hands behind my back, and put on the handcuffs.'

The following day was loaded. Besides the interviews at the mill that night, Emilio, who was a kind of cross between Ed Sullivan, a toastmaster, and a dentist, had set up all sorts of preinterview ceremonies that the New England Foundation representatives and I were to attend. It was all to begin at five o'clock, with cocktails at the Andover Inn, then more ceremonies at the high school, then dinner at the Lebanese restaurant again, and at last over to the mill for the interviews.

At five o'clock we all assembled at the Inn for cocktails and I ordered a scotch on the rocks. As soon as I put it to my lips, a school bus showed up and Emilio started herding us out. I stuck the scotch under my jacket and took it with me. We were driven to the high school in Andover to hear the New England Celestial Choir. Emilio asked me to leave the scotch outside – he said the sight of it might corrupt the students.

After three or four choral pieces, Emilio guided us down the main aisle of this huge, empty auditorium and up onto the stage, through the middle of a group of students who were rehearsing *The Music Man*. We strolled right through 'Cheep cheep cheep, pick a little, talk a little' and on into an unfurnished dressing room, where the school superintendent proceeded to deliver a rather dry lecture about how he had raised all the funds for the new auditorium, while we looked at each other reflected in the wall mirrors.

Then we were herded into the school bus again and driven to the infamous Lebanese restaurant for dinner. By now I was getting a little panicked that I wasn't going to get back to the mill in time to mix with the workers and get familiar with them before the interviews. So I ordered another drink, even though I never drink before interviewing. I ordered my dinner quickly, quickly, quickly, so I could eat before the others. But I could see the writing on the wall – the New England Foundation people were going to come over when they were ready.

When dinner arrived I wolfed it down and rushed over to the mill, leaving the others to finish. I was becoming aware of an underlying tension between the mill workers and the Arts Foundation. The workers wanted to show that they were artists, too, and they had prepared a display back at the mill of their ethnic crafts and pastries, as well as a brief performance of folk music and dance.

When I got there it was like a carnival. All the workers were there along with the boss, the PR agent, and the mayor of Lawrence. I started walking around, looking at the art and meeting people. By then I was pretty nervous because no one from the Foundation had arrived yet. At last, at about eight thirty-five, they showed up. Then it was time for coffee and dessert. Afterward everyone settled into their seats for the preinterview ethnic entertainment. Out came a Polish boy in traditional dress and black boots who did a boot dance while singing a Polish song. Then came a Spanish classical guitar player who did a few flamenco numbers. Finally, out came a Greek guy who played the theme from *Zorba the Greek* full blast on an amplified bazouki. By now it was getting late, and the following day was a working day for them.

Emilio was aware that it was time to get on with the interviews, and he got up and took the microphone in hand to introduce me. 'And now, for the highlight of the evening's entertainment. Some of you may have seen him walking around the streets. Some of you may have talked with him during his fact-finding mission. And some of you may have seen him over by the Robert Frost fountain. (Lawrence, like other towns in New England, wants to believe that Robert Frost was born there.) So here he is, the highlight of the evening, the world-renowned talk-show host, star of stage, screen, and television! I want you to welcome him and give him a big hand. Here he is, Mr Spalding Gray!'

I came on and sat down. Usually when I do interviews I like to start from a quiet, neutral kind of place, sit down and talk for 20 to 40 minutes with each person, really try to let something come out. But now it was a total carnival. People were talking and wandering between the interview room and the arts and crafts room. No one was paying much attention to the people who were being interviewed. But nothing much was going on in the interviews anyway. They were all talking about how much they loved working in Polo Mills. And why wouldn't they? The boss was sitting in the front row. They seemed to have no sense of their own contemporary history. The only sense of history they had went back to the days when people walked to the mill because there were no cars and the time when so many people were killed when the mill burned down and the time when the riots came. But now, there was no history – there was nothing to say. They were happy to have a job, come home at night, watch a little television, go to bed, and not dream.

So that's what was happening. Then I got the mayor of Lawrence up there. Now the mayor of Lawrence had been the mayor of Lawrence for 25 years, and he tried to use the interviews as a political forum. I was really trying hard to concentrate and listen to him because he was the mayor. Everyone else was getting up and going into the other room for more coffee and dessert. At last, trying to lure him off gracefully, I fell back on my old interviewing techinque – I asked him if he had any last words before he sat down. He did. He went on and on and on.

By the time I got the mayor off, the room had thinned out and quieted down. So I called up this Vietnamese man, a very gentle soul whom I'd met the day before working at his graphic computer. He began to tell me how he escaped from Vietnam by walking to Thailand through Cambodia and how he ate bark, bugs, leaves, and lizards to survive. Right in the middle, just as he was about to open up, Emilio broke in and whispered in my ear, 'Cut it! Cut it! You've gone on too long. The people have to work tomorrow, it's time to wrap it up!'

I left pretty depressed. My host and hostess drove me back to their home in Andover. On the way, my host said, 'A noble effort. A noble effort. But I prefer a Barbara Walters.'

On to the next mill in Irving, Massachusetts. This one recycled paper into paper party napkins. When I arrived I was issued a blue hard hat and taken on a tour. The paper was stacked up like mountains; some of the piles were close to 50 feet high. I was introduced to some workers who drove the forklifts that loaded the bales of paper onto the boxcars that would be brought up to the mill. They were real open with me and wanted to show me around. They told me there were some great pornographic calendars in some of the piles if I had the patience to sort through them. They invited me into their little shed, which had sayings on the wall like 'If you can't dazzle them with brilliance, baffle them with bullshit' and 'I must be a mushroom, because everyone keeps me in the dark and feeds me shit.' They, too, seemed happy and without any problems. Some of them had worked at the mill for 30 years. When I asked them why they felt so good, they said they liked working outdoors, living in trailer parks, watching a little TV at night, and not worrying about the bomb. They fished at a nearby stream at lunch and didn't remember their dreams.

After visiting with them for a while, I went for lunch at a little greasy spoon on the highway. While I was eating hotdogs and homemade pea soup, a mile-long freight train pulled up in the back of the diner. Three engineers got out, came through the back door, bought strawberry ice cream cones for each other, got back into their mile-long freight train and pulled away. I couldn't believe that such things still happened, or ever did. It was like a children's storybook.

During the interviews down at the mill I decided to try a new format. Searching through the paper stacks I had come upon a book called *How to Become a Writer*. Part of the book was a questionnaire which I thought I'd try out on the audience:

'*Do you believe in God?*'

'Oh, yes . . .'

'*What is the worst thing you can imagine happening?*'

'I don't know, something to my family.'

'*What is the best thing?*'

'Megabucks . . . I would win Megabucks.'

'*Do you think romantic love is a trap, a snare and an illusion?*'

A man said, 'You wanna run that by me again?'

I said, 'Well, first of all, have you ever been romantically in love?'

He said, 'Well, I . . . I've been married ten years. I'm still married.'

I said, 'And you're romantically in love?'

'I hope so.'

I said, 'Well, my Lord, what does she *do*, does she dress up in different gowns and that kind of thing when you come home?'

'Oh, no, nothing like that.'

'Well, what do you attribute this to? I mean all of you people here, you have good marriages, you enjoy your work, you seem happy, and you don't dream. What do you attribute it to?'

He answered, 'I don't know. Attitude, I guess.'

On from Irving to Shelburne Falls, a beautiful little town. It's known for its bridge of flowers, a concrete footbridge with flower boxes along the edges that spans the local river. Its sister city in Russia also has a bridge of flowers.

The first thing I do when I come into a small town like that is to check out the local bulletin board which is usually posted outside the drugstore, to see what's going on. This one read:

KARATE LESSONS

MAN/WOMAN/BABY SEEK LIVING SITUATION;

PREFER RURAL FARM, GARDEN, CAMPING – IF WATER AND OTHER FACILITIES AVAILABLE. BABY NO PROBLEM, WE ARE USED TO LIVING SIMPLY

WORKSHOP IN SAYING NO

RECORDER LESSONS
TOUCH FOR HEALTH *(I remember that one)*
PROTEST THE LAUNCH OF THE USS *Alabama*
FRESH RABBIT MEAT
SPRING CLASSES IN BLAZING STAR HERBAL SCHOOL
VAPASANA MEDITATION, SEE THINGS AS THEY REALLY ARE
SPALDING GRAY, WORLD RENOWNED TALK-SHOW HOST

Up until now, in these rural areas, I'd been playing to captive audiences. This was the first interview open to the public, at a Grange hall. No one was required to come, and I was a little worried that nobody would. And WGBY TV out of Springfield was going to videotape the interviews. Robin Doty, the producer, had his cameras follow me while I roamed the streets of Shelburne, asking natives if they would come to the interviews. Usually, they said, 'We'll see . . . we'll see. It's kind of late at night for us . . . ' But when they saw those cameras coming their way they would pull back, duck behind a telephone pole, or go into a store. And I thought: Why *should* they come? Why would they want to get up and repeat gossip they all already know in front of some city slicker who blows in from New York to ask them a lot of personal questions?

That evening at the Grange hall, no one had showed up by starting time. I thought I was going to have to interview the people on the television crew, but finally about eight people assembled. The only one who was really open to talking was a displaced Chinaman who was living in New England. I asked him what he felt about America, and he told me that he was upset about America because the first thing that happens when you sit down at a table is that you *do not* get served tea, as you do in China. We had a long chat about tea in America versus tea in China.

The next town, Hadley, Massachusetts, was a short hop from Shelburne Falls. I knew nothing about Hadley except that an ex-girl-friend of a friend of mine lived there. Tammy Mahoney had eventually married a local guy who would often beat her up. After she got out of the hospital, she'd come to Boston to read my copy of 'The Myth of Sisyphus', then return to Hadley for another beating. So I only knew Hadley as a place of existential battered wives.

When I got there, I went into a coffee shop and saw the *Hadley Reader* with a huge picture of me on the front page. It looked like one of those joke newspapers you pay to have made up, with a sensational headline containing your name. There I was, dressed in a tie and jacket, holding my hard hat in my arms, looking like Mondale-Gray-Hart. And underneath the photograph, a big, bold headline read: 'The Entertainer Has Arrived'. So I thought, Oh, boy, the place is going to be jumping, people are going to be hanging from the rafters! These are going to be the best interviews ever! Ten people showed up.

On to Portsmouth, New Hampshire. I was looking forward to Portsmouth. I had been there when it was a navy town, when I was working at Theatre-by-the-Sea and playing Edmund in *Long Day's Journey into Night*. In order to get into the role I was drinking Irish whiskey and not turning up the heat so that I had to pee on the ice that formed in the toilet each morning. 'Please turn up the heat,' my landlord pleaded, 'I'll lower the rent.' But I was too cheap.

Since then Portsmouth had changed completely. No longer was it a greasy-spoon navy town. It had become yuppie heaven, and it was raining white wine and broccoli quiche – you could eat it off the sidewalk. The old Rockingham Hotel had been turned into co-ops. All the bricks had been sandblasted. All the greasy spoons had been converted into boutiques and renamed Holy Macro, A Touch of Glass, Just Desserts, Sporting Lady, Marco Polo Incorporated, Grapes of Wrath.

I was staying at this wonderful old house, a big Victorian, with waterbeds in every bedroom. My host and hostess were an interesting couple with three children. The wife's grandparents had been among the original members of the Oneida Colony, that free-love, polygamous experimental group of the 1800s. She was very interested in Elisabeth Kübler-Ross and transcendental thinking. She was a great Amazon of a woman, a sort of contemporary New England Transcendentalist.

Her husband was quite the opposite. He was up working in the attic studio when I arrived, and we hung out down below with their little two-year-old girl (who was calling me daddy for some reason) talking about Kübler-Ross and death and dying and Jung and all that. Then I went upstairs to the pine-paneled attic where the husband was working on receiving visions for record jackets. He wanted to become a record-jacket designer and relocate the whole family to LA.

Between these two polarities was the spirit of the in-house guru, Dr Chuck Bisbano, who stayed there when he did seminars in the

area. Dr Chuck is a new-age therapist, and his followers were building an institute for him in Hawaii. He sells a set of 12 audio tapes
called *The Journey*. His healing process is quite simple. It's kind of
behavioristic, and it goes like this: All of us have had a major trauma
in our lives. We have to get in touch with that. When we meet reality,
we do one of three things – fight it, flee it, or flow. And Dr Chuck
suggests that we flow, by getting in touch with that first trauma and
reprogramming our memory to how we would have liked it to have
been, actually making up a new history. Dr Chuck does this in front
of a large audience. For instance, a woman will come out of the
audience and he'll ask, 'Now what was your trauma?'

And she'll say, 'I was four years old . . . '

'Yes . . . '

'And I was masturbating . . . '

'Yes . . . '

'And my mother came in and caught me . . . '

'Yes. And what happened?'

'She slapped me and said, 'You're a bad girl. You mustn't do that.
Don't touch your body in that way.'

'Good. Now, how would you like to re-image it?'

'I'm four years old . . . '

'Yes . . . '

'I'm masturbating . . . '

'Yes . . . '

'My mother comes through the door . . . '

'Yes . . . '

'And she says, "The body is a flower. It's a lovely instrument of
pleasure. It's a wonderful, wonderful machine. Enjoy!" And she
leaves.'

And the woman is healed.

So I was trying to think positively. God knows, I grew up in
Christian Science and a lot of this rang of that, so I thought I'd try to
get back to some of that transcendental thinking while I was in New
England and see how it might change my stay there.

Well, the interviews went wonderfully. The only thing I
remember was that I asked people about big mistakes they'd made in
their lives. One guy had shot down his own plane in World War II.
He was a tail gunner. He had a wonderful sense of humor about it.

Back at the house, I asked my host and hostess for feedback on the
interviews, because often people leave without talking to me and I

don't know how it's gone (particularly in New England). First, I went downstairs to my hostess. She said, 'You know, Spalding, if you were to go back to school, in two years' time you could become a wonderful therapist and healer.'

Then I went up to visit her husband in the pine-paneled room. He said, 'You know, Spalding, if you just learned how to stop on your laugh lines and not go any further, you could be a great comedian.' So no one was telling me how it went that night, and I felt a little depressed. I went down and got into my waterbed and put on Dr Chuck. He always put me right out. I listened to all 12 parts of *The Journey*.

The next day I decided I would hitchhike, just as an experiment. I was headed for Hardwick, Vermont, and I had a week to get there; so I'd start by hitchhiking from Portsmouth to St. Johnsbury. I thought of hitchhiking as a way to test the pulse of America, to get to meet people. But first of all you've got to get someone to stop for you.

Some months before, I had tested my luck at hitchhiking outside New Paltz, New York, that old hippie haven 90 miles north of Manhattan. I was sure someone would stop. I wanted to go to the Shawangunk Mountains to hike. They're a 15-minute drive outside of New Paltz. First thing in the morning, I took the bus to New Paltz, got out, and started hitchhiking. No one stopped. So I walked a little farther toward the mountains. No one stopped. Single men in station wagons veered around me. Hippies in Volkswagen buses, alone, veered. Farmers in pickups veered. When the sun started to go down and it began to get cold, I panicked and tried to flag people down with my hat. I ended up walking all the way back to New Paltz in the dark, mortified.

This time I thought it had probably been because I wasn't doing my positive thinking. Just before heading out, in the spirit of Dr Chuck, I sat in the backyard in the sunshine, thinking positively. I tried to image. I imaged a car stopping for me, the driver not talking my ear off, not trying to feel my knee, no accidents, just having a regular conversation. Then my hostess came out and said, 'All right now, I'll drive you out.' She was driving me out to hitchhike north on the Spaulding Turnpike. I thought: Well, that bodes well, even though it's spelled with a *u*. So we drive out to the Spaulding Turnpike, and just before my hostess let me off, she turned to me and said, 'Goodbye, Sterling. Good luck!'

It was a bright, sunny day. I had on my tweed jacket and tie, white shirt, gray slacks, Bass Weejuns. I looked like a New England businessman who'd just run out of gas and was trying to flag down a car. I got out on the road and stood there, trying to think positively. Not that the negative images weren't creeping in. I could visualize having to resort to the Great Western in Rochester, New Hampshire, at $85 a night. A few cars went by and all of a sudden this Subaru came screeching to a halt. The license plate read, 'Go For It', and under that, in small print, 'Live Free or Die'. I got in and the guy said, 'Hi. Welcome to my Japanese Cadillac.' He had a cigar, a fuzz buster, a CB radio. And we were off. He said, 'I'm off to St. Johnsbury.' 'Fantastic,' I said. 'That's where I'm going. What are you up to?' He said, 'I'm going up to fix computers at a bank in St. J. I'm a computer repairman.' I said, 'Well, that's great.' He said, 'Yeah, it's great. I like my work a lot, you know? Originally I was a shoemaker . . . ' And I had this vision of Joe Kallinger looking for delta fluid.

He said, 'I was making shoes and it wasn't very social. So I thought, I'm going to ask the next person who comes in to have a pair of shoes made what his job is, and if it's a social job, I'll do it. And it was a computer-repair guy. And, by God, I went for it! You know, like Rocky says in the movie: America's the land of opportunity – go for it! Go for it! And I did.'

It turned out that not only did he go for it, but he was also a born-again Christian. And I thought: Oh, Lord, now I'm going to have to convert to Jesus before I reach St. J. Well, at least he wasn't going to grab my knee. And I was interested in comparative religion, so I didn't mind philosophizing about Christ and all the rest of it. But before we could get into that topic, he went on to say, 'Shortly after I became a born-again Christian, I joined Amway.'

I told him I didn't know what Amway was and he was surprised. He went on to tell me it was a multi-level corporation. What is a multi-level corporation? The most I could figure out is that it meant someone's got to start at the lower level and I assumed that was me. 'Paul Newman and Joanne Woodward, couples like that, belong to it,' he said. Basically, it sounded like a Christian capitalist kabala club, where couples sell junk to other couples. He got out a huge catalog. It had laundry detergent, stain remover, silver polish, bug spray, mouthwash, bathroom freshener, toothpaste, smoke detectors. And I was trying to figure out how I was going to sell all this stuff to my friends in SoHo.

There were also pictures of all these smiling couples who had won prizes and were standing with silver-plated trophies against leopard-skin backdrops and artificial brick fireplaces. He said, 'Listen, don't think of Amway as only toothpaste and mouthwash. Look at *this* stuff!' He showed me an incredible gas barbecue and lawn chairs. And I kept trying to figure out how they'd fit into all those mini-malist SoHo lofts. All this time, we were riding through Franconia Notch, and I was looking out the window at the snowcapped Presi-dentials, torn between them and the Amway catalog. 'Now, all-righty, allrighty,' he said. 'Amway is my protection.' (He was always saying 'allrighty, allrighty.') 'Allrighty, say if I had a crash right now. Say the car just went *whoop*, right off the cliff here and I lost my arms and legs, my family would be completely taken care of by Amway.'

We got to St. Johnsbury and he said, 'Allrighty, I'm just going to fix the computer in this bank. Now, you take the catalog and go over to Dunkin' Donuts for a cup of coffee. I'll join you there and we can talk some more. I want you to come with me to Montpelier to an Amway meeting.' He almost had me convinced. I actually went into the Dunkin' Donuts with the catalog and began studying it. Then I thought: Good God, I've got to get out of here. This is ridiculous. But where will I go? I don't know anyone in St. Johnsbury. I need to be rescued.

Then I remembered my friend Jay Craven who runs the Cata-mount Arts Center in St. Johnsbury. I went to a pay phone and called him. 'Hi Jay, it's Spalding Gray. I just happen to be passing through town. I'm in a bit of a jam here, down at Dunkin' Donuts. I'm wondering if I could come over and see your space.' (Theaters and art houses are often called 'spaces'.) He said, 'Yeah, but we don't have a space. You can come over and we can chat in my office. We don't have a space yet, but we're working on it.' Just as I was about to go, the Amway man saw me escaping from the Dunkin' Donuts and cut me off. But he could see that I wasn't ready for Amway yet, so he handed me his card and said, 'When you're ready, call me.' The card had a picture of a bald eagle descending with its talons out, and under it his name and phone number in Franconia, New Hampshire.

I walked over to Jay's office and, by God, he did just what I hoped he would do. He invited me back to his home in Barnett, Vermont, just down the road. It was six o'clock in the evening, the sun was going down, and we were driving down Highway 91 in Vermont.

There were no billboards, no graffiti, no trash, no other cars – just this black macadam highway winding through lush green hills. It seemed like an animation of two men driving through the paradise that America once was.

His house was even more perfect, a salt-box up in the mountains outside Barnett. On a clear day you could see all the way across to Mount Washington. He had a beautiful barefoot wife from Cambridge, Massachusetts. She was cooking vegetarian pizza. Their son was four years old, with shoulder-length blond hair, and he'd never even *heard* of sugar. He doesn't know sugar exists. We were sitting at the table and the kid just gets up and *runs* across the room and Jay's wife goes, 'Did someone give him sugar today? He's kind of hyperactive, Jay.'

There was another guest, a parks planner from Burlington who'd been commissioned to go to a wonderful little four-room schoolhouse in Barnett and hang out with the kids, lecture on parks, and help them design their own park. They'd take bag lunches and go to the land allotted for the park, where they'd play games and define their favorite areas. I went along with them. The kids went wild, making little bark boats to sail in the stream and choosing the perfect tree to hang a tire swing from. Then we all sat around in a circle on the ground and told stories. Afterwards, one boy asked me where I came from, and when I told him New York City, he got very excited and wanted to come home with me. I asked him why, and he told me that he came from a family of 12 and all they did was run a giant dairy farm. He was up at five-thirty every morning, milking cows, all year round. He didn't even get a summer vacation. When I asked what he wanted to do in New York, he said, 'I want to hang out with the guys and play basketball in the streets.'

The whole stay was so great I couldn't stand it. I had to get back on the road. I was really looking for some misadventures, and so much wholesomeness was making me claustrophobic.

I decided to try my luck at hitchhiking again. Hardwick was half an hour away and I had two days to get there. I was wide open to whatever might happen in between. I thought: Now what will I image today? I was standing on the road, it was up to about 80 degrees, and it was only May. I had a case of spring fever, that last-day-of-school feeling, itch at the base of my spine. I thought, I've got two days, why not image a single woman? A single woman who will come by and pick me up and take me to a pond, a perfect pond. We'll frolic naked all day.

I was standing there visualizing this when a woman, alone, went by in a 4x4 Toyota pickup. She stopped 300 yards down the road, turned around and started back. I was really getting scared – I don't want that kind of power because I don't want that kind of responsibility. But she pulled up and I hopped in. We drove off, and I said, 'So, what are you up to?' She said, 'Oh, I'm taking a "well" day.' I'd never heard the expression before. I thought she meant that she was going divining for water. She said, 'A well day is the opposite of a sick day.' I said, 'What are you going to do on your well day?' And she said, 'Well, I'm just going to have a good time and frolic.' She had been born on the Upper East Side of Manhattan and was convinced New York City was crazy. In 1965 she decided that she wanted to hitchhike to California, but since she was afraid to hitchhike across America, she decided to do it through Canada. She got as far as Vermont and had been there ever since. Now she had a couple of children and was a water analyst for the local waterworks. She said she knew that she was really a rock star but that was a future incarnation she hadn't reached yet.

I said, 'So what are you doing on your well day, frolicking and all that?' She said, 'Do you want to know the truth?' I said, 'Sure, why not?' She said, 'I think I'm going to take some hallucinogens; I'm going to take some magic mushrooms.' This little two-year-old inside me was going, 'Me too! Me too! Me too! Me too!' But it wasn't coming out. I was just acting cool. 'Oh, really? Magic mushrooms, huh? Where are they from?'

She said, 'Listen, babe, I *know* you'd love to do them with me, but it's been so long since I've done them, I just want to go into myself and be alone, you know? Some other time. Maybe I'll have you up for a drink, get you out of Hardwick . . . look out for *that* town. But I'll take you to a pond, if that's what you want.'

And she did. She left me off at a pond right on the outskirts of Hardwick. It was kind of a man-made pond, not my idea of the ideal pond. There were three guys with huge beer bellies and tattoos, fishing. They had a gallon jug of Seagrams 7 and plastic bottles of 7-Up, and they were *bombed*. They had their wives with them. The wives were in pin curlers, with cigarettes dangling from their mouths. One of the wives was pushing another one into the water, yelling, 'Shelly, you *fuckin' slut!*' A little boy, one of their children, ran up to me with orange Popsicle smeared all over his mouth and gave me the finger. He just stood there shooting the bird. And I realized that I had arrived in Hardwick, Vermont, soon to become the place of Jim Fixx's untimely death.

In Hardwick, for the first time on the tour, I was put up in a motel rather than a private home. I never understood why, but I was aware of a good deal of tension between the two people who had invited me to perform. Later I heard one of them, a woman who ran the local newspaper, had changed her mind at the last minute and tried to book a production of *The Fantasticks* instead of me. But Larry Wood, the town manager, insisted that it was too late to cancel.

I had also heard that some of the townspeople were a little reluctant to have me. An investigatory reporter had recently come up from the *Boston Globe* and had found out that the Hardwick police didn't get along with their chief, whose name was Don. He wrote an article on the town in which he referred to the police as 'Don's Whipped Dogs'. Many of the farmers in the area had read the article, and some of them had gotten together and silk-screened T-shirts that read 'Don's Whipped Dogs'. They had been bringing the shirts in from their farms and selling them on the streets on Saturdays. So the town was on edge.

The first thing I did was to go out and buy a fifth of Murphy's Irish whiskey, which I brought back to my motel to sip while I watched 'The Waltons' on TV. I missed Jay Craven's family, and the Waltons reminded me of them, only they had more kids. I sat there drinking Irish whiskey and cried when the last light went out in the Walton house. Then I went into town in search of the appropriate bar in which to continue the cocktail hour. I found it right away. Walking down the main street, I heard a ruckus coming out of a place called Bennie's Pool Hall. A guy came out and yelled to his friends in a pickup, 'He'll be right out, he's just in there shrinking his carrot.' I thought: This is the bar for me. I'll give it a try. I pretended I was just a drifter, just passing through, a kind of macho, fly-on-the-wall-type guy, hanging out in the corner, drinking myself into oblivion because I'd been jilted by my gal, that sort of thing. I pretended I wasn't listening to anything anyone was saying. They were cautious. They knew damn well I was a stranger in town because everyone knew everyone in there.

But I was listening with my peripheral hearing. There was a cancer collection box for a local person and everyone was talking about him, and cancer. A woman put a quarter in and said, 'By God, if I found out I had cancer, you wouldn't see me around here at all. I'd just go go go like a lawn mower.' And the guy next to her said, 'By Jesus, your ass is grass. You don't *bite*, do ya?' Another guy was saying, 'Well, I've been working on my refrigerator since January.' His friend said, 'I think you should come over to my place and do some work. I could use someone so consistent.'

I was just hanging out with my Venus-flytrap ears, picking up on it. A guy said, 'Well, I bet Maude a six pack of them pigs' cocks I could sleep with her the whole night without touching her once.' Now, pigs' cocks, as they're known in Vermont, are those stubby little beer bottles. In the old days they used to be tall and slender, but they knocked them down in size so they could fit a bunch of them in the icebox. The guy went on, 'Next morning I bought her a six pack of pigs' cocks. *Hahahahaha*!'

There was a round table with a whole bunch of guys sitting and talking about golf. They were all wearing golf hats that read: 'Old Golfers Never Die, They Just Lose Their Putters'. One said, 'You know something it is about golf that makes a cheater out of an honest man.' Another guy said, 'Well, that's a good story, but is it the truth?' And a third said, 'Oh hell, no, Howard, you know the truth's no story t'all.'

Then I noticed a real outspoken guy at the far end of the bar. I moved in on him to talk. I was kind of hoping I could get him to be interviewed the following night. I said, 'I see cocktail hour's in full swing.' And he said, 'I should think so. Cocktail hour begins 'bout nine o'clock in the mornin' 'round here.' We fell into talking about life plans, future goals, that sort of stuff. I said, 'What's *your* plan? What would you really like to do with your life if you had the choice?' He said, 'I got a plan. I'll tell you 'bout it, straight out. I'm gonna get the railroad reactivated, get those tracks runnin' up to Canada. I'm gonna get it going and I'm gonna have a big engine. Then we're goin' to have a diner car, a bat car, a sleeper filled with a whole bunch of beautiful whores, and a caboose right in the back all for me. And we're goin' to get that thing runnin' and I'll come up and tell your audience about it, by Jesus I will!'

Then the janitor from the local high school started quoting to me from Cicero – he was trying to get me to memorize Cicero's definition of virtue, but I'd had too much to drink and I couldn't remember a word of it. He told me if I paid him $5 he would recite the first and last names of all the presidents of the United States in one minute. I said, 'Listen, I don't have that kind of money. I'm just a drifter, I'm just passing through.' He said, 'Oh, looking for adventure, are ya? Well, you can tell when you're having a real adventure when you wished you were home in bed. But I'll tell ya, if you're looking for something realistic and off camera, you've come to the right place.'

For the following day the town manager had scheduled a series of meetings with different town organizations. In the morning I was to visit the grammar school, then have lunch at the Golden-Age Drop-in Center, and that evening I was to attend a town selectman's meeting at which they were going to discuss the rebuilding of the sidewalks.

At the school I observed a square dance demonstration. Then on to the second floor, where the principal pointed out a whole row of plants hanging from the ceiling. 'Look, look at these plants. None of them has been vandalized! This is proof that we have no juvenile delinquency.'

The first thing I saw at the Golden Age Drop-in Center was an old man wearing a golf cap that read 'I'm *not* as good as I once was, but I'm as good once as I *ever* was – and that's a fact!' The young woman in charge took me around and introduced me to golden agers who had lived in Hardwick for a long time. Most of them were reluctant to tell me their stories. They said they hadn't lived in Hardwick long enough to talk about it, only 30 or 40 years. Seeing that I wasn't getting any information from the old-timers, the young woman took me aside and said, 'You know, Mr Gray, I haven't been here that long, but my husband and I have a dairy farm and we were always taught that you've got to work hard in order to get what you want. Well, it's just the opposite as far as I can see nowadays. We're only getting two cents on a gallon for milk and we can't even afford to have children to help us work the farm.'

When I went back to have my Irish whiskey with 'The Waltons', the woman at the front desk handed me a note that read, 'Mainard Coombs called. Please call back'. I couldn't recall anyone named Mainard Coombs, but I went to my room and called the number and got this guy's wife who claimed that Mainard and I had gone to college together. I said, 'Hmm . . . that's strange. I don't remember any Mainard Coombs.' She said, 'Oh, you'd remember him if you saw him. He hasn't aged a bit.' I said, 'Really? How did he manage that?' She said, 'We don't know. We talk about it a lot. We make jokes. We think it might have something to do with his pipe: He never takes it out of his mouth. He takes a bath with it, he sleeps with it, he swims with it, he never takes it out of his mouth.' I said, 'What's he smoking in that pipe? And is he inhaling?' 'Oh, no,' she said, 'I don't think so.' Then she said, 'We both know what Hardwick is like and we figured you needed a break. Why don't you come out to our house for dinner? It's right on the outskirts of town.' I said, 'Oh, thanks, I'd love to, but I have to attend a town meeting tonight. But why don't we meet tomorrow? They're having a benefit lasagna dinner to raise money for the Buffalo Food Co-op. Why don't you come in and we'll meet there?' She said, 'Oh, that's a good idea. We're planning to go anyway, so we'll see you there. But I don't know if we'll be able to attend the interviews because of the kids.' I said, 'OK. See you then.' I hung up and caught the end of 'The Waltons'.

After dinner, I went off to the town selectman's meeting. An architect from Burlington, Vermont, was showing slides, close-ups he had taken of the Hardwick sidewalks. I was overwhelmed. Up until then I hadn't noticed anything wrong with the sidewalks. They seemed fine. But my God, they were a mess! They were overflowing into the streets. At some points they were two inches high, at others, six inches. The next morning when I walked out into Hardwick, I was tripping, slipping, falling down. I said, 'My God, this town needs Federal relief!'

That day the woman who ran the local newspaper showed up early at my motel with a gift of a loaf of store-bought Italian bread. I told her I was feeling kind of claustrophobic and asked her to drive me out into the country so I could walk back. It was quite a sensational drive. She drove real fast like a racecar driver, slamming through the gears in silence. At last when we were way out in the hills, she stopped the car, turned to me and said, 'All right, will this do?' I spent most of the day walking back.

That evening I skipped the cocktail hour and 'The Waltons'. I wanted to be completely sober for the interviews. I went over early to the lasagna benefit dinner, where I met Jay Craven sitting outside on the steps. He'd come over from Barnett for the dinner and to watch the interviews. Inside, the place was filled with Vermont ambience. It was like the Waltons – families with lots of kids, pregnant mothers, and fathers in long Rip Van Winkle beards, sleeping right through the seven-year itch. While I was talking to Jay, a youngish guy with curly hair and a pipe in his mouth turned to me and said, 'Are you Spud Gray?' I said, 'Yeah, but I left that name behind in Boston. You're not Mainard Coombs?' 'That's right.' 'I never knew you were Mainard Coombs. I remember you as Gideon.' It turned out to be Gideon from Provincetown, who had been the night manager at the The Breakers Hotel and had let me use his bed. 'My God, it's good to see you again! What happened? You haven't aged!' 'Yeah, I know,' he said. 'Well, you know, I . . . I moved up here. (Pause) Sesquash moved up here. (Pause) He's living in a teepee. We do carpentry work. You know it's tough to make a living up here. But I like the quiet, you know? I've always liked the quiet and I sit by the fire and I (Pause) smoke my pipe and I (Pause) sit at night in the quiet by the fire and I (Pause) sit at night in the quiet and read. I read at night.'

'OH REALLY, READ? WHAT DO YOU READ?'

Now, up until then, I had thought of myself as a type-B person. But right then I realized that Gideon was type-B and I was *definitely* type-A. Slowly he turned to his wife. 'Um . . . honey? What's that book I'm reading now? I like to read history books. You see, I see Vermont as something like Brittany after the Romans left.'

'WHAT DO YOU MEAN?'

'Well, the Vermonters used to be sinewy and tough and courageous, with good teeth. Now they're soft and fat, their teeth are dropping out, they have pimples, and their diet is bad. So it's like that for me. (Pause) So what happened to you? How'd you get so old?'

I said, 'Well, I've been through it. I haven't been sitting by the fire reading, that's for sure.'

And just as I was about to tell him my entire life story, I bit into the health food salad and chipped a tooth on an organic stone.

That night the interviews were super good. One woman came up glowing. She was sending off so much energy, her whole face lit up. She was about 52 years old and had on ski boots. I said, 'What's your background? What have you been doing for a living?' She said, 'Well, for 32 years I lived and worked in Southern California.' I said, 'What did you do there?' 'Guess.' I said, 'I have no idea.' I went through all the southern California clichés – lifeguard, working in a health food store, massage therapist, things like that. She smiled and said, 'Nope, none of the above. I was a nun for 32 years in Southern California and then I dropped out and became a cross-country ski instructor.' Having tired of that, she was thinking of changing professions and was consulting 9-years'-worth of dream journals to help guide her in making a decision.

My next engagement was to be in Montgomery, Vermont, 10 miles from the Canadian border. I was excited because I thought I was going to do interviews at the People's Prom. Montgomery is a town of about 630, and they don't have enough seniors graduating from high school each year to have a prom so the entire town has a prom and everyone comes. They call it the People's Prom, and they have a different theme every year. This particular year it was 'Ain't Misbehavin''.

I was planning to hitchhike there, but someone from Montgomery was kind enough to drive all the way to Hardwick to pick me up. Along the way he gave me a brief history of the town. It seemed it was made up of Vermont natives and Harvard dropouts. Being so far away from any big cities, the people tried to make their own culture, creating events like the People's Prom, casting life masks of all the people in the community, and rewriting Shakespeare to make him topical and reflective of ongoing life in Montgomery.

I asked him how the interviews were going to work at the prom and he told me that they wouldn't be *at* the prom, they were to take place at the Montgomery Historic Society (the townspeople called it the Hysteric Society) the following day. But he was driving me up early so I could attend the People's Prom. All I was required to do was to come in the costume of my choice and dance my ass off.

The following evening I arrived at the Historic Society and outside was a sign that read: 'Spalding Gray: Artistic Storyteller, Philosopher, Family Fun. (They had me covered this time.) Adults $2. Children $1'. There was a pretty good turnout, but everything that I said in the interviews kept provoking laughter, in-house giggling, and whispering. Then I realized that all the questions I was asking, everyone already knew the answers to because it's such a small town. They have no newspaper, so they depend on a kind of creative gossip. So the interviews were beginning to backfire on me.

Then Maggie Sherman came up. Maggie was one of the fiery, creative spirits of the town. During one long Vermont winter she got bored and decided to do life masks of the entire town. She did almost 600 people and had each of them decorate his or her own mask. She told me how her husband Joe would often suggest weird practical jokes and she would decide to act them out for real. Once she had to have all her pubic hair shaved for a hernia operation. And Joe said, 'Wouldn't it be funny if you had grown feathers there by the time you went in to see the doctor again?' She said, 'Great idea, Joe!' and she built an entire mirkin out of chicken feathers and put it on before her next appointment. The doctor took down her pants and screamed. Which of course reminded me of the time at Emerson College when I came back from sunbathing and put a piece of burned chicken skin on my shoulder and cried, 'Melanie, Melanie, I've got a bad burn!'

But we had trouble talking because the Irish contingent, who had been drunk since the prom, were in the back carrying on. I realized they were in competition with me. I had made a faux pas with them when I first arrived in town. I had walked into a bar and sat down, and one of the Irish contingent yelled, 'Hey Spud Gray! They're still talking about you over in Burlington!' I thought: How do they know I used to be called Spud? And how do they know anything about me and Burlington? The only time I had been in Burlington was in 1965 when I went to act in the Champlain Shakespeare Festival. My roommate and I were both interested in the same girl, but he got to her first. Now, she was living in Montgomery, Vermont, it turned out, and she had told the Irish contingent all about Spud Gray. So I had offended them by treating them like wise asses and just brushing them off.

The other thing they were pissed about was that I was hanging out with my hosts, Joe and Maggie Sherman. I was tired, and I didn't feel like socializing. Also, Maggie and Joe lived next door to an idyllic dairy farm run by an old Vermont farmer and his son. The farm was like this incredible circle: The cows would eat the grass, then they'd shit, then they'd put the shit on the grass, the grass would grow; the cows would eat the grass, the cows would shit, they'd put the shit on the grass, the grass would grow; the cows would shit . . . and in between they would milk them. They didn't have to buy any extra feed. I was fascinated by this. There were geese, too, and little puppies and kittens. I spent a whole day there, just wandering.

But the Irish contingent thought I should have been hanging out and drinking with them. I said, 'Listen. Please, please, you people in the back. I'm trying to do interviews up here. People are making a lot of comments back there. I would like to be let in on what's going on because I feel really left out. And nothing can happen up on stage as long as you carry on, so would you guys please elect a representative and send him up.'

This led to a loud discussion, after which they chose a representative and thrust him out of the flock. Up comes one Tim Kelly, drunk and boisterous. He says, 'All right, Mr Spalding. All right. Philosopher – maybe. Storyteller – maybe. Artistic – maybe. Family Fun – maybe. What we all want to know, and I'm speaking for the Irish contingent, is what are you doing here acting like total-in-control Mr Know-It-All Mr Dick Cavett in a necktie and jacket? You've got everyone in the palm of your hand. The undertaker doesn't even wear a necktie here in Montgomery. We also want to know how much money you're making tonight.'

Now I would answer that question in any city. I would answer it in Portland, I would answer it in Providence, although in Montgomery, where most of the people were on welfare, it was another matter altogether. But I pride myself on telling the truth and had made it a condition that I would honestly answer any question that came up. So I simply said, 'I'm making five hundred dollars.'

'Five hundred dollars! Oh my God! Hey, Pete! Peter, how long does it take you to make five hundred dollars? Maggie, come on, five hundred dollars? When was the last time . . . ' And he went through the entire audience and asked each of them how long it took them to make five hundred dollars, or if they'd ever seen five hundred dollars before. Then he turned to the Irish contingent and said, 'Let the doors be locked!' They got up and shut the doors, pulled the shutters closed and stood there with their arms akimbo, like in a grade B horror film. And he said, 'Now, bring on the deer guns. We're going to make sure Mr Spalding Gray earns his money tonight!'

It turned into something like a Liddy-Leary debate, in which Tim accused me of manipulating the audience. '*Me*?' I said. 'How 'bout you? You've had me in the palm of your hand all night. I haven't been able to get a word in edgewise!' He ended by saying, 'We want you to earn your money by moonwalking,' whereupon everyone began to clap and shout. When I told him I didn't know what moonwalking was, there were hisses, murmurs, and laughter. Tim finally got up to demonstrate a moonwalk, and the crowd went wild. We had to adjourn the whole thing and go to a bar across the street to work it out.

The last stop, Willy Loman's last stop, was Portland – Portland,

Maine. Like Portsmouth, it also had recently been gentrified – cobblestones polished, sidewalks swept, historic this, historic that. I came upon a street singer in the square, clean and sober, singing, 'Lock up your booze and hide your daughters/Because I'm gonna bathe their feet in champagne water/'Cause I'm a tiger on the loose, oh yeah/I'm, a tiger on the *looooose*.' People were just *fleeing* from him. But I saw him as this wholesome American guy. I felt like I was in a Bing Crosby movie: 'Hi! Going my way?' I said, 'Hi, my name's Spalding.' And he turned to me and said, 'Well, hi, Spalding. It's good to meet you. I've played with your balls many times before.' It was the first time I'd heard that one in 42 years. I'd heard every other variation.

It turned out that he was one of those guys who can't strike a balance between creativity and self-destructiveness. Every time he got very creative, he tried to destroy himself. He had been just about to cut a record in LA when he went off to Mexico for a vacation with $2700 in a brown paper bag, got beat up, got drunk, got robbed and left for dead hanging in a tree, was put in a hospital where he read nine volumes of C. G. Jung, got out of the hospital, started drinking again, decided to commit suicide aesthetically by throwing himself under the wheels of a maroon '49 Packard, did it, didn't succeed, went back in the hospital, got out, and started drinking again. He said, 'If you drink long enough and hard enough you're sure to end up in Washington County, Maine.'

He stopped drinking in Machias, Maine. Now this guy *had* to be a powerful man to stop drinking in the winter in Machias. And when he stopped drinking, all sorts of Jungian visions came out of his unconscious, and he started painting them. He rolled out these beautiful paintings he'd done in Machias and tried to sell them to me. He said, 'Do you want me to demonstrate to you how the pure animal being can be drawn out of a child? Look over there at that little boy.' He picked up his trumpet, aimed it at a little five-year-old boy, and blew a loud, clear bell tone across the square. The boy's face came alive in total rapport. I said, 'This is wonderful! You've got to come up and be interviewed.'

And he did. He came in carrying his guitar in a case and a knapsack on his back, all dressed up in suspenders, with a red bandana around his neck. Everyone had lots of great Down East stories, and it was a wonderful evening. The only problem was that the microphone wires from the PA system were picking up the news and the weather, which was broadcast as a kind of white noise under it all.

But at the end of it, everyone just left without saying anything to me. They thought I was this famous busy person, some world-renowned talk-show host who needed to be left alone. I felt distraught, like after a very good one-night stand. I ended up going out for drinks with the stage manager and the producer, and the stage manager walked me back to where I was staying. My hostess had promised to leave the back door unlocked so that I would be free to come home at any time. When we got there it was two in the morning, and the back door was locked. I said to the stage manager, 'What'll I do?' I was ready to sleep in the bushes. He said, 'Throw stones at the window.' I said, 'I'll wake them up.' He said, 'You're the *guest*! You're the guest of honor. Do it.' I thought, I should have had him along on the whole tour with me as my manager.

We threw stones at the window, and the hostess came down and let me in. We talked for a while at the kitchen table. The next day I got on People Express and flew back to Manhattan, that island off the coast of America.

TERRORS OF PLEASURE: THE HOUSE

A couple of years back Renée and I rented a little cabin for two summers in a row in Krummville, New York. Upstate. I had never been in the Catskills in the summer and I felt a little displaced. I never thought that I could spend a summer away from the ocean because I'd grown up in Rhode Island. So it was a whole new experience for me, and I was a little panicked. It was a perfect cabin built in the late seventeen hundreds. The owners, Howie and Francine, said that we could use it every year if we wanted, they would keep it open just for us. And the price was right. The only water around was a man-made pond out back that happened to belong to the neighbors. But they let us use it. It tended to scum over, and I'd heard there was a snapping turtle in it – so it wasn't exactly my idea of a fun place to swim. You wouldn't want to lie around on its muddy edges to sun yourself, and there was no crashing surf, not even a ripple. I found that I was constantly being drawn to a small town called Phoenicia – about a 25-minute drive from where we were – because of the Esopus River, a very beautiful, clear trout stream that flows into the Ashokan Reservoir. I was excited about river swimming because you can enter a river at many different points. Also, the Esopus is so swift that you're mainly swimming in place against the water, like a salmon fighting its way upstream. Somehow that sort of fit into my summer anxiety, and the river would give me a chance to work it out. The only problem with the river as I saw it was the tubers.

People were tubing in flocks on that river. There were great oversized men and women and children in oversized tubes, the grown-ups drinking Budweiser beer. They would just sit with the six-packs right in their laps as they floated down. Some thirstier men would rent an extra tube and put a net in it to carry their beer. Once, when Renée and I were up hiking in the nearby mountains, we came down to the Esopus to take a dip, and this ice-cold can of Budweiser floated by, unopened. Renée just reached out, opened it up, and chugged it. It was just like a commercial. I mean, we were actually thinking of trying to sell it to Budweiser as an idea, a 'This Bud's for you' type of thing. But we didn't go through with it.

I was thinking that we should buy a house because renting wasn't enough for me; I wanted to have the sense of *ownership*. I thought it'd be kind of like growing up, like having a child, if you *owned* your own house. And I wanted a house with rooms because I'd grown up in a house with rooms and I'd been living in a loft in New York City with *no* rooms for too long. I was beginning to have dreams of houses where you go into one room and that particular room has some character, and then this other room has a different character. You might read in one room, then go into another to eat, and yet another to sleep. Fantastic!

I began to go around with a real estate agent in that area. I knew I wanted a house near a body of water, but there was always something that wasn't quite right, and I would keep looking around. This went on for about two years. After a while I found that I was getting addicted to just going out with her because I liked to see the inside of other people's houses – how they lived, what they had on their walls, the *chachkes*, what family intrigues were going on. I was also getting on better and better with this real estate agent. Once she showed me 80 acres of undeveloped property for thirty thousand. We went charging into those 80 acres, and I thought, this is it. I felt like a pioneer. The further we went, the more I thought, well, I will buy the property, turn it into an art park as a tax write-off, and I'll spend my life putting little paths through it so my friends from New York can come up and just wander blissfully. When I have the money for the house, I'll build one (in a hundred years), but now I can just *dream* about the house. It seemed perfect. But as I charged into those acres, I began to look around me. And the more I thought about owning the property, the more I saw all these rotten logs on the ground and I began to think about gypsy moths and what would I do, and the whole thing just started to crawl, rot, and steam before my eyes.

I was feeling a little guilty for going out with the same agent and not buying anything. I mean, it was like we were going steady, but I had no intention of marrying her. So I shifted to a new agent, a man this time. One day we were driving and we turned down this side road. We crossed a narrow old iron bridge over the Esopus River and wound down through this sweet little valley right in the heart of the Catskills. We stopped at this bungalow-type cabin on top of a hill with a great view. We went into the house and I found myself in the middle of this crazy domestic scene. The kids were running around, yelling, while Mom was making blueberry pancakes. When they saw me, the kids just stopped and stared me down in silence. And the real estate agent, who I didn't like as much as the woman, perhaps because he smoked cigars, pulled me aside and whispered, 'Look, you can probably get this house for twenty-six. The guy's daughter needs some sort of operation and he needs some fast money up front.' So I decided no, not good, I'm not going to get involved with that kind of karma. As I was leaving, I noticed this little red Adirondack-style cabin up the hill. It had rough-cut siding, a nice porch with screens that were rusted and ripped, and a pine tree nearby. It was up on a small embankment and looked over a pretty rolling mountain. No houses across the way at all.

I said to the real estate agent, 'What about that place? It doesn't look lived in. Is it for sale?'

And he said, 'Oh, we can't get near that. The guy and his wife are indecisive. They're divorcing and we can't get any reading on whether they even want to sell at all. One day one of them wants to sell and the other doesn't, and so on and so forth, so we can't help you there.'

That winter I was back in New York City and one day I saw an ad in the *Village Voice* for an Adirondack-style cabin in the Catskills for thirty-five thousand. And I thought, oooh, I can't imagine what could be going for that price because I hardly ever saw anything for under fifty. It was an owner's listing, he was trying to sell it privately.

So I called a Far Rockaway number and the owner, Carlo Carbone, began to describe the house, 'Well it's a nice little house with a . . . well, it's not exactly, a lawn, we left it natural. It's sort of a hill-and-dale affair.'

And I said, 'Well, I think I've seen the house before, I think it's the very cabin I saw last summer.'

It sounded like at last he was ready to sell. I figured I could afford thirty-five thousand. I had some savings and I wanted to spend it all, just *all* of it, on a house and not have to carry any mortgage. I had saved about twenty-five and I had inherited about ten from my Gram

Gray when she died. I felt like blowing it all at once if I could get Carlo down to maybe thirty. We decided to go see the house, but he had problems with his Buick and couldn't get the keys over to us. Renée and I were so anxious that we drove up without him. Sure enough, it was the very house I had seen, the one next door to the man whose daughter needed to have the operation. It was the house that couldn't make up its mind. The screen porch was open, but we couldn't get into the house, so Renée just broke in. She found a rusty saw on the porch and stuck it in the crack of the door and kind of wedged the latch open. And we walked in.

It was basically a one-storey house with a central room and a nice fireplace built with stone from the Esopus River. There was a kitchen area to the left and three small bedrooms tacked onto the back. The bedrooms were really like closets, which was fine with me because it meant there was no room for furniture to collect, no room for clutter. The house was furnished in a tacky kind of Sears Roebuck, Ethan Allen decor. American eagles on all the lamps, American eagles everywhere. I thought it would be a cozy place to write the Great American Novel, you see. There was artificial brick linoleum on the floor, but we thought we could tear that up and maybe find wood under it, or maybe put wood over it. But the best thing about the house were the wooden ceiling beams. They were actual logs, they weren't even hewn. Renée said, 'I think we can do something with this. Let's get out the Polaroid.' So we did, we took a few Polaroid shots – including one of what she discovered was a problem with the foundation. The house didn't really *have* a foundation, it was built on cinder blocks. They had kind of caved in under the house and did not look too solid. She took some shots of the trout stream right across from the house, and I began keeping these Polaroid pictures in my desk drawer back in New York City. I would pull them out, and it would make me feel very secure because I began to think that the photographs *were* the house. You can sometimes mistake a picture for the actual thing; I mean, you can even think a Polaroid *is* your girlfriend. And I said, now this is a nice little house, look at the size of it. I can fit it into the palm of my hand. There shouldn't be any problems with this.

So I decided to try to bargain with Carlo Carbone. First of all, we were supposed to go up to see the house. He was going to show it to me for the first time – he thought.

He calls me and says he'll pick me up at the coffee shop on the corner of West Broadway and Canal Street and that I'll recognize him by his dark purple '76 Buick. He arrives on time and I recognize him instantly. He's short and balding and he's wearing a couple of gold chains around his neck. First of all, he insists on splitting the gasoline because his Buick burns so much and he's a little low on cash. He also insists on taking Route 17 through New Jersey, not exactly the scenic route, but he's into speed.

Carlo asked me what I did for a living, and I said, 'Oh, a little acting, a little writing.'

And he said, 'Oh, I'm in the creative arts myself, I'm a florist, have been for years.'

Then he launched into his life story. He told me the reason he was selling the house was that he had had a skiing accident up there about six years ago. He took a tumble. When he got back up on his feet, he looked down and saw that his skis were headed in a direction they should *not* have been pointing while they were still attached to his body. After his friends helped him down the mountain, he realized he had fractured his leg in three places. He wanted to go to the best doctor possible. He heard about the man who had invented an artificial leg bone, who just happened to be living in Albany. So Carlo went up there. But when he arrived, he found that the doctor was now 80 years old and senile. Carlo claimed, 'They didn't even give me any anesthesia when they operated. They put a nut-and-bolt affair in three places in my leg to hold the bones together. Then when I went to have them taken out, the doctor came at me with something that looked like a wood bit, again without any anesthesia, and the nurse threatened to hit me over the head with my cast if I yelled. It was just a nightmare, the guy was completely nuts. Not long after the second operation, I was driving in my car and I began to smell this horrible stench wafting up from my leg. It turned out I had gangrene. I couldn't go to work and I was on crutches for months. My wife was fighting with me the whole time because I wasn't bringing in any money, and we have three daughters. Once, while we were fighting, I bumped into a pot of boiling water on the stove with my crutches and knocked it over. It spilled all over my wife, it scalded her. She sued, got full control of the house *and* the flower shop. My daughters wouldn't speak to me, and soon I was living in a storefront in Queens with orange crates and beach chairs for furniture, if you can imagine that. Shortly after that, I had a heart attack. And I really couldn't afford the bypass, so now I'm taking these heart pills.'

By now I was ready to jump out of the car, and we were only in New Jersey. What were we going to talk about the rest of the trip? What we talked about mainly was how I should buy a Buick (maybe his) if I bought a car. He said never buy a foreign car because they're not safe. Then we get farther north on the Thruway, and riding out of Kingston I see the Catskills like I've never seen them before. They are all snow-capped and it is one of those clear bright blue days and the snow is blowing fresh and powdery and it's deep and it's fantastic and we roll down the country road and Carlo turns into where the driveway is supposed to be. He plows into a huge snowdrift and the snow bursts over the Buick like a wave. We're stuck; we have arrived. He sits there with the tires spinning. I'm afraid he's going to have a heart attack before he sells the house.

We just leave the car in the snowbank and charge into the house to look at it. It's quite cold, so the first thing Carlo does is throw a switch on the wall to get the heat going. The furnace is in the attic because there's no basement; the heat comes out of little ducts, goes up, and kind of ripples across the ceiling, just hanging there. Meanwhile, Carlo's telling me that the house is totally winterized. He wants me to taste how wonderful the water is. The well pump is turned off, but he's got a thermos with some of this sweet well water in it. I'm trying to act as though I know something about house buying and I say, 'Look over here, the floor looks a little slanted – and how come this door doesn't close properly?' I really don't want to ask. I'd rather go back outside and see the view because Renée had said over and over again to me, 'You can change the house, but you can't change the location.' So we set out over this hill-and-dale affair, which is completely covered in deep snow – it's way above my knees. I head down toward a huge sycamore tree right next to a rushing trout stream and I turn around to see Carlo, panting, behind me. He says, 'I haven't been in any deep snow since I had my heart attack (*hack, hack*). My doctor says I shouldn't do this.'

I say, 'Slow down!' I'm beginning to feel enormous sympathy for him and I want to buy the house right away before he dies. I'm getting obsessed with the house. He finally reaches me and we stand there looking out over this fantastic vista of the Catskills, and the wind is whistling through the sycamore tree, and he says, 'Isn't it beautiful? Wasn't I right when I told you that you had to buy this house because of the view? Look at it.'

And I turned and looked at him standing there, panting, with his eyes all watery. And I thought, this man is a modern-day King Lear. He's a blue-collar King Lear. He is standing here misty-eyed in the wind, his three daughters have left him, how could a guy like this sell me a bad house?

On the way back to the city we talk money. I'm trying to get him down to twenty-seven thousand, but he can tell my heart's not in it. He keeps saying, 'Look, Spalding, buying a house is like taking money out of one pocket and putting it in the other.' At last, after much talk, he promises to fix the foundation, which he assures me is only a $1,200 job, and he'll put it in writing. But he doesn't want to take money off what I'm paying him, he wants to pay for the new foundation out of his own pocket because he claims to know how to deal with the locals.

In the following days, I try to negotiate with him over the telephone. I'm constantly calling him up. I also don't believe that he's really in touch with the contractor, Ned Perkins, who is supposed to fix the foundation for him. So I'm also calling Ned, I'm kind of bugging him, too, to see if he actually is going to do this foundation. And Ned thinks he's in great demand because *two* people are calling him up.

Every time Carlo calls me Renée stands by and whispers in my ear, 'Don't deal with him anymore. I don't like it, I don't like it. He sounds exactly like my father. You can take it in your own hands if you want – you're stubborn as a goat.' But she did convince me to at least hire a local contractor to appraise the house. We drove up and met him in front of the house. Carlo still hadn't given me a key, so Renée had to break in with the saw again. He took a quick look and then said, 'Where's the insulation? I thought you said this place was winterized. And what's the furnace doing in the attic? Listen, if I were you I'd offer the guy twenty-six thousand. He needs the money bad. Then I'd hire someone from New York City for fifty dollars to come burn it down so I could collect the fire insurance.'

Finally, Carlo started to get angry about my checking up on him and he called Renée. No one was home, but her answering machine recorded this message:

Hello, this is Carlo Carbone calling. I received your message about Ned Perkins. It's the second message I've received. I'm very perturbed about the idea of you calling upstate constantly and spoiling it for me with these people up there, who now think that they're the only people in the world that can do the job for me. I gave you a written agreement and signed it, and there's no reason in the world why you should doubt my integrity. I intend to follow through. There has been a great deal of rain up there, and they cannot work when it's so wet. It will be taken care of, but please do not call any more up there because you're spoiling it for me, and you're making it cost. It's costing me money. I've agreed to pay for this one out of my own; I think I should be the one to deal with them, don't you?

(Pause).

Please go along with the fact that I did sign an agreement with you, I have a written agreement with you, and there's no reason in this world why you should constantly think that somebody's trying to put something over on you. (Oh, really?)

I don't intend to do that. And I would appreciate it if you would leave this job to me of having the foundation work done, since I'm paying for it. It will be done. Rest assured.

And if it's not Ned Perkins, it'll be someone else. But it'll be someone of my choosing, I will take the trouble to find out who is gonna do it and when they can do it, when it's feasible for them to do it. They cannot work when they are up to their ears in mud and expect the foundation to stay. They have to wait until the situation dries up, and if they can't do it by June 1, it'll be done a month later. But it has to be given the time to dry up. The extent of the amount of rain upstate has led to this kind of a thing. We've had an excessive amount of rain and I'm sure you read the papers and know what's happening upstate. I will take care of it.'

Renée was furious after hearing this. She was convinced he was a supersleaze. I wanted to believe him. I wanted to go ahead with it and needed a lawyer for the closing. I'd never been to a closing before and didn't have time to find a lawyer, so I called up Carlo to ask if he had any suggestions. And he did. He happened to know a lawyer in his area, another Italian guy, maybe a goomba. I actually called him up and hired him, sight unseen.

Here was the plan: I was going to buy the house for thirty-one thousand, but four thousand would be put in what I was calling 'escarole'. I asked Carlo's lawyer to hold the four thousand in escarole in his own desk drawer. (They must have thought I was a real rube.) And that money was not to be spent until the foundation was fixed. That was the agreement.

So Carlo arrived at the lawyer's office for the closing, panting, watery-eyed, like he was on the verge of another heart attack, which really made me want to rush it through. My lawyer was late, but everyone was very cheery. I signed all the papers while they sat around trying to convince me how lucky I was to get a house in the heart of trout-fishing country.

Moving in was no big deal. I drove up, walked into the house, plopped down on the coffee-stained, gold-flecked Castro convertible surrounded by Ethan Allen furniture and just sat there waiting for the feeling of ownership to wash over me. Nothing came. Renée wasn't even there to help me out because she was working on the movie *Insignificance* down in the city, so I just sat there alone. And I realized that I *had* no sense of ownership. Someone had lived there before me. Someone would live there after me. I was just passing through. Now I had to worry about making a will. Also, the house was *full* of somebody else's life. Somebody else's flatware, blankets, sheets, towels, pots and pans. There was even one of Carlo's hunting jackets hanging in the closet.

The first thing I do to try to make the house my own is to call my friend Howie over to help me move out all the furniture into a little shed in the back – I'm thinking of saving it in case one day it becomes antique. Howie says, 'Spalding, you know, there is some furniture that just *never* comes into vogue. I think a yard sale is in order.' And I'm thinking, one step at a time, one step at a time. Do something to make yourself feel a part of the town. Go down and rent a post office box.

So I go downtown and the first person I see is this guy wearing Bermuda shorts, about 30 years old with a crew cut. He's completely mad, as far as I can tell. He comes up to me and says, 'HAVE YOU EATEN YET? HOW'S THE APPETITE? WHAT'S YOUR ATTITUDE? ARE YOU READY FOR A TRIP TO OUTER SPACE? YOU CAN GO TO A DOCTOR. I KNOW TWO DOCTORS RIGHT BEHIND THE FUNERAL PARLOR, I'VE BEEN TO THEM BOTH. GO FOR THERAPY, GO FOR A WALK, JERK OFF BEHIND A TREE. HEY, I WAS A BOY SCOUT! BOY SCOUT TRAINING GOT ME THROUGH TWO FRENCH MENTAL INSTITUTIONS. TWO OF THEM. YEAH. HAVE YOU EATEN YET? HEY! SCHWARTZE! SCHWARTZES GONNA TAKE OVER THE WORLD! WHITEY'S HAD HIS WAY TOO LONG. TIME TO GAS WHITEY! LOOK OUT FOR SCHWARTZE. WHERE YOU COME FROM? CALIFORNIA?'

'No, Rhode Island.'

'YOU'VE GOT A GOOD TAN. RHODE ISLAND, GOOD. LOTS OF
GOOD JEWISH TEMPLES THERE. LOOK OUT! WRITE YOUR SIS A POST-
CARD, WRITE YOUR DAD A POSTCARD, WRITE YOUR MOM! GOTTA
GO – CATCH YA LATER.'

So I staggered into the post office and reserved a box. I felt
somewhat like I'd landed. Since my refrigerator was broken I had my
first meal downtown and afterwards took my first long night walk
down my country road. *Now* I knew why I moved to the Catskills.
All I could hear was bears and mountain lions rustling, water dripping, and psychopathic killers stalking. It's fantastic to be living in
the country. Soon I became frightened by the darkness and started
back. On the way I saw a great white glow, which I assumed was the
full moon. When I rounded the corner I noticed that Carlo's next-
door neighbor (who happens to be his brother) had one of those
incandescent lamps that light up automatically to keep prowlers
away. The entire neighborhood was lit up. You couldn't see any stars
or planets, let alone comets.

The next day I hire two local carpenters to come up. I figure maybe
cosmetics might solve the problem. If only the house could *look* like
the ideal cabin, maybe I'd be satisfied. I could get rid of the horrible
sliding windows and get four-pane Andersen thermal windows, get
some boards down over the brick linoleum. The carpenters tell me,
'It will be five thousand dollars just to put down planking and new
windows. Maybe you'd better think it over before you spend that
much on cosmetics.'

That night it rained and I discovered my first leak. Rain is leaking
in onto the big log ceiling and I think, my God, if this keeps up that
beautiful beam is going to rot. At that point I realized I didn't need a
five-thousand-dollar cosmetic job. What I really needed was a basic
handyman, an honest fellow who would come up and do maintenance whenever I needed him.

The next morning at breakfast I asked around and found Coot
Dunbar. He gave me his card, which had a picture of him at 8 years
old, sawing a board on the edge of a Hires Root Beer crate. His head
is completely shaved, like he had ringworm or something. The card
read, 'Coot Dunbar, Entrepreneur'. He was an ex-hippie from Ten-
nessee, living off the money he made from odd jobs. He didn't want
any hassle at all. He didn't even want to make a lot of money from
me. He just wanted, he said, to turn me on to life.

I brought him up to the house and said, 'Now I think the leak is coming from the chimney.'

He said, 'Yeah. I can grok that.' He rushed up onto the roof with some tar and slapped it on the chimney. (I didn't realize it was next to impossible to stop a leak if it's coming from the chimney.) He charged me $20 for that, and then he fixed my porch screens for another $100. That was very important because I was spending a lot of time out on that porch. It was the one place I felt at ease. I was cooking meals out there. When I could sleep I was sleeping with a big knife by the bed, because of the silence. Every morning I'd wake up with this incredible anxiety about what to do next. And part of the way I would alleviate this anxiety was to call various service people, using a responsible voice. You have to act normal on the telephone if you want them to come up and fix stuff.

The first service person I called was a refrigerator man, Starky Jakes. I said, 'Hello, Mr Jakes. This is Mr Gray, the new home owner up on the hill.'

'Oh, yes, we know all about the houses up there. We can come up, we've been there many times before.'

'I need you to check my refrigerator. I think it has a little freon leak.'

So I hang up and I'm kind of pacing around barefoot on that cool brick linoleum when there's a knock at the screen door. I peer out and see what look to be my first visitors – maybe the neighbors have come to welcome me. They're not bearing cakes or pies, but there are two women and a little boy with a string tie tight around his neck standing there.

One of the women calls out, 'Have you heard about the Great Crowd yet?'

'Nope, not yet.'

'The Great Crowd is everyone born after 1914 who has joined the Jehovah's Witnesses. They're going to live forever.'

'I've never heard about that, that's incredible. Isn't it going to get a little crowded?'

She goes on, 'We will all sit in his glorious throne, and the Lord will divide the sheep from the goats.'

She opens up her Bible and quotes from Matthew 25:30, something about the gnashing of teeth. Then she says, 'When you call on your neighbors with the Kingdom's message, you may find some who display a goatlike disposition. This they do by showing indifference or rudeness or by outright opposition.'

By now I'm trying to be sheeplike and open and listen to her, and she continues, 'Isn't it a lovely thought that we're going to live forever? And it's just around the corner. Adam and Eve didn't have children before they sinned, and until you understand that, all of your prayers will be useless. It will be like putting paint on a house that is falling down.'

I thought, she's got my number. She must have chosen this text when she first saw the house from the road. She sold me a book called *Let Your Kingdom Come*, and that got rid of them for the time being. I read the entire book while waiting for the Speed Queen man to come. It had this wonderful picture showing the Great Crowd. There's a leopard in a tree, smiling, content, not ready to jump. There's a little black girl holding a baby leopard in her arms. There's a little white boy standing between two loving parents, the mother carrying a Thanksgiving-style fruit basket and the father holding a garden hoe and a rake. Then there are some blacks with fruit baskets on their heads behind him, and there are houses with perfect foundations under them all around.

Shortly after that Starky Jakes arrived, with Speed Queen written on the side door of his pickup. He jumped out with a young boy trailing behind him and strolled right into the house as though he owned the place. He told the boy to stand in the corner and *stay* there. He said, 'By Jeezum crow, I hope you didn't buy this house, did you? If you did, I hope you didn't pay more than twenty-six dollars for it!' He had one of those horrible thin wrap-around beards, with no moustache. I noticed that he looked a little bit like a goat.

'I'll tell you why I know about this house. I helped build it. And you know who I worked under? Old Diefenbach. Old Boss Diefenbach. I bet you don't know about him, do you? He owned all the property up here, was what you'd call an Adirondack-style developer. Well, he's dead now, he died of a stomach ulcer, but he used to come up on this big hill, fold his arms, and say, "By Jesus, there's a sucker born every minute." '

During this diatribe, the boy, who I took to be his son (I was never introduced) began to wander around in a naturally curious way. Jakes yelled to him, 'You watch it or I'll bash you like you've never been before. You stay where you're put!' Then he smiled again at me and asked, 'Whatcha got for a problem here?'

I said, 'Well, actually . . . before you look at the refrigerator, could you take a look at the chimney?'

'Oh, the chimney. This thing is *sinking*, this house is built on clay. We didn't put no proper footings under there, you know. There's no footing under the chimney and there's no footings under the house. Of course it's gonna drop!'

And I walked over, and sure enough you could see that it had sunk a little, but I figured that it had stopped years ago. Now, I wasn't so sure. I said, 'While you're at it, what are those little holes up there? You see the holes in my ceiling beams?'

He said, 'Those little pin holes? Oh, them. Them's powderpost beetles. Boy, they do a job. Well, they been eating in there since 1957. We call that cancer of the house. But aren't those beams lovely? In fact, that's how Old Diefenbach figured we'd sell these houses to city slickers. They'd come up and that's the first thing they'd look at. They'd buy it every time.'

So I said, 'Why don't you try pumping up the refrigerator with the freon, see if it holds.' And he does and says, 'Looks like it's not holding.'

He charged me $30, grabbed his son and left.

I was spending a lot of time now just drinking out on the porch, taking it 'one day at a time', as Alcoholics Anonymous says, just sitting outside and cooking on my hibachi.

I decided to call a chimney sweep because I really wanted a fire in the fireplace. That was a big part of the reason why I bought the house. I called Jiminy Sweep, and he comes over wearing one of those black chimney sweep hats and gives it a careful examination.

'Don't light a fire in that chimney. That thing is pulling away from the house. If it's not stopped, the chimney will pull the whole house down with it.'

And I said, 'Can't you put a metal sleeve in it for the time being? Just so I can make a *little* fire?'

'Oh, noooo,' he says, 'you can't do anything until you right the house. Don't you know it's the foundation, not the location that counts? Until you get a proper foundation, nothin's gonna be right. The doors won't close, the windows won't fit, so you can't rebuild the chimney until you do something about that foundation.'

So now I'm thinking only about foundations. I see them every-where I go. And I decided that since Carlo wasn't coming through, I'd take care of it myself and then bill him. I called two young locals to come up, a neighbor gave me their number. They were both about

thirty years old. One talked and smoked a lot. The other one, a stone
mason, was dark and dour. He hardly ever spoke but seemed certain
he could rebuild the chimney, and his price was right. They said the
reason the cinder blocks were cracked and pushed in under the house
was because there wasn't proper drainage for the rain water. The
water collected and then froze around the blocks. They told me it was
a badly constructed house. I told them I was beginning to realize
that.

For twenty-five hundred, give or take a little, they were going to
jack up the house, remove the cinder blocks, and then dig down 4 feet
by hand, which would put the blocks below the frost level. Then they
could put in a whole new drainage system. The only problem was
that they still couldn't guarantee that the earth wouldn't freeze and
shift again because the house was built on clay. That's why everything including the chimney (and the old family barbecue in the yard,
which was now at a very disturbing angle) was that way. Essentially,
this lovely hill-and-dale affair was a big mound of wet clay moving
toward the trout stream on the other side of the road. Nature was
taking its own course. The thought of the house in perpetual motion
was too much. I wanted a house that would stand still for years. The
only way to ensure that was to have the house jacked up and a full
concrete foundation poured under it. They didn't have the equipment to do that but gave me the number of a guy who did, Franz
Klinger.

I didn't waste any time. I called Franz from my front porch during
cocktail hour that night, and he said he'd be up in the morning. I
didn't know where I was going to get the money but I figured I could
pay in installments.

As soon as I saw Franz, I knew he was the right guy for the job. He
was very Germanic, stood with his arms folded like an ancient
plowman and said, 'I can do the job for you for eight thousand
dollars, but the porch *has* to go. There's no way I can get underneath
to do my digging.'

Now I'm thinking, if there's a sucker born every minute, I should
be able to sell this house. I drop in on Micky Micadella, a local real
estate agent, and Micky looks more like a spider than a goat. He gets
me into his web and says, 'I would never never never buy a house
unless it was through an agent. If you go through a private owner you
have no protection. And besides, what's a guy with a name like
Spalding Gray doing up there on that back road? With a name like

that, you should be governor of the state of New York, I mean, after all.'

Now I was beginning to think of changing my name. Maybe that was why people were charging me so much.

When I woke up the next day, Sunday, all I could hear in my head was Harry Belafonte singing, 'House built on weak foundation, will not last, oh no, oh no.' Over and over again. I went outside to get into my van to go downtown for breakfast and my van wouldn't start.

So I call up the service station and no one can come up, but they happen to know a mechanic who's at the coffee shop. So I call him there and he comes right up. He charges me $35 just to cross two wires because it's Sunday. While he was getting the van started, I talked to the plumber who had ridden up with him. He asked, 'This house winterized?'

So I get real proud, because it's the last good feature of the house left. Maybe I couldn't have a fire in the fireplace, but at least I could turn on the heat. I said, 'Yes it is. As a matter of fact, I've got a furnace in the attic.'

'You gotta be shittin' me. Don't you know heat rises? You got an oil burner up there? That's totally against regulations. You can't have liquid fuel in an attic. If the stuff leaks through and this house burns down, you couldn't even collect the insurance.'

So now I was thinking of running away. I sat on the porch that evening counting my blessings: nice porch, good well water. . . I called Renée in New York and she was no help. She said things like, 'If you had taken that thirty thousand dollars and invested it in vaginal sponges, you'd have three hundred ninety thousand dollars by now. You should be reading the *New York Times* business section, not the real estate section. If you just wanted to throw your money away, you could have bought me a bulletproof chinchilla coat.'

I had supper on the porch and went out for my evening walk, by now a kind of drunken weave through the neighborhood. I went up and turned left this time and walked onto that hill, the infamous lookout where Old Diefenbach first stood. And I saw an entire community of unbelievably tacky little bungalows, just like mine, except that they'd all been redone. Some of them had new foundations, some had hurricane fences with barbed wire around them, pink flamingos and Humpty Dumpties in the yards, with camouflaged jeeps parked out in front. It looked like a community of retired survivalists, which depressed me enormously. I came back down and sat on the porch thinking, how did I inherit this karma? Because I certainly believe in karma – not exactly Buddhist karma, but earthly karma. What you reap you sow; what goes around comes around; the consequences of actions. I thought, really, am I a loser? I didn't look at myself that way, but I never really had the go-for-it spirit.

I remember the first time I didn't go for it. I was in camp up in Maine. I must have been 8, 9 years old, and this cat sauntered by with a chipmunk in its mouth. I knew it was going to take it under one of the cabins and eat it. The chipmunk was hanging from the cat's mouth like a kitten, and it made eye contact with me. It looked right into my eyes and seemed to be saying, 'Help! You can save me if you go for it!' That stayed with me for years.

Until I was appointed captain of the soccer team at Fitchton Academy, probably to help me develop the go-for-it spirit. Our team got as far as the championship playoffs with Holderness Academy. Just before the game the whole team lined up for the big pre-game pep talk. I just stood there, my words barely audible above the wind, and said, 'Okay, guys, you want to win, right? Well, let's win then. Let's go go go for it.'

More recently, my friend George Coates came to visit me from Berkeley. Whenever George comes to New York City, he wants to take me to a part of the city I haven't been to in a long time. That way we can be on equal terms, experientially. We were walking in the East Village and he became very frightened because it looked wild to him and he had two hundred in cash in his pocket. I said, okay, I'll take you over to my neighborhood, we'll go down to Surprising SoHo, it's completely different on Sundays. We start down West Broadway and walk by a gray Cadillac with chrome-spoked wheels, and the thing is talking. It's going, 'Burglar. Burglar. Burglar. Burglar'. And all the bridge-and-tunnel women in their bulletproof chinchilla coats are looking at the car, saying, 'Who, me?'

We pass the car, and a little farther down we see a group of people standing in a circle on the corner of Spring Street and West Broadway. A woman is saying, 'Whoa! What should we do? What should we do?' Everyone is looking down as if there was a hole in the sidewalk going down to the golden city of El Dorado. George and I join the circle and look down to see this money blowing in circles, like leaves. There were hundreds, fifties, uncountable tens. George just reaches down and picks up a twenty. A woman says, 'What are you doing?'

And George goes, 'You know what I'm doing.' And he put the twenty in his pocket and walked away.

I said, 'George, George did you see the hundreds? Why'd you just pick up a twenty?'

'There were hundreds?! No, that would be greed, wouldn't it?' And we walked on. I didn't pick up any of it. And it was *my* neighborhood.

Just last year I was taking a bus from Springfield to Hartford and I felt all this energy in the back of the bus, not from the engine, but sixties-type energy: sex, drugs, rock and roll. There's this black guy playing the shell game. He's trying to get anyone to bet on which shell the pea is under. I sit down (why not?) and take a look at it. The guy next to me won't play. He says, 'That's just a trick, y'know, the guy'll get you every time.'

So this woman with a handful of money moves in and starts playing. The bus driver is watching the whole thing in his mirror and I figure he's going to bust this guy any minute. And the woman, who seems quite drunk, starts losing money like crazy, and I asked her, 'Hey, you ever win at this?'

And she says, 'Aah won a whole lot, and then I lost it.'

I thought, well, she's just a stupid drunk. She doesn't know when to stop. Once when the guy was looking away she actually picked up the shell to show the onlookers where the pea was. I didn't bet on it because I didn't want to cheat. I only played twice and lost both times. Forty dollars later, I got off the bus. On my way out I realized that the bus driver had been watching the whole thing because he was getting a cut. It was a rolling gambling casino between Springfield and Hartford.

I began to read self-help books, which I borrowed from the Phoenicia library (*The Age of Anxiety*, *The Road Less Travelled*, etc.), because I couldn't get any radio or television reception. The first book I read was the most beneficial to me. Somehow it explained why the house was the way it was. The book was called *Entropy*, and it was about the second law of thermodynamics, which states that matter and energy can only be changed in one direction, from usable to unusable, from order to chaos. So this puts me at some ease. I find passages that help me get to sleep:

Consider for a moment the numbers of each species that are required to keep the next higher species from slipping toward maximum entropy. 'Three hundred trout are required to support one man for a year. The trout, in turn, must consume ninety thousand frogs, that must consume twenty seven million grasshoppers that live off of one thousand tons of grass.'* Thus, in order for one human being to maintain a high level of 'orderliness', a thousand tons of grass must be used.**

I turned to a more comforting passage:

It should be emphasized that entropy law deals only with the physical world where everything is finite and where all living things must run their course and eventually cease to be. It is a law governing the horizontal world of time and space. It is mute, however, when it comes to the vertical world of spiritual transcendence. The spiritual plane is not governed by the iron-clad dictates of the entropy law.***

Spiritual transcendence? I thought it might be possible to shift my attention to a more metaphysical state. So I picked up Walt Anderson's *Open Secrets,* an interpretation of Tibetan Buddhism. The Tibetans emphasize the Vajrayana path to enlightenment: in their view there is nothing so negative that it can't be turned into something positive. I was really considering running away to become a Tibetan monk. There are three paths, according to this book: the path of renunciation, of celibate, Spartan, vegetarian living (I thought that was out); a life like other people's – get married and obey the laws; and the Vajrayana path – the diamond vehicle, the Tantric path – for the wild outcasts, who become free of lust through satisfying it. All the no-nos are praised: sex, alcohol, and meat eating.

This led me to one of Bhagwan Rajneesh's books; his photo stared up at me from the book like an Indian Rasputin. It was like he was hypnotizing me, beckoning me to come on out to Oregon to his Rancho Rajneesh, the ultimate place of no-nos. I pictured this as the perfect escape because a friend of mine had told me that she had been out there and she'd never been approached so many times by men.

* G. Tyler Miller, Jr. *Energetics, Kinetics and Life* (Belmont, Calif.: Wadsworth, 1971, p.46).
** Jeremy Rifkin, *Entropy* (New York: Bantam, 1980, p. 54)
*** Ibid, p.8

She felt no paranoia at all. Male *sannyasins* would just come out of the bushes in their flowing orange robes (all followers of Bhagwan have to wear orange) and say, 'Do you want to do it?' She had the choice to say yes or no, but no one ever accosted her. There were naked people in the bushes, all around, squatting and humping without guilt or fear. I saw myself out there, swinging naked and tan through the trees, my entire body turned into one big peener chasing after a dripping cooz, all out of time, no thought, complete immersion in sex. She told me that one night in her tent she overheard a couple making love. Just as they began to peak, the other tents joined in, all breathing in unison, until the entire Rancho Rajneesh came together in one big climax. It all changed by the end of the summer. She told me that Rajneesh had proclaimed AIDS as the next plague and he now required all the *sannyasins* to wear orange condoms and orange surgical gloves, and I knew those free-love days were over.

I went back to *Open Secrets* and read that from the Vajrayana point of view, you are perfectly welcome to pursue worldly success while on your way to enlightenment. Aha, spiritual materialism . . . maybe instead of going to Rancho Rajneesh, I should go to Hollywood and do a few sitcoms and make enough money to restore the house to perfection. I had to put my house in order before I could save the world.

I approached Renée with this idea: 'This is it, we'll go to Hollywood. Going to California is like panning for gold, only the gold today is in TV sitcoms. I'll go out and make enough money so we can come back and fix up the house.'

I'd been out to Hollywood once before. I was a runner-up for the role of Patty Duke's husband in 'Hail to the Chief', a new sitcom about the first woman president – the president has been fatally stung by a bee in the Rose Garden, so the woman VP becomes president. The casting director had auditioned me in New York and the Hollywood people had liked the video so much that they flew me out and put me up in the Beverly Hilton. If I got the role it would pay fifteen thousand a week; all I had to do was sign a six-year contract.

I said, 'Well, there's no way I can do that. I can't think that far ahead.'

And my agent said, 'Don't worry about it. That's what lawyers are for, understand? That's why you're making all the money, so you can buy your way out of the contract. Sign it, do it. The show probably won't run that long anyway.'

I heard they had boiled it down to Dick Shawn and me, the dark horse from the East. I was sitting in a giant stone-and-leather room in Century City waiting nervously for my audition, going over lines like: 'Honey, honey. Why do you *think* I can't make love to you anymore? Do you know what the guys down at the Pentagon are calling me? They're calling me the First Lady! How do you expect me to get it up?'

Then the casting director rushed up to me and said, 'You're on!' and she led me by the arm swiftly down a long, carpeted corridor. She told me to prepare myself to enter the producer's bullpen, which seemed to me like a torture arena. When we got to the door, I heard Dick Shawn carrying on inside while all the producers laughed. Worst of all, he was saying all *my* lines. Somehow I had developed a fantasy that I was the only one who would be speaking those lines. I could see Dick Shawn through a crack in the door and to my horror realized that he was not on book. He had memorized all his lines and was spewing them forth with great ease while the TV execs just rolled in the aisles. I was mortified. When he was finished, I walked through the side door and onto the stage. I looked out at all the executives sitting in the dark and I was introduced to everyone, including Patty Duke. I felt better when I noticed that she was using a script, but I was pretty stiff. When I put my arm around Patty, it felt like an artificial limb. I heard all my lines coming out of my mouth in this flat, understated Boston accent. I sounded like one of the Kennedys. I think Dick Shawn got the role.

Renée and I got a cheap flight to Los Angeles on Tower Air. It was so cheap that it made me a little nervous. I was afraid the pilot wouldn't really be concentrating. During the flight, I see this guy in line for the bathroom who looks familiar. He's about 6 foot 3, with overalls on, and he looks like a big Yogi Bear. I keep wondering, 'Who is that guy?' We arrive at the airport and as he is walking off the plane with us I realize that he's the SoHo bum, the only bum in SoHo, the one who's always standing outside the Cupping Room on West Broadway, going, 'Ya gotta nickel for a cup of coffee, nickel for a cuppa coffee?' He has no teeth.

I said, 'You're the SoHo bum! What are you doing on our flight?'

'I saved up all my nickels. Are you from there? I'm going to miss all my SoHo friends.'

And I said, 'What are you doing out here?'

He said, 'I'm panning for gold. I've come out here to search for gold.'

I said, 'Renée look! He's panning for gold. That completes the metaphor. We're on to something.'

The first audition my agent sends me up for is for a role on 'St. Elsewhere'. I'm supposed to play a bum. The character is a very intelligent businessman who has simply gotten sick of the corporate world, drops out, and becomes a bum. The casting agent had requested that I not eat for about 5 days, let my beard grow, and come dressed as my idea of a bum. I said, 'Well, I'll let my beard grow, but I'm not going to stop eating until I get the role.'

It's not very hard to dress like a bum in Hollywood, even a secondhand raincoat will do. I wore a T-shirt, my own raincoat, and a light growth of beard. When I rounded the corner to enter the 'St. Elsewhere' studio, all these other bums converged on me, and I realized it was an open call. It was like arriving at a costume party to find that everyone is wearing the same costume.

I'm sitting next to a guy who tells me that he had been on the bottle for 2 years until finally his agent called him up, offered him a loan of two thousand dollars plus a rental car, and flew him out to Hollywood on Christmas day (he wanted to fly on Christmas because there's never anyone on the planes then and he could get some sleep). He'd been off the bottle ever since. And I thought, gee, he's perfect for the role, let him have it.

When I got into the office, I was thinking so much about his story that I wasn't very convincing. They gave me the perfunctory, 'Thank you *so* much for coming in.'

The next thing my agent sent me to was an audition for 'Mr Sunshine', which was being co-produced by Henry Winkler. Henry had seen me before and thought I'd be perfect. It was a show about a college professor (I could relate to that, I'd been teaching at Columbia) who had just gotten divorced (I could relate to that – I've never been married, but I've been separated) and who had just gone blind. This was a sitcom! My lines went something like:

'I don't want to get involved with any more women, I've had it, all right? All right, I give in, send me a seeing-eye hooker.'

'I'm going into this situation with my eyes wide open.'

'I'm going out on a blind date – that'll add new meaning to the whole situation.'

I drive over to the studio in my little rented Nissan Centra and park it. I look to my right and see a man going by with a knapsack on his back and one of those white sticks. He's actually blind.

I go into the audition and Henry says, 'Here he is, folks, here he is.' Henry had seen me do *A Personal History of the American Theatre*. He says, 'This guy is incredible. He stands naked in front of the audience with a box of little cards.' Now, people in Hollywood are quite literal-minded. Slowly, everyone in the office turns around to see if I'm dressed. I say, 'Sit, Henry. Sit. I sit. Behind a box of cards.'

So we went through the audition and Henry's co-producer said, 'Well, I think that's a little soft. I really don't think a college professor would be that soft-spoken.'

I said, 'That's strange, because I teach college and I do speak at that level.'

And he said, 'Yes, but you're not blind, and I think you'd compensate for your blindness.

So I yelled, 'ALL RIGHT, SEND ME A SEEING-EYE HOOKER!'

'Well, maybe somewhere in between those two. Thank you very much for coming in.'

On the way back to the Highland Gardens Hotel, I turned on KPFK, the listener-sponsored radio station. They had been broadcasting Shostakovich's diaries every day at noon, and that particular day they were reading the entry that describes how Stalin had all the blind storytellers and poets lined up against a pit and shot them.

The next thing I was considered for was 'The Tonight Show'. The producers wanted to screen me first, so one of Johnny's representatives called me in for a rather intense 2-hour interview. He got me rolling on all of my stories and said, 'Oh, very good, very good, but you're a little dark. Try to censor yourself a little more.' The one he liked the best was about Adriana Glick, my first sensual girlfriend, at Emerson College. We used to make love in front of my fireplace in which I burned the leftover set from a college production of Molière's *The Misanthrope*. When I finished the story, he said, 'Oh, I like that very much, but listen, don't say words like "misanthrope". Johnny hates theater. Basically you're playing to a bunch of not overly intelligent people who want to go to sleep. You get too high-falutin. You go light and then you get heavy, you're not a good self-editor. But I love your stories. Do you have any more? Do you have any good therapist stories?'

'Oh, yeah, I have one about my first therapist. I was always trying to make him laugh or make him talk or just get him to react to me in some way. He was a complete stoneface, the kind of guy who if you didn't speak to him, he wouldn't speak back and you could sit for the entire session in silence. But one day I happened to be telling him a story about my father, who is a creature of habit. He has little bedtime rituals. He's not a very metaphysical man, nor is he in any way superstitious, but he always puts his slippers right by the bed, just so, and then he hops into bed. One night my brother Rocky was hiding under the bed (Rocky must have been about 14), and after my father parked his slippers, Rocky just reached out, grabbed the slippers and threw them straight up in the air. My father yelled to my mother, "Betty, come quick! My slippers are flying! My slippers are flying!" And my therapist laughed.'

Johnny's rep said, 'Oh, that's good, that's good, love it, have you got any more?'

I said, 'I do, about my second therapist . . . oh, wait, wait a minute, no. That one starts funny but it ends with Auschwitz.'

'No, thank you. Listen, Spalding, really, I love you, I love you really, I think you'd go very well on "The Dick Cavett Show".'

I said, 'Yeah? Well, I'd love to be on it.'

'It hasn't been on for *years*.'

I said, 'Oh, really? I didn't know that.'

He said, 'You didn't know "The Dick Cavett Show" was off the air? I love it, I love it, but I don't *believe* it. Listen, you've got to realize that being on the Johnny Carson show is not a whole lot of fun. You can't go out there and just chitchat. You'll be on the spot. You gotta go for the jugular. Doc Severinsen and Ed McMahon and all the rating people will be there watching you like a hawk. And Johnny's going to be interviewing *you*. He has to know all the questions as well as the answers before you go on. He's got to be in control. For starters, you should prepare five questions for him. Okay? You've got a TV, right?'

'Yeah, we've got one.'

'Well, would you watch the Johnny Carson show for the next week? And get a feel of how you might fit in? Would you promise me that? And then let's talk again at the end of the week and see if you can come up with those five questions.'

So I gave it a try, but unfortunately I fell asleep almost every night before Johnny came on. It wasn't that I didn't want to get on the show, I had nothing against it. I would love to capture the American imagination. Who wouldn't? It's just that everyone goes to bed early in LA.

Johnny's producer called and said, 'Have you thought of the five questions?'

And I said, 'I really haven't given it much thought. But I did come up with a good opener.'

'What is it?'

'Well, the first question might be, "Why is this night different from any other night?" ' He didn't laugh, he was Italian.

Renée said, 'Enough of this depending on other people. We've got to put together our own package.' And she comes up with the idea of trying to sell my life story to Warner Brothers for a feature film. And, by God, they're interested. We condense my stories *Sex and Death to the Age 14; Booze, Cars, and College Girls;* and *47 Beds* for the film: it will be about this character, Sterling Gray, a Huck Finn–Candide-type who gets into all these weird situations. And he doesn't know whether he wants to get married or not. He thinks he does, but he's got to have a Perfect Moment first, right? So they call us into the studio to pitch it – Renée, who's going to be the producer, Adam Brooks, who's going to be our director, and me. I get very confused and keep saying, 'And then I – I mean Sterling – I mean I – I mean – me . . . ' Basically, I'm going through the monologues. The Warner people seem interested, but they want to know if the character gets married at the end. I said, 'Well, I don't know if he does.'

'We can't buy it until we make that decision.'

I said, 'I can't even make that decision with Renée, how're we going to make a decision on the script? I mean, let's make it later. Do you like the story?'

'Well, we have to have it completely clear.'

They sent it 'upstairs'. (I was surprised. I never knew Warner Brothers had an upstairs. It looked like one giant ranch house to me.) Then the writers' strike came. And right in the middle of the strike, they called me and said, 'We can give you the report on it: you've got Recognition Factor. People upstairs at Warner Brothers know who you are, but I can't tell you if you have the green light yet.'

Renée got tired of waiting for the green light and flew back to New York City. I was determined to stick it out. A few days later, my agent called to say that Simon Ballsner, a major TV director, was interested in me, and only me, for a TV movie-of-the-week called 'Leftover Life to Kill'. This looked like it could be the Big Break. Simon was going out on a limb with this one, taking a big chance by trying to cast what he referred to as two very talented unknowns, Sandy Struggles and Spalding Gray. If I did the movie, my agent said my name would soon be a household word. The story went like this: I was to play Scott, a New England sculptor who has fallen in love with one of his students and married her. The relationship is perfect except that my mother, one of those classic domineering types, is always interfering. About three-quarters of the way into the script, my mother has a heart attack and I insist on keeping her at home rather than putting her in the hospital. I'm finding it difficult to deal with the situation, so the burden of responsibility falls to my wife, Dale. And Dale is trying to get me to confront my mother and tell her that I love her despite what a dominating bitch she's been. That was basically it. I would get thirty-five thousand for four-weeks' work. No six-year contract. I could just take the money and run.

Simon Ballsner set up the first big meeting between Sandy and me at his office. I didn't know what to wear. I rushed out and bought an Yves St. Laurent shirt and some baggy, but well-tailored, designer pants of light cotton, because by now it was close to July and an outrageously brutal heat wave had descended on LA. I was nervous about meeting Sandy and Simon. My agent told me that Sandy was a beautiful and talented soap opera star and that doing this movie could also be her big break.

I arrived at Simon's office early and instantly felt at ease. It was one of those big solid rooms with white walls that came together at perfect white right angles, with a sweeping view of palm trees out the window. I was surprised to find Simon dressed only in a T-shirt, shorts, and sandals. 'Come in,' he said. 'I've heard so much about you. I've called you in today because I just want to see you and Sandy together for the first time, see what the chemistry between you is like.'

Then in comes Sandy and she sits down right next to me on this huge white couch, the kind of couch that if you sit back in it and relax it will devour you and someone will have to help you up. So I was sitting forward on the edge of it and rolling up my shirt sleeves into perfect squares, just above my forearms. Sandy was tall, thin, blonde, and smiley. I tried not to stare at her. I felt like I was being scrutinized by her father on our first date. But I didn't feel much of anything else.

Simon looked across at us and said, 'Good. Beautiful, I love it when the stars first meet. You look splendid together. Just splendid.' And that was it for the first day.

After Sandy left, Simon sat back in his chair and began playing with a basketball, rolling it around in his hands. 'Now, tomorrow you're going to come into Century City and read for the Network Maven and all of her cronies,' he said. Oh no, I thought, it's going to be another bullpen. But Simon kept assuring me that as far as he was concerned I had the role, reading for the network was just a formality. Also, he told me that Sandy wouldn't be there. She hated the network people and had enough LA power points not to be present for the audition. I would be reading opposite the free-lance casting director who had first brought me to Simon's attention. I was going to have to prove myself again. The dark horse from the East. To reassure me that I had the role, Simon sent me off with Silvio, his private driver, to get my insurance physical. On the way over, the driver told me he was also from the East and wanted to move back, because it was the only place where people still told the truth.

The physical was brief and chatty, performed by a Doctor Feelgood-type who basically checked to see that my heart was beating. When my agent heard about the physical he said that it looked like I really had the role. It was a Hollywood rule that once you had your physical you were 'in like Flynn and that's no sin'. He also said that there were sleazy agents who would hold Ballsner to it.

Silvio drove me back to Highland Gardens while the huge sun, a deep smoky red from all the surrounding brush fires, was sinking at the end of Sunset Boulevard. I sat there in silence, fantasizing about joining the Peace Corps.

Back at the hotel, I decided to spend the evening going over the script and staying out of the heat. Simon warned me not to study the script too hard, and most important, not to push at the reading. Just be relaxed and neutral. That night around cocktail hour I got a call from Simon. It sounded like he was coming over the transatlantic cable. Actually, he was on Hollywood Boulevard, calling from his car telephone.

'Keep up the good work, Spalding. Stay off any drugs and start working out. You should be running every day and playing basketball. I hope you know how to play because there's a big basketball scene in the movie. (My heart sank.) Also, why don't you buy one of those pull-up bars to firm up your pecs. After all, we don't want you to look like a self-defeated shlub, do we?'

The next day I dressed again in my Hollywood audition outfit, sprayed myself with a heavy dose of Right Guard and waited for Silvio to pick me up. We rode with both the air conditioner and the radio going full blast. The only thing Silvio said was, 'Looks good. I've seen a lot of them come and go, but Simon is really hot for you, I can tell.'

We arrived at Century City and I went into an office with Simon and the casting director to wait for the Maven. I sat down and again rolled up my shirt sleeves into perfect creaseless squares just above my forearms. Four of the cronies had already arrived and were sitting quietly, collating the sides. Then the Maven came in, a great matronly lady of about 57 who looked like the Duchess of California. She was wearing pearls and a giant designer muumuu that rippled like an elegant tent and veiled the mystery of an unimaginable body.

Simon stood up. 'Allow me to introduce you to Rhoda Flemenstine, the Maven of Century City.'

Rhoda smiled and said, 'How do you do, Mr Gray. Do you even know what Maven is?'

Now the only maven I'd ever heard about was the Vita Herring Maven on the radio, so I said, 'Isn't a maven someone who makes schmaltz?' So we were off to a good start.

I read opposite the casting director and didn't push it in any way. I just read flat and understated, with my New England accent coming through. The scene was the one with my wife after I have tried to tell my mother that I love her:

> Dale, it's no good. Words can't change what's gone down between us. What just happened in that room was a total farce. I stood at the end of my mother's bed and felt nothing. No remorse, no compassion, not even that old familiar guilt. I felt dead inside. Dale, Dale, you've got to help me. I feel like I've lost it. I feel like a piece of the pie is missing. I'll do whatever I can to help you deal with my mother, but please don't send me back into that room again. Please.

Silence prevailed. 'Thank you very much,' the Maven said. Simon asked me to please wait outside while they discussed my audition. I felt like a little kid being sent from the room so the grownups could talk. I went out into the giant over-air-conditioned windowless waiting room with devouring leather chairs and huge clearglass coffee tables empty of all magazines and books and just sat there staring at an abstract purple acrylic wall-hanging, waiting. About 10 minutes later, Simon came bursting out with the casting director trailing behind him. 'The ball's in my court. The ball's still in my court. We haven't got the green light yet, but it looks good.'

'Well, what seems to be the problem?'

'They didn't think you were passionate enough. You were a little low-key.'

And I said, 'Wait a minute! I'll show them. Let's go back in there. I can be passionate! "DALE, DALE, YOU'VE GOT TO HELP ME! I FEEL LIKE I'VE LOST IT! I FEEL LIKE A PIECE OF THE PIE IS MISSING! I'LL DO WHATEVER I CAN TO HELP YOU DEAL WITH MY MOTHER, BUT PLEASE, PLEASE DON'T SEND ME BACK INTO THAT ROOM AGAIN!!!!" '

Simon said, 'No, no, Spalding, calm down. They'd rather see you on tape. They want me to shoot some footage of you first. They want to see if the camera loves you. We're going to get together with Sandy tomorrow and put the honeymoon scene on video. Then I'll edit it and screen it for the Maven.'

The next day I decided to wear a T-shirt and dungarees, loosen up a little. When Simon saw me he said, 'Oh, so you've decided to go "cazh". That's great! You look great.' And he shot me a quick pass with his basketball (a Spaulding, I noticed), which bounced right off my fingertips and broke a fingernail.

'Looks like it's been a while, hey, Mr Spuds. Haven't you been out there practicing?' I wondered where he'd picked up my nick-name. I thought I'd left that identity behind in Rhode Island.

In the corner of the room, Silvio was setting up the video equipment and Simon was squinting at me through the view finder. 'Oh, yes, it does!' Simon cried out. 'The camera loves you, I can tell already. But the question is, do you love Sandy? I've got to capture that chemistry on tape. You see, that's one of the problems. You're not acting like you're really in love with her. You're holding back. Don't you think she's luscious?'

I lied and told him I did. If I told him the truth, I knew I wouldn't get the role. The truth was that I felt no attraction to Sandy. The truth was that I felt Simon was in love with her. Also, the whole idea of falling in love on camera was very confusing to me. Wasn't *acting* like you were in love to a certain extent *being* in love? I mean, I often act like I'm in love with Renée, so what's the difference? If I act like I'm in love with Sandy won't that, in fact, put me there?

Actually, the whole issue of character had always been confusing for me. When I see glamorous stars from 'Dynasty' or 'Dallas' being interviewed on TV, it strikes me that they are always hiding behind this giant myth of character. If the interviewer asks, 'You play such a backstabbing deceitful bitch. How do you feel about that?' the stars usually say, 'Oh, I don't know. It's very difficult because I'm not anything like that in real life.'

Simon told me that Sandy was meeting us for lunch so we could get better acquainted in an informal sort of way. Then afterwards we'll come back and play the big honeymoon scene for the camera.

We decide to lunch at this fantastic sushi place just around the corner from Simon's. It's too hot to walk, so we all pile into Sandy's black BMW. By now the outskirts of LA are really burning, and the whole city is encircled by a ring of fire. The chaparral is bursting into spontaneous combustion like the burning bush in the Bible. Fourth of July is only a few days away and certain demented patriotic pyromaniacs are setting random fires all over town. White ash is falling like hot snow. The BMW is so hot that you could fry an egg on the hood.

Inside the cool restaurant, Simon orders a huge platter of yellow-tail sushi. I have never tasted such plump and succulent yellowtail in my life. But I was not at ease. I didn't know what to talk to Sandy about, I didn't want to pry. We talked a little about her childhood in Kentucky, about an oil well she had invested in that had just gushed, and whether or not mosquitoes carried AIDS.

I couldn't get enough of that sushi. I felt like a bear storing up for hibernation. We must have left sixty-dollars' worth behind on the table. I was tempted to ask for a doggy bag, but a voice inside me said, No, Spalding, don't appear too needy.

Back at the office, Simon and Silvio were setting up for the big love scene. We are supposed to have just finished making love and are now lying naked under blankets in front of a fire. I am supposed to get out my sketch pad and begin to sketch Dale. Simon put down a paisley spread and asked Sandy and me to get comfortable on it. The honeymoon scene went something like this:

SCOTT:
    Got your eyes full honey? What are you looking at?
DALE:
    You.

SCOTT:
   What do you want?
DALE:
   You.
SCOTT:
   But haven't you had enough of me?
DALE:
   No, not enough. Never enough of you.

Then I'm supposed to move in on her and sing 'As Time Goes By' in her ear; then we kiss and collapse in laughter.

I really try to find my way into the character. I'm using my notebook as a sketch pad and I'm holding a paper clip, which I am pretending is a piece of charcoal. I'm just sketching away as we go through the lines.

All of a sudden Simon yells, 'Cut, stop! Cut it. Spalding, the sketch pad is just a *prop*. Don't worry about it. You really want *Dale!*'

And I said (slightly taken aback, because I thought I was in character), 'Oh, you mean I'm not really an artist?' Because any real artist would rather sketch than make love.

After rehearsal, I stuck around to see the video. Sandy rushed off to another appointment. I was amazed at how busy my face was and how still, almost blank, Sandy's was. In fact, my features were in constant motion, like amoebas under a microscope. Simon thanked me. He said the video looked great, just great, but that he needed time to edit it and get it over to the Maven. He arranged for me to fly back to New York City first class, promising to call me as soon as anything broke. We'd most likely begin shooting at the end of August or early September.

Things were going so well I couldn't believe it. I figured the plane would crash in the Grand Canyon. Here it was the Fourth of July and I was flying first class over the whole country. My friend George Coates had told me that the best time to fly over America was the night of the Fourth, so that you can see the entire USA lit up like a big firecracker. I was flying during the day, but I had a clear view of the desert and the stewardess came by with a full pitcher of Bloody Marys to start the 1984 celebration off right. And because it was a holiday, hardly anyone was in first class and I almost had the whole thing to myself. I already felt like a real star.

Renée picked me up at Newark Airport and we headed straight to the Catskills to open the house. I told her we would soon be rich. 'Fat chance,' she said. 'Don't trust those guys until you sign every line.'

The house was its same old collapsing mouse-ridden self. Little nuts and little shits were everywhere. Renée cleaned up while I got on the phone to find a plumber. The water was turned off because a pipe had burst at the end of the previous season and I hadn't had time to find someone reliable to come up and fix it.

Simon called the next day while the plumber was trying to dig his way under the house to get to the pipe. He told me that he hoped he could find someone as good as I was for the role. He said that some of the moments on tape were 'transcendent', but that I had to realize that I was rusty as an actor. I was hesitant and didn't have that go-for-it spirit. He told me I had to decide between performing my monologues or going back into acting in a serious way. He also said he could always see something that he could only describe as thinking pass over my face every time I made a move. He felt my love for Sandy/Dale was ambivalent. He wished I could have just gone in there and grabbed her. He ended on a more encouraging note. 'We will work together one day. Have a good summer.'

Well, I was disappointed, but not surprised. I decided to go out on the porch and recount my blessings. After all, I had a fantastic girlfriend, a porch with a good view of state land, and some pure, wonderful well water (as soon as the pipe was fixed). Just then the plumber called out, 'Mr Spalding, go try the water now.' I rushed back into the house, turned on the tap and the water burst forth, smelling of death. The whole room filled up with the smell of a dead animal, but I was in such a hurry that I drank half a glass before I realized it. I spat out what was left in my mouth and went out to search for the well. When I found it, I noticed that the hygenic seal had popped off the metal sleeve (like everything else on that property, it was not up to code) and the top of the well was wide open. Maybe some depressed raccoon had committed suicide during the February doldrums.

Well, I thought, how bad could it be? What possible lethal disease could a dead animal carry . . . ? 'RABIES!' I screamed, and rushed out to Renée, who immediately called the Board of Health. She was lucky enough to get the rabies specialist on the line and I told him the whole story. Then he said, 'Listen, Mr Gray, do you know what rabies is? It's hydrophobia. And do you know what hydrophobia is?

It's fear of water. Now, what would an animal with a fear of water be doing jumping into a well? If you really want to begin a series of very expensive and very painful rabies shots into your stomach, we can do that this afternoon. But you know, Mr Gray, life is really too short to be worrying about catching rabies from a well.'

And a lightbulb went on in my head and I thought, Wow, he's right. He's really right!

Now, where do I go from here?